Shoshone Tales

Shoshone Tales

Collected and Edited by Anne M. Smith,
assisted by Alden Hayes

Foreword by Catherine S. Fowler
Afterword by Beverly Crum

University of Utah Press
Salt Lake City

Volume 31 of the University of Utah
Publications in the American West

Map on page xxxv reprinted from *Handbook of North American Indians, Volume 11: Great Basin,* ed. Warren d'Azevedo; gen. ed. William C. Sturtevant (Washington, DC: Smithsonian Institution Press, 1986), 1b-264, by permission of the publisher. All rights reserved.

Library of Congress Cataloging-in-Publication Data

Shoshone tales / collected by Anne M. Smith ; assisted by
    Alden Hayes ; foreword by Catherine S. Fowler ; afterword by
    Beverly Crum.
        p.   cm. —(University of Utah publications in the American
    West ; v. 31)
        Collectd 1939.
        Includes bibliographical references.
                        (alk. paper)
        1. Shoshoni Indians—Legends. 2. Gosiute Indians—
    Legends.   I. Smith, Anne M. (Anne Milne), 1900–1981.
    II. Hayes, Alden C.   III. Series.
    E99.S4S47   1993
    398.2'0899745—dc20   93-2944
                                                                          CIP

Contents

Foreword

This collection of Western Shoshone tales (including Gosiute) was gathered by Anne M. C. Smith with the assistance of Alden Hayes in September and October 1939 at various sites in central and eastern Nevada and western Utah. Smith (all of her friends called her "Nan") had just completed her doctoral dissertation in anthropology, "An Analysis of Great Basin Mythology," at Yale University, and she was determined to fill in the gaps in the record on Western Shoshone traditions that had become apparent during her research. To accomplish her task, she asked Hayes and Douglas Osborne—students at the University of New Mexico and previous companions on a field trip among the Northern Ute people in eastern Utah—to "wrangle car and camp" on a trip over countless miles of dirt and gravel roads, mostly in remote areas in Nevada (Alden Hayes, personal communication, March 25, 1991). They were able to find and document materials from twenty narrators, fifteen of whom are represented here. Nan and Alden recorded tales, while Doug looked for archaeological sites. Nan kept a field diary for much of the trip, in which she detailed some of the party's adventures on the road, her impressions of the country, and some of her observations of the Indian people she met and the conditions they were living under.[1] Nan wrote with particular admiration of narrator and interpreter Anna Premo of Owyhee, Nevada. Mrs. Premo's daughter, Beverly Crum, a scholar and teacher of the Shoshone language, has added an Afterword to this collection, giving some of her thoughts on her mother as storyteller, the role of Western Shoshone myths in the lives of the people, and various linguistic aspects of the stories. This collection—too long unpublished—amply attests that Nan successfully met her research goals. It adds immeasurably to the record of Western Shoshone oral tradition, from a time when that tradition was still a lively art form and played an important role in the culture.

Anne M. Cooke Smith

Anne Milne Millspaugh was born in New York City on October 20, 1900. She received an A.B. degree from Cornell University in 1922. She returned to New York City and married a stockbroker named Cooke, who had been a flyer during World War I with the Lafayette Esquadrille. The marriage broke up after a few years, but Nan retained his name during her years of graduate study. In the early 1930s, Nan spent a vacation on a dude ranch in Wyoming, and fell in love with the West. She determined to continue working there, and entered graduate school at Yale University in the fall to major in anthropology. She participated in archaeological excavations in New Mexico in 1934 and 1936 during her graduate studies (Alden Hayes, personal communication, March 25, 1992).

The Yale Anthropology Department in the 1930s was an exciting place for students interested in North American Indians and comparative cultures. Leslie Spier, who had worked among the Yuman-speaking peoples of the Southwest and California, was there, as was Edward Sapir, renowned expert on American Indian languages, including those of the West, Southwest, and California. George Peter Murdock, who had conducted fieldwork on the Columbia Plateau, was also an important force in the department.

Both Spier and Sapir were deeply interested in the Indian cultures of western North America—particularly those of the Great Basin, which at that time were not well known. Spier, through his ethnographic studies of the Havasupai in the years shortly before and after 1920, became very interested in comparisons among them, southern California tribes, and Great Basin peoples (Spier 1928). Along with Sapir, who had already written extensively on the Southern Paiute language of the Great Basin (Sapir 1930–31), Spier directed several graduate students at Yale to begin ethnographic studies on that region. They included Willard Z. Park, who worked among the Northern Paiute of western Nevada; Maurice Zigmond, who worked among the Kawaiisu and Panamint Shoshone of California; Beatrice Blyth, who worked among the Northern Paiute of Oregon; and Edgar Siskin, who worked among the Washoe of Nevada. Nan began her research among the Northern Ute of Utah in 1936 and continued in 1937. In 1937 she completed a master's thesis under Spier entitled "The Material Culture of the Northern Ute." As her work involved general ethnography, Nan apparently gathered several mythological tales among the Northern Ute along with her other data. She credits Anna Gayton, Spier's wife and a distinguished California ethnologist, with turning her attention to the analysis of Great Basin mythology for her doctoral dissertation (Cooke 1939, preface). Her task was to determine if the Great Basin constituted a single culture area in terms of the myths told by its people, even though some, like the Ute and Northern and Wind River Shoshone, were now far removed from Great Basin lifestyles. Her two-volume work—an important contribution to Great Basin studies as well as to the analysis of folklore—included one entire volume of Ute myths that she had gathered in 1936 and 1937 (see Smith 1992). For the remainder of the analysis, she used the collections of tales made by her fellow Yale graduate students then working among the Great Basin peoples, and the meager published and unpublished literature available at that time. An intent to expand and revise her analysis may have led her to the field in 1939.

After her brief reconnaissance among the Western Shoshone, Nan returned to Albuquerque, New Mexico, where she married fellow Cornell University graduate Eastburn Smith in 1940. They apparently spent the war years at Sacaton, Arizona, where East was superintendent of the Japanese relocation center. After the war, they returned to New Mexico, where East became regional director for the Soil Conservation Service, the Bureau of Land Management, and later the New Mexico State Parks. They lived in Santa Fe with their two sons after 1952.

During her years in Santa Fe, Nan retained various contacts with her anthropological colleagues, including Alden Hayes. She also remained active in the field of Indian affairs, as well as in local and national scholarly societies and environmental groups, and was a force in the New Mexico Democratic Party (*The New Mexican*, June 19, 1981). She compiled and published an extensive report on the condition of New Mexico's Indian population for the New Mexico State Planning Office (Smith 1966), and also took an advocacy role for the Ute in early hearings before the Indian Claims Commission (Jorgensen 1992).

In the early 1970s, Nan turned to her large body of unpublished data on the Ute and Western Shoshone people. She began reworking these materials, and finished her master's thesis on Northern Ute lifeways (Smith 1974). Although the death of her husband, her own ill health, and various other tasks often intervened, by 1977 she had managed to prepare the Ute tales and the Western Shoshone collection for publication (see Smith 1992 for the Ute Tales). She died at her home in Santa Fe, New Mexico, on June 18, 1981.

Nan Smith was highly regarded by a host of friends, both for her academic work and her many endearing personal qualities. Alden Hayes, who remained close to her after their 1939 field trip and visited her many times in Santa Fe, writes: "Nan was a handsome woman with so much animation—such vibrant charm—that it was hard to realize that such positive opinion, love and energy could come from that tiny figure of barely over a hundred pounds. She was an effective fighter for causes she thought just and worth the effort—and there were many of them. Her opponents knew they'd been in a fight, and though they were frequently exasperated, always respected her, and I think sometimes felt some pride at having been engaged by her" (Alden Hayes, personal communication, March 25, 1991).

The Western Shoshone, 1939

When Nan Smith and her companions visited the Western Shoshone people in 1939, they were living in various locations throughout eastern Nevada and western Utah. They had only one large reservation—Duck Valley—established in 1877 on roughly 290,000 acres near the Nevada-Idaho border, which Nan, Alden, and Doug visited. Of two smaller reservations for the Gosiute people, located at Deep Creek and Skull Valley, Utah, they visited only Deep Creek.[2] The other people they located were on reserved lands numbered more in the tens and twenties of acres rather than the thousands, and most were adjacent to towns such as Ely, Elko, and Battle Mountain. The people they found near Wells, Tonopah,

Manhattan, and Beatty were living where they could, but not on reserved lands. They learned of people who were in more remote locations, especially on ranches, but declined for the most part to spend the many hours' travel time it would have taken to locate these persons or families.

During the late 1930s and early 1940s, reservations were purchased and established for some of these scattered and landless families. Yomba, South Fork, Ruby Valley, and Duckwater reservations were all established and occupied between roughly 1937 and 1940 (Clemmer and Stewart 1986, 533; Rusco 1989). Nan indicated in her field diary that she was aware of these activities, but apparently she and her companions did not spend any time attempting to reach these locations.[3] Given that they had only minimal funds—enough to cover roughly one month's field time if they camped out—they concentrated on better-known locations. There is good evidence from Nan's field diary that she was also seeking specific persons who had previously given materials to fellow anthropologists Julian Steward, Jack Harris, and Omer Stewart, all of whom had been in the field in the mid-1930s. The timing of their fieldwork would have precluded any of them from working with persons at these newly established reservations.

Even in 1939, reservation confinement was a relatively new experience for a number of Western Shoshone people. Before the disruption of their lifeways by Euro-Americans, they had lived by hunting large and small game animals, gathering many types of plants, and fishing where possible (Steward 1936). They covered a large territory in order to accomplish their subsistence tasks, often in small, family-based groups. They followed specific seasonal rounds that took them from lowlands in the spring and parts of summer to highland and mountain locations in the fall. They came together in larger camps in the valleys in the late fall and winter, and there celebrated the events of the year in song, dance, and story. During this time, they lived on produce cached in previous seasons, supplemented by some hunting and fishing.

Although by 1939 non-Indians had been coming into Western Shoshone territory for more than a century—first to trap for furs, later to make traverses as emigrants, and ultimately to settle—for a good deal of that time the Western Shoshone people had been able to occupy many of their traditional lands and make at least a partial living by hunting and gathering. They had been involved in

Duck Valley, 1890. Northeastern Nevada Museum, Elko.

skirmishes with miners and ranchers in the 1860s, leading to the Treaty of Ruby Valley in 1863. In the treaty they agreed to allow passage of the railroad, telegraph, and roads, and limited exploration for mining, but they did not knowingly give up aboriginal title to most of their lands.[4] The Duck Valley Reservation was created at Owyhee in 1877 with the goal of consolidating all of the Western Shoshone people in one location, but many refused to go, preferring to remain close to their aboriginal holdings and free of the ultimate confinement of reservations (Crum 1983, 93). They had adjusted to the new and alien presence by learning to be wage laborers on ranches, in mines, and in towns, by trading and selling craft products, and by cutting and selling wood and a favorite food product, pine nuts. In 1939, with the exception of the federal reservations and colonies near some towns, Western Shoshone people were still living over a widely scattered area.[5] The people who had gone to Duck Valley or moved to lands near towns still retained ties to their larger lands, as well as various cultural patterns from pre-Contact times.

Nan Smith's field diary attests to the conditions for Indian people in the late 1930s. With the exception of Duck Valley, where she felt most people were reasonably well off, she found the conditions for many colony residents and landless people to be quite poor—in some cases appalling. Her observations can be supplemented with a small but growing body of literature about the same period in Nevada, which is of particular interest because it was the time when some major changes in federal Indian policy were implemented. This was the period of policy development spawned by the Indian Reorganization Act of 1934 and by various New Deal programs of the Roosevelt administration. Although Nan did not see that they had much effect except at Owyhee, she documented some of the conditions that these were designed to combat. Some of her observations are worth noting.

Duck Valley Reservation

Nan and her companions reached the Duck Valley Reservation on October 8, 1939. She described the valley as "good cattle country," irrigated by the Owyhee River, "and a good clear mountain stream it is." She was told by the agent, a Mr. Beck, that there were 950 Indian people on the reservation, of whom 95 were Northern Paiute and the rest Shoshone or mixed Shoshone-Paiute. She was told by the agent that most of the Indian people were ranchers, running 3,390 head of cattle. The cattle were owned by individuals, but were herded in the mountainous summer range communally, with the owners taking turns. In the winter, they were brought down to the valley and each person took responsibility for feeding his or her animals. Nan noted that there was considerable irrigated land in the valley for this purpose, with a good system of ditches carrying water to hay fields from the Owyhee River. She was told that the surplus grazing land (2,300 acres in 1939) was leased to non-Indians. She noted other recent improvements on the reservation, including a new hospital, a large gymnasium at the school, and new roads. Some people were in "good" housing, while others still occupied wall tents, albeit usually with interior stoves and wooden floors. She noted further that the school was run by the state, and that the teachers thus were not federal employees— a departure from other reservation situations.

Whitney McKinney (1983) and Steven Crum (1983) have written about Duck Valley during this period, providing details as to how and when some of the improvements noted by Nan came about. In 1937, after several decades of struggle, a large dam was completed on the Owyhee River for the purpose of irrigating Duck Valley lands (McKinney 1983, 128). Until that time the cattle enterprise was limited to the number of cows that could be fed through the winter on the limited hay raised. The dam impounded enough water to irrigate 13,000 acres of reservation land (McKinney 1983, 128), and the ditches Nan saw were part of this water project. By 1939, 5,650 acres were under cultivation, the hay crop nearly doubling from the production of 997 tons of alfalfa in 1935. The increase in cattle had been somewhat modest (roughly 300 head since 1935), but cattle would increase by another 1,500 by 1941 (Crum 1983, 79).

The Duck Valley Irrigation Project was a New Deal program, as were the several projects that provided the new hospital in 1936, the new gymnasium in 1938, reservation fencing for cattle, and improved roads (Crum 1983, 80–82). As also observed by Nan, though, not everyone was involved with cattle, and the number of people who made a good living in this way was still small. Only about 10 percent of the reservation's families were able to subsist by livestock alone, while most depended on wages in addition to cattle sales (Crum 1983, 80). By 1939, some Social Security benefits were available on the reservation, but many people worked at more than one job to make a living. In the mid to late 1930s, New Deal programs resulted in jobs for a few local people, and the reservation population had benefitted (Crum 1983). The new hospital had significantly improved the health of reservation residents, particularly those with diseases such as trachoma (Crum 1983, 82). The new gymnasium received mixed reviews; apparently by rule of the agent, "Indian events" could not be held in the new facility—only dances with non-Indian music, movies, basketball games, and Christmas plays (Nan and her crew attended a movie during their stay). In retrospect, this situation was indicative of the assimilation pattern being fostered at the time, a pattern that led to considerable erosion of certain cultural features within a few years (Crum 1983, 83).

The Colonies

Nan found people at the Elko, Battle Mountain, and Ely colonies less well off than at Owyhee, but placed these sites well above others where landless Indian people were living. She described the housing at Elko: "Most of the cabins are made of railroad ties laid up with a line of cement between them—not a bad effect, architecturally. The Indian colony here is much better housed than at Ely or Wells." Battle Mountain, too, had new housing, the result of rehabilitation monies made available to the Indian Office (Crum 1983, 89). Nan remarked, "I imagine that the government has built the houses. They are alike save for a few which are larger. They are nice little cottages, yellow with white trim. The interiors are clean and tidy, quite different from Wells and Ely . . . but the Indians complain that they are very cold houses in winter." But of Ely she observed, "On the side of a hill above the town are a group of one-room unpainted, tumble down shacks where the Indians live. Such poverty and such squalor!"[6] She noted that the economy of all of these locations was mixed—mostly wage labor for men and women, some profit from the sale of craft items and other commodities such as firewood and pine nuts—but most people were quite poor.

In the 1930s, few colonies benefitted from New Deal programs, although a few jobs had been made available. According to Crum (1983, 87), two women at Ely had been given jobs as domestics. Nan may have visited them.[7] A few other jobs were made available elsewhere. Craft sales (gloves, baskets) apparently earned little, as it was estimated by others that the people were working for only pennies a day (Steward 1936). With reference to the recent effort to relocate some people from Elko on the new South Fork Reservation, Nan noted that the move had apparently been successful, and the agent told her that they were "doing pretty well" at ranching and farming.[8] But he added, "The Wells and Ely Indians don't want to be resettled, they prefer the fringes of town, with WPA, drink and movies."[9]

The Landless People

Far worse conditions obtained for the people who were living on the outskirts of towns but not on reserved lands. For the most part, these Western Shoshone people were not entitled to any federal assistance, and they were involved in few New Deal programs. Although there was supposed to be an effort on the part of state and county managers of some of the programs to reach landless Indian people and provide them jobs and better housing, local efforts were usually bogged down in politics, and there was open discrimination against Indian people (Crum 1983, 88 f.). Nan described conditions at the Wells camp: "The Indians live just beyond the shanty town on the outskirts of the village in a collection of disreputable huts and broken down tents surrounded by garbage, tin can dumps, parts of old cars, and refuse of every description." One of the residents immediately complained to her that the people received poor to no services from the government, including the Public Health Service, that they were not being educated, etc. Of the conditions at Beatty, another place where Indian people did not have reserved lands, she says little; other sources, however, indicate that Indian people had small farms near a series of springs immediately north of the town, and although their housing conditions were poor, they were able to sustain themselves with produce supplemented by hunting and gathering (Hamby and Rusco 1987). At Tonopah and Manhattan, Nan and her companions tried to locate some specific Indian people, but were told they had gone into the hills to harvest pine nuts. Their one trek to a ranch (at Cloverdale) to locate someone recommended to them as a good narrator netted only disappointment, as this person, too, was away at the time. A general survey of landless Western Shoshones in 1935 conducted by the Indian Office concluded that as a class they were "a people without a country... the most maladjusted, helpless, and poorest of the entire picture" (Crum 1983, 91). This may be a bit overstated and melodramatic, but nonetheless, efforts in the late 1930s and early 1940s were under way to remedy this situation and buy reservation lands at South Fork, Yomba, Duckwater, and elsewhere for the landless Western Shoshone. Within a few years of Nan's visit, many more Western Shoshone people were on reserved lands and beginning to herd cattle and harvest hay and other crops. Conditions elsewhere would not improve until much later.[10]

Fieldwork in 1939

Nan Smith and her companions spent approximately a month in 1939 traveling through extreme western Utah and much of eastern Nevada. It was the fall of the year in fairly high country (base elevation ca. 5,000 feet) and although days were relatively warm, the nights were quite cool or cold. Their limited funds would cover the fieldwork (including paying narrators and translators) only if they camped out and cooked most of their meals over an open fire. Nan wrote in her field diary about the harshness and beauty of the high desert, about some of the people they met and with whom she and Alden worked, and occasionally about personal loneliness and her

Owyhee Reservation. Northeastern Nevada Museum, Elko.

other feelings. She expressed gratitude for what Alden Hayes and Doug Osborne did for her during their travels, for without them, she would not have been in the field. [11]

The Country and Camping
Western Utah and eastern Nevada in 1939 did not have miles of paved roads or improved campgrounds. Nan remarked, "The only good roads in Nevada are the east-west transcontinental highways [U.S. 40 and U.S. 50]. North-south there are only the dirt roads going down the valleys between the mountain ranges." They traveled north-south in Nan's coupe, covering nearly 600 miles (from the Idaho border to Las Vegas), so they spent a good deal of time on roads Nan regarded as "poor" and "impassable when wet." These phrases were repeated with emphasis to describe most roads to ranches, mining towns, and reservations. The trio usually just drove up into the hills at night to camp, spreading their bedrolls around a cook fire. Nan came to look with favor on gas stations, as she wrote, "I never really appreciated gas stations until this trip. When we are camped near a town we buy a couple of gallons of gas every morning and use the rest rooms. I have a good wash then. Gas stations with hot water are very rare and a great treat."

Temperatures and weather conditions occasionally drove them indoors, straining their budget. Near Ely they sought shelter from rain and snow for two nights in a small cave about 10 miles north of town. They finally gave up on the cave for one night and rented a cabin in Ely for $1.50. It had a rickety stove, but Nan was able to cook a stew and they dried out their clothes and bedrolls.

Food cost about $2.50 to $3 a week each, provided they cooked it themselves. Occasionally they treated themselves to a breakfast or dinner out, and less occasionally, a movie. When camping, they were usually in bed by dark (six to seven o'clock at that time of year), although Nan occasionally read or worked on her notes by candlelight—if her fingers weren't too cold to write. Alden was always up before sunrise to make a fire and boil water, so that all Nan had to do was "dump in the coffee." She did most of the cooking. She wrote, "Breakfast consists of cereal and coffee, bread and jam and the remains of last night's dinner. Lunch when we are travelling is usually bread and peanut butter, jam, cheese and apples or bananas. Dinner—beans and chile or potatoes and onions; cocoa, sometimes soup, and sour dough bread. Meat is a luxury. I make stew once a week and it does for two days."

Most of their camps were dry camps, the exception being the week they stayed at Owyhee and camped along the Owyhee River—true luxury. She wrote of the usual conditions: "I wash my face with a piece of cotton and witch hazel, and brush my teeth with a minimum amount of water. The boys feel that washing clothes is silly and they haven't the slightest objection to cooking cereal in a pot that had beans and chile in it the night before." Wood was another problem, and in some places it took them an hour or more to find enough to cook dinner. They usually moved camp each night because of that factor.

According to Nan, the Indian people with whom she worked were quite surprised by their way of life. She wrote: "The Indians are always amazed at our style of camping... they wouldn't think of sleeping and eating out the way we do. When they go up into the mountains for wood or pine nuts they always take a tent and a cook stove along. They can't understand how we get along as we do."

In spite of the hardships, Nan took time to observe the beauty of the country. While camped near Ely she wrote: "Woke up this morning about five and watched the dawn, one of the most beautiful sunrises I have ever seen. There were lots of clouds in the sky and they took on beautiful colors... I have never before seen a sunrise on a snow capped mountain and I was enchanted by the rosy glow and beautiful shadows." On another occasion she recorded: "The sky is absolutely cloudless, a brilliant blue and the air so clear you can see tremendous distances." She was impressed by the night-time sky, with stars "more brilliant than I have seen them any-where else," and regretted she did not know more about constella-tions when questioning the narrators.

Working with the People

Generally, most of the Western Shoshone people Nan was able to find were willing to work with her and Alden. Occasionally, people refused, or she had to talk long and hard to convince them of the value of her research. A few persons she contacted had forgotten most of the old stories, and several people she had heard about from Julian Steward, Jack Harris, or Omer Stewart had died in the interim between their work and hers. Nan worked with several men as well as with women, and notes that only at Owyhee would she have to work exclusively with women, while Alden worked with the men. She was careful about her field attire, as she re-marked, "Indians don't like gals in pants." She wore a denim suit, long boy's stockings to keep her legs warm, a bandanna, and a tweed overcoat. On one occasion she wrote that in this attire, she was quite a sight, and "felt like Gladys Reichard indeed."[12]

Nan did not attempt to write down any of the stories she heard in the Shoshone language, although she occasionally transcribed a Shoshone term or phrase. Because of this, she probably missed some content as well as considerable style (see Beverly Crum's comments on language in the Afterword).[13] A number of the narra-tors gave the stories in Shoshone while an interpreter (apparently simultaneously) rendered them into English. She paid both narrator and interpreter at the rate of $.50 an hour, but occasionally a per-son refused pay, apparently not defining the task as work. On a few occasions, she worked with the narrator directly in English, some-times to her distress. She noted that "Indian English, even the best, is none too good."[14] As to the sexual and scatological content of many of the tales, she remarked that most of the time she did not feel that narrators or interpreters were cleaning them up for her benefit. Some of the narrators and interpreters were a little embar-rassed by the content, remarking that "they don't sound dirty in In-dian, but they sound pretty dirty in English." Nan added, "And they sure do. I don't know that I'll ever get them in shape to publish."

Nan occasionally commented in her field diary on the storytelling context and how she went about requesting tales. In Ely, she apparently read some of her Ute tales to Mary Stanton to get her started. She then remarked, "Finally we got under way—Old Mary shouting, two of the girls interpreting and the rest of the family interrupting whenever old Mary forgot some detail. They were all quite anxious to make sure that I got everything straight. Got a good long story and lots of ethnographic information along with it. More and more people kept coming in until finally there were sixteen people in that one room and the confusion was incredible. When the story was finished Mary said she was so confused she could not think and I quite understood for I was in the same state myself." Most other storytelling sessions were less taxing, although she sometimes complained of being very tired at the end of a particularly good session. A modern alternative field procedure is to use portable tape recorders, letting the narrator finish his/her story in the native language, and then carefully reviewing it later with an interpreter. This better preserves both content and style and minimizes the confusion Nan describes.

Brief biographical sketches or notes on the narrators appear in Nan's field diary, although she did not rank them all in terms of storytelling ability or style. An examination of the tales transcribed from each person gives a feel both for the repertoire of some individuals and their abilities. She was particularly admiring of Anna Premo of Owyhee, for the number of tales she could recall, as well as their content. She also spoke very highly of Tom Premo as an interpreter. Of one session that Alden recorded while she listened, she remarked that the narrator, Herbert Holly, was a "very dramatic story teller and Tom an excellent interpreter. Everyone enjoyed themselves hugely."

The repertoire of Commodore (from Deep Creek) was very extensive, and Nan remarked on his ability to tire her out. On one occasion she wrote steadily from 9:30 A.M. until 1:00 P.M. Lily Pete, who acted as interpreter for Commodore, was regarded by Nan as excellent, "better than I ever had in Utah" [among the Ute]. Mary Stanton of Ely was apparently a good storyteller, in spite of the confusion in her household and her occasional moodiness. Nan reported that she was also a shaman, and wrote down considerable material about her life. Bill Dock of Beatty impressed Nan with his repertoire, although she had a good deal of trouble following his English, which he felt was excellent and did not require an interpreter.

Certainly the collections from these individuals are the largest, although occasionally a lengthy tale was recorded from another narrator (see Versions under *The Tales*, below).

Overall, Nan was most favorably impressed by the Western Shoshone people she met. In spite of the poverty under which some were living, she found nearly all of the people honest, hard working, and enjoyable during their work sessions and visiting afterward. She felt that the materials she gathered were made the more valuable because of this, for as a woman from Ely remarked, "You must not tell them [stories] if you can't tell them straight." Early in the trip she already felt that the field situation was quite different from what she had encountered among the Ute. She wrote, "Lord how different these people are from the Utes. Information fairly pours forth from them. It would be no job at all to get a good ethnography done here." The rest of Nevada and Nevadans also received praise: "It is difficult to describe the friendly attitude of these Nevadans. There are so few people in the whole state but by gosh they *all* are friendly." Good fieldwork among interesting people, good companions, and not too many "adventures" provided Nan great pleasure.

The Tales

The collection of tales supplements a rather meager published literature on Western Shoshone oral tradition. The first documented materials from Western Shoshone people were from John Wesley Powell, who interviewed a few Gosiute and Nevada Shoshone men in Salt Lake City in 1873 as part of his larger study of the conditions of Great Basin Indian people (Fowler and Fowler 1971). Working through an interpreter, Powell recorded six tales, at least two of which were lengthy.

Powell's efforts were followed by those of Julian Steward in the 1930s (Steward 1943). Steward recorded 36 stories, from Panamint country in California on the south to Owyhee, Nevada, on the north. He made his unpublished materials available to Nan in 1938 for her dissertation, and his list of consultants and their locations helped set the itinerary for her 1939 field trip. In the 1940s, Carling Malouf and Elmer Smith gathered a few partial tales from a single Gosiute narrator and prepared a brief analysis of some of their themes (Malouf and Smith 1942). Wick Miller (1972), the only person to publish Gosiute tales in the Shoshone language, gathered his materials from the mid-1960s to early 1970s, and continues to collect materials today.

The majority of Western Shoshone tales take place in "The Time When Animals Were People"—the mythic past, when animals had the power of speech and, through their adventures, set many human customs. Nan's dissertation, along with the work of her fellow ethnographers, has tied many of the incidents, motifs, and elements reported in these tales to others in the Great Basin. Some aspects are more widespread, making tales told by Great Basin peoples part of a larger body of oral literature with even broader ties (Hultkrantz 1986; Liljeblad 1986).

Although Nan did not provide an analysis of this collection, she undoubtedly felt that it fit well with the other Basin materials she had used for her dissertation. In that study, she compiled distribution tables of the principal themes, and it is quite clear that she was able to fill in missing themes for the Western Shoshone based on these new data. The only statement in her field diary about receiving unfamiliar materials was at Beatty, in southern Nevada, where the narrators might well have been relating some tales with California influences. Even though she had heard or received a tale from other narrators, she was always careful to seek out more local versions, so that she could study variation—both geographic and among the narrators.

Great Basin Tales

Common general tale types identified by Nan as characteristic of Great Basin mythology include (1) creation and origin tales, (2) etiological tales, (3) trickster tales, (4) cannibal tales, (5) test, contest, and conquest tales (involving culture heros), (6) novelistic tales, and (7) miscellaneous tales (Cooke 1939, 15 ff.). Of these, by far the most common are the trickster tales, and this feature in and of itself is a major characteristic that sets Basin traditions apart from those of surrounding areas. Trickster tales, usually with Coyote as the main character, are well represented in this Western Shoshone collection: "Coyote Marries His Daughter," "Coyote Learns to Fly," "Coyote Plays the Hand Game," "Coyote Races Frog," etc. A subclass of these, the so-called Bungling Host tales, is also characteristic and includes in this collection "Coyote

Avenges Wolf's Death," "Porcupine Tricks Coyote," "Cannibal Bird," and "Theft of Pine Nuts." Although Coyote is the most common actor, he is by no means the only trickster, nor is he portrayed consistently as one. He may also be an innovator, establishing cultural conditions for humankind; and he may be the dupe of other actors—although one feels that perhaps he deserved his fate in the end.

Nan characterized Basin mythology as less interested in matters of origins, culture heros, and novelistic tales, although examples of all of these are found in collections from each tribe, including the Western Shoshone. Most of the concern with origins is general: Great Basin narrators will sometimes localize a tale to include their specific tribe, but the tale also accounts for the origin and dispersal of other people (see, for example, Jim Tybo's "Origin Tale"). Unlike the Southwest, where stories are more specific about the adventures of a single tribe in pre-existent and often layered worlds, Basin concerns with origins are more general and rarely set out a specific charter for a group or tribe.

Culture heros, likewise, are uncommon in Basin folklore, although Coyote is sometimes portrayed as such, particularly when something he suggests ultimately benefits humankind. For example, in Commodore's tale "Controversy over Death," Coyote favors the finality of death, as opposed to his brother Wolf's idea of continued life for all. The narrator thus suggests, "If it were not for Coyote, there would be too many people now." Another culture hero is Cottontail ("Cottontail Shoots the Sun"). If it were not for Cottontail, the sun would shine too hot and burn everything as it used to do. Interestingly, however, culture heros in Basin tales often go back and forth between a series of what might be considered positive and negative actions for themselves and later humans. Sometimes their deeds are mischievous, sometimes downright deceptive. They are not distinctly positive personalities. They are perhaps much more like real human beings—both good and bad.

Novelistic tales—ones involving a long and distinct series of incidents leading to an endpoint—are uncommon, but a few examples are included in the collection. Among them are "Coyote Avenges Wolf's Death," "Owl's Widow," and "The Theft of Pine Nuts." These are not made up of a series of isolated incidents strung together, but form coherent units in and of themselves. Some narrators may leave out or add a specific incident, but a story line definitely develops. Smith (Cooke 1939, 194) notes that in contrast, short tales formed around a single incident, or at most a couple of them, are more typical. Although it may appear in this collection that some narrators are better than others based on the length of the tales they tell, this may not be a valid criterion given Smith's observations (contrast Commodore and Arthur Johnson, for example). Other factors, such as narrator style, may come into play. Only in a few instances did Smith have any hint that certain tales or incidents were told in some type of cycle or cyclical order (see, for example, "Coyote and His White Relatives," by Commodore, and "Eye Juggler," by Johnny Dick).

Cannibal tales in the Basin, including the several represented in this Western Shoshone collection, tend not to focus on human cannibals, but rather on nonhuman forms that prey on human beings. This feature also sets the tales of the Great Basin apart from ones told in neighboring areas (the Northwest Coast, for example). The Cannibal Bird (see the version by Commodore) is a good example—he is a creature that captures human beings to save for later meals but is tricked by a young boy. The several Cannibal Giant ("Tso'apittse") tales are in the same category.

Etiological tales, including "just so" stories, have come out of the region, but are more prevalent in surrounding areas, according to Smith (Cooke 1939, 32 f.). Tales well represented and included in this collection are "How Fire Started," "The Theft of Pine Nuts," "Council on the Seasons," and "Owl Kills Birds by Naming Them." Subthemes in several other tales account for other minor features of the present world, such as how several mountains were made from one ("Owl's Widow," by Commodore), why Coyote has little eyes ("Coyote and Bear," by Commodore), the origin of a certain rock formation ("Tso'apittse," by Herbert Holly), and why some plants are bitter ("The Race to Koso Springs," by Tom Steward).

A final feature that tends to unify Great Basin tales and set them apart from those in surrounding areas is a consistent attempt at humor, with obscenity and a blunt manner of speaking being the common humorous devices. Smith observed that many Great Basin tales are told for their entertainment value. People derive an enormous amount of pleasure from the stories of a good narrator. Although there is little doubt that the tales instruct in proper behavior, this is often accomplished by illustrating the consequences of its antithesis—Coyote ends up eating his own penis after engaging in incest with his daughters ("Coyote Eats His Own Penis"). Coyote's misadventures become exceedingly funny—if not painful—under such circumstances. But as Smith (Cooke 1939, 169) reminds us, obscenity is culturally defined, and many things that are labeled obscene in one culture will be inoffensive in another.

Style

There is little doubt that individual Great Basin narrators differ in their ability to tell stories and tell them in a manner that is consistently pleasing to their listeners. Sometimes a narrator uses special language, clever phraseology, or unusual words. They may add extra incidents or adventures to prolong the action. Sometimes they involve the audience in participation, so that the tales become performances. These and other features can reflect individual skills, but they also reflect cultural norms as to what constitutes a good telling. Smith (Cooke 1939) considered several features of Great Basin folklore that she felt were stylistic, although she was probably hampered in her determinations by not having the tales in the native language.

Smith concluded that in the Basin, whether a narrator chose to add more or less specific cultural detail (ethnographic information) to stories appeared to be a matter of style (Cooke 1939, 146 f.). She notes that a good deal of cultural knowledge is often assumed between narrator and listener, so that providing extensive background may not be necessary. Detail that forms part of the plot is essential, as in Mary Stanton's tale about setting menstrual customs ("Coyote Learns to Fly"). But as narrator, Mrs. Stanton also tells nonessential details, such as what seed crops Wolf planted and what type of food the young girl wanted to eat. Anna Premo apparently liked to add detail to enliven her stories (see "Porcupine Tricks Coyote"). On the whole, Smith found that stylistically Basin stories were not characterized by a good deal of cultural detail (Cooke 1939, 146).

Heavy localization—establishing a setting in terms of specific places or placenames—is uncharacteristic; only occasionally does a narrator mention the name of a local mountain, river, or other feature. A narrator who appeared to favor this device was Mary Stanton (see "Cannibal Bluebirds").

The use of song recitatives appears to have been at least in part up to the narrator, although certainly within the Great Basin, tribes and groups differ in their use of these. Sapir (1910) was the first to define this feature for the region—short, highly patterned songs interspersed throughout a tale. He noted that characters in Southern Paiute tales often sang characteristic songs and spoke in characteristic voices, a feature also seen in certain areas of the Southwest (especially among the Yuman-speaking groups). Nan had not heard these tale songs among the Northern Ute, but one of her colleagues at Yale, Willard Park, had noted that they occurred in some Northern Paiute tales, and Julian Steward had noted them among both the Owens Valley Paiute and the Western Shoshone. Nan heard them fairly frequently from her Western Shoshone narrators, although she did not attempt in most cases to transcribe the songs or their music (see "Coyote Plays the Hand Game," by Commodore, "Coyote and Mouse," by Arthur Johnson, "Coyote Marries His Daughters," by Anna Premo, and "Coyote Learns to Fly," by Mary Stanton). Smith also found that Basin folklore did not use patterned numbers to any appreciable degree (for example, three incidents and then a final one) nor magical devices (for example, having a body part advise the main character, although Coyote does sometimes consult his tail), or several other features.

Versions of Tales

Nan was careful to record different versions of the same tale from narrators she visited across the whole of Western Shoshone territory. In fact, she tried to record each narrator's entire repertoire, which often meant that she obtained several versions of the same story. Comparison of versions from different narrators can contribute to the study of individual narrator style, but it also can reveal the possible origin and development of a particular story. In the 1930s and 1940s, and persisting to a certain extent to the present, folklore studies were much concerned with the distribution of tale types and motifs and the question of origins (Liljeblad 1986). The data in Nan's dissertation, as well as her collection of tales from the Ute (Smith 1992) and this Western Shoshone collection, all contribute to those ends.

Some of the tales Nan collected from different narrators include "Coyote Marries His Daughters," "Cottontail Shoots the Sun," "Theft of Pine Nuts," "Cannibal Giant," "Coyote Avenges Wolf's Death," and "Owl's Widow." In terms of overall content, some of the versions are remarkably similar—a testimony to the strength and power of oral tradition to those who might think that only written traditions can survive through time. Some differ in ways that could easily be seen as a matter of narrator style. Others display differences in cultural-historical reconstructions of a particular story or its motifs. Only much more lengthy analyses of these data would determine which aspects best fit which versions.

Another aspect of comparative versions is made available to Great Basin scholars in the publication of this collection: the comparison of versions through time. Three of the tales collected by John Wesley Powell in 1873—"Owl's Widow," "Cannibal Bird," and a short version of "Cottontail Shoots the Sun,"—are among the tales also recorded by Smith. Nearly seventy years intervened between these two collections, yet the similarities are obvious. Powell visited the Western Shoshone people at a time when many people were still living who remembered life before the white man; Smith's visit came after a time of major disruptions, but at a point when some people still retained a good deal of their cultural oral traditions. A comparison of versions collected by both illustrates this point.

Strength and persistence of tradition continue today, as more tales are recorded. Although there are few people living today who can tell the stories in their native language (but see Beverly Crum's Afterword), some younger people are helping to perpetuate the traditions by telling the stories in English. They, too, add considerable style, humor, and grace to their presentations. Although Western Shoshone storytelling has changed considerably in the more than fifty years since Nan Smith was in the field, it does still exist and, one hopes, will continue to undergo a revitalization. This collection may contribute to that revitalization.

—CATHERINE S. FOWLER

Notes

1. Anne Smith's field diary is presently in the possession of the University of Utah Press. It will eventually be deposited in the Special Collections of the University Library.

2. Nan and her companions apparently entered Deep Creek Reservation from the Utah side and worked with people in both Utah and Nevada. They may have visited Skull Valley before going to Deep Creek, but the

field diary does not record such a visit; however, the diary does not seem to start at the very beginning of the field trip.

3. Yomba and South Fork reservations were occupied by the time Nan and her companions were in the field, although people were just beginning to settle there, especially at Yomba. Families were in the vicinity of Duckwater as well, but full settlement had not taken place.

4. For a more detailed account of the Treaty of Ruby Valley see Rusco 1989. The Western Shoshone National Council, an overarching political structure made up of constituent member groups from various reservations and nonreservation communities, has been fighting for the return of public lands under this treaty for nearly twenty years.

5. The term *colony* is more common usage in Nevada than elsewhere in the Great Basin. Colonies are federally recognized groups, but usually with a land base of only 20 to 30 acres. They are located near Nevada towns and cities.

6. It is possible that Nan is speaking here not of Ely Colony, but of housing built by a few individuals on nonreserved lands. Not all Indian people elected to move to colonies once they were established in local areas.

7. The women Nan visited in Ely were consistently washing a considerable quantity of clothes, thus suggesting that they were working for someone. The WPA domestic jobs were apparently as laundresses (Crum 1983).

8. The agent Nan spoke with at Owyhee, Mr. Beck, had charge of all Indian people in northeastern Nevada and adjacent Utah, including Gosiute people at Deep Creek and at Skull Valley. It is doubtful that some people saw him or any services with any frequency.

9. Nan noted that people at Ely were having considerable difficulty with bootleggers and that alcohol was causing fights at night. She also indicated that Indian people there were going to the movies. It is doubtful that WPA employment was much of an economic factor, as so few people were involved (Crum 1983).

10. Wells Colony did not become federally recognized until 1977 (Clemmer and Stewart 1986).

11. Throughout her diary, Nan stresses the importance of the assistance given her by Alden Hayes and Doug Osborne. Although they were junior to her by about fifteen years (she calls them "the boys"), they all got along very well and enjoyed each other's company.

12. The comment about Gladys Reichard undoubtedly refers to Reichard's "conservative" field apparel. Reichard worked among the Navajo people where, again, a woman would not have been seen in pants in the 1930s or until many years later.

13. Native languages, with their own narrative and stylistic features, are much preferred for recording tales. Like many of her contemporaries, Nan apparently did not have a tape recorder.

14. Nan made some interesting observations on the Indian English she heard: " 'He' and 'him' are the only pronouns they know and are used to re-

fer indiscriminately to singular and plural, masculine, feminine and neuter. 'Pretty' is the one adjective and is used continually. 'Pretty soon he go,' 'pretty soon he said,' 'pretty long road,' 'pretty bad man,' etc." These observations are in line with conflicts in certain grammatical features in the two languages; the phenomenon remains little studied.

References Cited

Clemmer, Richard O., and Omer C. Stewart. 1986. "Treaties, Reservations, and Claims." In *Handbook of North American Indians*. Vol. 11, *Great Basin*, edited by Warren L. d'Azevedo, 525–57. Washington: Smithsonian Institution.

Cooke, Anne M. M. 1937. "The Material Culture of the Northern Ute." Unpublished master's thesis, Yale University, New Haven.

–––. 1939. "An Analysis of Basin Mythology." 2 vols. Unpublished Ph.D. dissertation, Yale University, New Haven.

Crum, Steven J. 1983. "The Western Shoshone of Nevada and the Indian New Deal." Unpublished Ph.D. dissertation, University of Utah, Salt Lake City.

Fowler, Don D., and Catherine S. Fowler, eds. 1971. "Anthropology of the Numa: John Wesley Powell's Manuscripts on the Numic Peoples of Western North America, 1868–1880." *Smithsonian Contributions to Anthropology* 14. Washington.

Hamby, Maribeth, and Mary Rusco. 1987. "Native Americans and Yucca Mountain: Socioeconomic Perspectives." Submitted to the Nevada Nuclear Waste Projects Office by Cultural Resources Consultants, Ltd., Reno.

Hultkrantz, Ake. 1986. "Mythology and Religious Concepts." In *Handbook of North American Indians*. Vol. 11, *Great Basin*, edited by Warren L. d'Azevedo, 630–40. Washington: Smithsonian Institution.

Jorgensen, Joseph G. 1992. Foreword, xi–xxviii. In *Ute Tales*, by Anne M. C. Smith. Salt Lake City: University of Utah Press.

Liljeblad, Sven. 1986. "Oral Tradition: Content and Style in Verbal Arts." In *Handbook of North American Indians*. Vol. 11, *Great Basin*, edited by Warren L. d'Azevedo, 641–59. Washington: Smithsonian Institution.

McKinney, Whitney. 1983. *A History of the Shoshone-Paiutes of the Duck Valley Indian Reservation*. Salt Lake City: Institute of the American West and Howe Brothers.

Malouf, Carling, and Elmer Smith. 1942. "Some Gosiute Mythological Characters and Concepts." *Utah Humanities Review* 1(4): 369–77.

Miller, Wick R. 1972. "Newe Natekwinappeh: Shoshoni Stories and Dictionary." *University of Utah Anthropological Papers* 94. Salt Lake City.

Rusco, Elmer. 1989. "Western Shoshone Land Claims and the Western Shoshone National Council." Prepared for the Nevada Nuclear Waste Projects Offices by Cultural Resources Consultants, Reno.

Sapir, Edward. 1910. "Song Recitative in Paiute Mythology." *Journal of American Folk-Lore*, 23(90): 455–72.

——. 1930-31. "The Southern Paiute Language." *Proceedings of the American Academy of Arts and Sciences* 65(1–3). Boston.

Smith, Anne M. 1966. *New Mexico Indians: Economic, Educational and Social Problems*. Santa Fe: Museum of New Mexico.

——. 1974. "Ethnography of the Northern Ute." *Museum of New Mexico Papers in Anthropology* 17. Santa Fe.

——. 1992. *Ute Tales*. Salt Lake City: University of Utah Press.

Spier, Leslie. 1928. "Havasupai Ethnography." *Anthropological Papers of the American Museum of Natural History* 29(3): 81–392. New York.

Steward, Julian H. 1936. "Shoshonean Tribes: Utah, Idaho, Nevada, Eastern California. A Report to the Commissioner of Indian Affairs." Unpublished manuscript, Special Collections Department, Getchell Library, University of Nevada, Reno.

——. 1938. "Basin-Plateau Aboriginal Sociopolitical Groups." *Bureau of American Ethnology Bulletin* 120. Washington.

——. 1943. "Western Shoshone Myths." *Anthropological Papers* 31. *Bureau of American Ethnology Bulletin* 136:249–99. Washington.

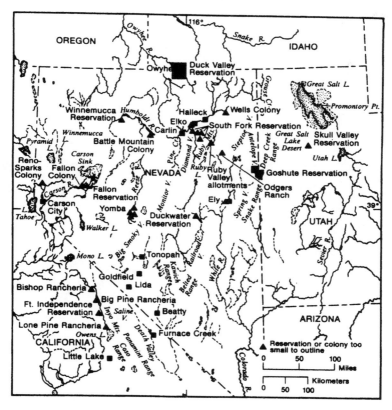

Lands of the Western Shoshone and Gosiute Peoples, Twentieth Century.
Smithsonian Institution Press.

Gosiute Tales

Deep Creek, Utah
1939

Controversy Over Death

A long time ago people never used to die. Coyote's brother, Wolf, said, "When people die they will get up after two days." Coyote didn't like that. Coyote said, "When we die, we should die forever." Wolf didn't like that. Coyote kept on asking his brother why the dead should get up. He didn't like that, he wanted them to die forever. After that Wolf wished that Coyote's son would die. Coyote had Magpie for his son. After Coyote's son died, Coyote went to his brother's place and said to him, "Raise my son to life after two days." Wolf didn't answer for a long time. Then he said, "You, Coyote, said that people should die forever." Wolf told him to burn all his clothing, and cut off his hair and burn it. Wolf told him that dying forever was what Coyote wanted in the first place. If it weren't for Coyote there would be too many people now.

After Coyote burned his clothing he lay down flat on the ground and looked up at the sky. Soon he saw lots of black birds up there. They were crows. They belonged to his big brother, Wolf. Coyote wished that one of them would fall down. Coyote heard them cawing. He saw one coming down. It sat down on Coyote's feet. It hopped up to his face. Coyote caught it. He tore the crow to pieces and scattered the pieces on the ground because he was angry at Wolf. Coyote had a funeral service for his son. He sang all night.

—COMMODORE
(Lily Pete, translator)

Controversy Over Conditions of Life

Coyote and Wolf argued. Wolf said that women should have babies in their arms. Just shake their hand and the baby would come and the baby would stand up when the woman shook her arm. Coyote didn't like that. He said the woman should have the baby inside her and should suffer. Wolf said the mothers should not have to nurse babies, they should be well grown when they were born. Coyote wanted women to nurse babies.

Wolf wanted everything ready for people to eat. There should be no hard times for people. Coyote didn't like this. He wanted the people to work.

Wolf said there would be no winters, no snow. There would always be berries and seeds for people to eat. Everything would be plentiful. Coyote objected to this. He wanted winters and snow. Coyote told Wolf that his father told him that.

—Commodore
(Lily Pete, translator)

[When asked who was Coyote's father, Commodore replied, "Nobody knows his father."]

How Fire Started

There were no matches in those days to start fire with. Crow smelled smoke somewhere to the east. They were cold. When they smelled smoke the birds flew up toward the sky to see. Coyote was the doctor. Coyote made them fly up to see where the fire was. Chickadee flew up and got tired and fell down to the ground. Every time a bird tried it and fainted and fell, Coyote put water on its head. All the birds tried it. Woodpecker and Blue Jay tried it. Hummingbird was the last one to go up. He slept on a tree way up in heaven. He saw fire to the east. They were cold. They went after the fire when Hummingbird came down and said he had seen it in the east. They all went after the fire, all of them went. Bald Eagle carried Snake on his back. All the birds went. They were all humans at that time. They ran all the way. They went up to the mountain peak and stayed there all night and the next day they started on again. They stopped at another mountain peak the next

night. They started again the next day. They went over ten mountains to get to the fire. They rested on every mountain peak. They
kept on running, they did not walk. They got there.

They found people there dancing around the fire. There were
lots of people there. The chief told them to rest and then to dance
later. After a while they all started dancing. There were several old
ladies who were talking about Coyote. They said he was after the
fire. Coyote had long hair, down to his knees. Coyote was the
leader of the visitors. Coyote danced near the fire and the old
women knew he wanted to steal the fire. Coyote carried the fire off
in his long hair while they were dancing. He carried it away and he
looked like a person carrying a lantern at night. The other people
knew which way he went by the light. They chased him. The other
people killed Coyote when they caught up with him. They killed the
rest and they wished that Coyote would get stuck in the snow.
There was lots of snow and Coyote crawled into a cave. He killed
Rabbit and roasted him. Rabbit was a human, too. He roasted Rabbit. He also killed Rat; he went to Rat's home in the cave and killed
him. He slept in the cave that night-and in the morning when he got
up, there was lots of snow. He turned into a seed. He wished himself to be in Rat's nest. The wind blew him on the snow and blew
him over the snow. He got stuck. The wind blew him very far and
then blew him to dry ground where there was no snow and then he
went home from there.

He remembered his friends; they were all dead. When he got
home all his friends were there. They had come back to life and
then gone home. They started to make a fire. That happened a long
time ago.

—COMMODORE
(Lily Pete, translator)

Coyote Marries His Daughters (1)

Coyote had a wife and five children, four daughters and one son.
His mother-in-law also lived there. Coyote told them they were going to have a dance, just Coyote and his family. They danced the
Circle Dance. They danced all night. Along toward morning the
wind was blowing hard and their skirts blew up and Coyote looked
under them.

In the morning he took his mother-in-law out to get willows to make a basket. Coyote fooled his mother-in-law and told her there were enemies out that way that might kill her, so he went along to protect her. They were on their way. The old woman saw a rabbit and called to Coyote to come kill it. He told the old lady not to call him Mister White-Face-Paint-Clay. He told the old woman to stand in front of him. The rabbit was under a bush and Coyote said that bush killed his father. He made the old woman stand in front of him and then he wanted to have intercourse with her. The old woman started scolding him and Coyote said he didn't know what he was doing. But Coyote got his own way.

They got to the willows. The old woman made the fire and Coyote was going to roast the rabbit. They slept there that night. They had roast rabbit for supper. The old woman didn't like the smell of the rabbit but Coyote let her eat it. Coyote told the old woman to save all the bones. He told her to save the hip bones. He tied them all together and tied them on his feet. They slept in a cave that night. Coyote told the old woman all kinds of ghost stories when they went to bed. He wanted to scare her. He tied the rabbit bones on his legs and rattled them and scared the old woman with them. The old woman got so scared she slept with him. Coyote told her that the cave had many ghosts in it. It was Coyote's father's cave. The old woman slept with him. He had intercourse with her and he killed the old woman.

Coyote made a wound in his belly. He stuck an arrow in it and put the rabbit guts around the arrow. On his way home he made a fire. His daughters knew there was something wrong when they saw the fire he made out on the plains. The oldest daughter went after him. She tried to carry him but he kept trying to have intercourse with her. The daughter got mad and threw him down. He was pretending he had been wounded. Then the oldest girl went home and told the next oldest girl to go get him. So she went away to carry her father and he did the same thing to her. She ran away from him and went back home and told the next oldest daughter to go get him. He did the same thing to this girl. Then she got mad and sent the youngest girl out to get Coyote. He did the same thing to the youngest daughter. She ran away from him and Coyote said, "Ouch, my wound hurts." He said that his daughters did not treat him well. They should carry him even if he did try his tricks on them.

The youngest daughter went home and told her mother that Coyote was sex crazy. She sent her mother, Coyote's wife, to get him. The mother got mad and said they wouldn't be here in this world if Coyote hadn't done things like that. When his wife got to Coyote, he told her about her mother, saying that the enemy had killed the old woman. He said he had no mother, no father, no grandparents. So his wife carried him and he had intercourse with her while she was carrying him. Coyote told his wife to carry him around the house twice so his daughters could see him. He told his wife to put him down on the east side of their camp. She put him there. She kept going to look at him to see if he were dead every once in a while. When he was about to die, he told her to give his daughters to a certain man to marry—a man who would come from the west. He told his wife to give the two older daughters to this man who would come with a pack on his back, accompanied by a dog. He told her to burn his house when he died and then to go away.

So it happened. They went away (after Coyote's death) and were camped in the mountains. After his family had gone, Coyote crawled out and went and got the old woman's meat. Then he went off with a pack on his back and his dog. He pretended to be the man his daughters were to marry. When he came to his family's camp, they boiled the meat. The two oldest girls made a house not far off from their mother and slept there that night with Coyote. He did not let them have a good look at him. He told them if they had a good look at him they wouldn't have any noses. Coyote's son took a good look at him and thought that this man looked like his father. When night came the mother told her son to go out with his new brother-in-law when he went to urinate. The little boy knew by the way the man acted that his brother-in-law was really his father.

All night long Coyote made a lot of noise while he was having intercourse with the girls. He tied the girls' legs together. His tail thumped. It sounded like someone pounding something. When morning came the old woman told her little boy to go have breakfast with his sisters. She thought the noise was that of pounding meat. So the little boy went over and saw the old Coyote's tail thumping away. The boy knew it was his father. That day the boy and his new brother-in-law went hunting rats together. The boy saw Coyote's teeth and knew it was his father. When he saw the teeth he ran home. The boy told his sisters that they had their own father for a husband. The mother said to look under their husband's pillow for something that he used on the girls (extra penis). His daughters found it under his pillow and knew it was their father. The old woman threw her daughters in the ashes and squeezed them for they were already pregnant. Both of them were pregnant. The old woman wondered what they should do. They could go up to the sky and be turned into stars. So they did. They are the Pleiades.

Coyote came home and looked for his family. They laughed at him from where they were up in the sky. They had roasted that extra penis he had hidden under his pillow—roasted it in the fire. When Coyote came home he looked all over trying to find their tracks. When he came near the house he heard something sizzling in the fire. He took it out of the fire and put it away. Then he came back again and ate it. It was his penis. He returned to the house and the head dropped off the end of the penis so he knew what it was. His family in the sky all laughed at him. Then he told them to come back to life again. He told them to come down and get him. He tried to climb on the cedar trees and get up to them but he couldn't. They told him everyone would call him bad nasty names. He said, "Don't talk to me like that. Come down and get me." They told him to be a coyote, a worthless creature who howls around in the mountains. He answered and called them Many Stars.

Then he went on his way. He howled as they had told him to do. He had his rabbit-fur blanket with him. His daughters and wife made fun of him. He was a human at that time.

—COMMODORE
(Lily Pete, translator)

Coyote and Sage Hen's Children

Coyote kept going on his way. He heard a voice calling him bad names. He looked all over to find the person who was calling him bad names. He couldn't find him. When Coyote went back again the voice said the same thing to him and he looked again but he couldn't find him. He looked a third time and then he found him. It was a little red wood tick. Coyote quarreled with him and then he went on his way. Wood Tick had called him, "He who had intercourse with his own daughters." Then Coyote came back the fourth time and trampled Wood Tick to death. After he killed him Coyote went on his way. He looked back and saw a big red thing—Wood Tick, who had grown big after Coyote killed him. Coyote kept on running.

While he was running he heard a voice. He found some little children. He asked them whose children they were. They didn't answer. The youngest boy answered and said that they were Sage Hen's children. Then Coyote urinated on the children and went on his way. The mother hen came back and asked them what had happened. She did not like the way they smelled. They didn't answer their mother. The youngest one told the mother what Coyote had done. She asked them which way Coyote went and they told her which way he had gone.

Sage Hen flew after Coyote. She got ahead of him and sat down by the lake. There was a trail by the water, which Coyote was following. When Coyote got near the water, Sage Hen flew up and scared him and he fell into the water. His rabbit blanket got wet. After a long time Coyote got out of the water. Coyote got mad and called Sage Hen names and spoke of her gray neck. When he got out of the water he wrung out his rabbit-fur blanket. He lay down by the lake and put his blanket on the sagebrush to dry, then he went to sleep. He had a lot of lice, Coyote did.

He had a belt with lots of knots in it. He remembered what his father had told him a long time ago when he was a little boy, about how to make cattails out of his belt. He put his belt in the water and went to sleep again. When he woke up he heard a bird in the cattails. When he woke up he stretched his leg out and felt the cattails with his feet. He got up and pulled out one cattail. He ate some. It had little things like berries at the roots. They were close together when Coyote pulled it up but he stretched it and put it back in the water again. He made a home there. He called his house "Cattail House." He ate cattails every day. He pounded them and roasted them in the ashes. After they were cooked he made a rope out of the cattails. He had a piece of stick to dig out the roots with. (All this happened out here at Fish Springs.) Coyote dried the cattails by the fire. After they dried up he pounded them. He made a pot out of clay in which to boil the cattails. He boiled cattails for supper that night. When he was ready to eat, a lot of warriors came. Coyote got scared and hid in the cattails. He took his wooden spoon with him. After a long time he tasted the cattails he had boiled. They tasted good. So he went home then and there wasn't anybody

there. He pounded some more cattails. The people had eaten up
the cattails he left there so he had none and so he pounded some
more. He heard somebody whisper something. A man was calling
Coyote and showed him his penis. He said he had killed Coyote's
mother with it. Then Coyote cried and cried.

Coyote got mad then and pulled all the cattails out of the water.
He ate some more cattails that night. The same voice said the same
thing to him again and Coyote cried again. Coyote then got after
him and trampled him to death. (The man was the little bird that
lived down by the water.) It was the same little bird who had eaten
up Coyote's store of cattails. He had turned himself into a band of
people to scare Coyote. Then Coyote killed all the warriors except
the one that was the little bird. Coyote called him by that name and
told him that he would always live in the cattails.

Coyote had a hut made out of willows. He hung some cattails
to dry in his little hut. Every time he got up in the morning he found
the best of them gone. He asked his ears what was stealing his cattails. The ears didn't answer him. Then he asked his eyes and they
didn't answer him. Then Coyote got mad. He asked his mouth, but
his mouth didn't answer him, it chewed. He asked his feet but they
didn't answer. Coyote got mad again. He asked his tail but it didn't
answer him. He asked his penis. It didn't answer him, just acted
funny. Then he asked his extra penis (the one his wife had roasted)
and that one answered him and told him it was the little mole who
lives underground.

Coyote got mad. Then he went to get some more cattails. He
found the little bird there. The little bird was not afraid of him.
(After Coyote had trampled the little bird, he had come to life
again.) Coyote hung the cattails low so he could catch the mole
when he came to steal. He had his rock knife that he used for killing
rabbits and other things. He didn't sleep that night, he watched. He
used the knife on Mole that night when he came to steal the food.
He stuck the knife in Mole's stomach and then he ran away. Pieces
of Mole's fat got stuck on the knife and in the morning Coyote
licked the knife. Then he made a fire. Little Mole didn't come the
next night. He was sick. He wanted his mother to ask Coyote to
come and doctor him. The mother came. Coyote wasn't a doctor,
but the mother came and asked him to come doctor Mole. The old
woman didn't know he was Coyote. She told him, "Coyote stuck
his knife in my son's stomach." He asked who Coyote was. He kept

on asking who Coyote was. Coyote told her he never heard of that man Tukkupittseh. Coyote told the old woman that his name was Tukkupittseh. He said that he didn't know the name. Tukkupittseh means "wildcat." Coyote told the old woman to pick up two pieces of sharp stone on her way home. Coyote went at night to doctor the boy. The fat was sticking out of the wound. Every time he put his mouth at the wound he ate some of the fat. The little boy knew that Coyote was trying to eat him. Coyote got mad and told them to hire another doctor. He kept on doctoring him. He doctored him all night long. Coyote had those two sharp pieces of stone in his hand. The old woman got scared of Coyote. She knew he was up to something. All night long Coyote tried to kill the old woman with the rock. Toward morning she went to sleep. When she went to sleep, Coyote killed her son with the rock and then he killed the old woman, too. He carried them home after he killed them. Then he ate them up when he got home. He stayed there for a long time. He made his home there.

While he was still living there, a girl came to him. She asked him where Wolf lived. Coyote told her he didn't know anyone by that name around there. The girl said her mother told her that Wolf was a coyote. She told him her mother told her to go and get Wolf. Coyote said he had traveled all over the world and never heard of anyone by the name of Wolf. He also said he knew no one named Coyote, that he was not Coyote. The girl wanted Wolf, not Coyote. She didn't like Coyote. Wolf had created the earth. Coyote told the girl he did not know anyone by that name of Wolf, but that his big brother called him by the name of Wolf. Then the girl told Coyote to come with her. She took him home with her. Coyote was so glad that he ran, kept running all the way. When the girl got behind, Coyote came back to her again.

They were going on their way. Coyote got tired and thirsty. The girl told him to go straight ahead, she was going to look for water. She told him there was water there. She drank from the water herself, but she wouldn't let Coyote drink. She wanted to find out if he was Coyote. She knew that if he were really Wolf he wouldn't get thirsty. Every time they got near a spring she told him to go straight ahead, that she was going to look and see if the spring was dry. She told him there was another spring and she went first to look at it. She went to the spring and found water there. She ate her dinner there. Coyote was so tired that he used his bow and arrow for a walking cane. After a long time Coyote caught up with her. She was eating her dinner at the spring. The girl gave him water to drink when he got there. The girl told him to wash his face, it didn't look good it was so dirty. There wasn't much water in the spring. Coyote wanted to drink all the water. There wasn't much. He didn't want to waste it in washing his face. He drank and drank. After he got through drinking he washed his hairy face.

The girl gave him boiled duck to eat. She told him not to break the bones but to save them all. Coyote saved all the bones. After he finished eating he gave her the bones. The girl picked them up and put them under her. She sat on them. The girl's vulva chewed them up. Coyote was surprised.

Then they went on their journey again. The girl told Coyote not to run. They were going on a long journey. The girl told him not to run so fast. When they were still going, Coyote got tired. Then after a while they reached the ocean to the west. The girl told Coyote to wait for her. She was going to an island. She went flying over the water. She was a goose.

The girl flew over the water to the island and told her mother that she had brought Coyote with her, not Wolf. Then she came back to where she had left Coyote. There appeared dry land straight to the island for Coyote to travel on. Coyote got there.

The old woman and her daughter boiled meat for Coyote. They all had supper together. They told Coyote to save all the bones. Then they put the bones under them. Coyote got scared.

Then they went to bed. They told Coyote to sleep apart from them. Every time Coyote moved, he moved toward the girl, getting closer and closer to her. He kept on moving closer to her and slept with her. The girl told him not to do anything to her, just to sleep. He kept on trying to have intercourse with her but she told him not to do that. When he tried to have intercourse with her the girl's vulva got after him and tried to bite off his penis. Coyote got scared and hollered. The girl told him to go back to sleep in his own bed, but he didn't want to sleep away from her.

They had boiled meat again for breakfast. After breakfast they told him to hunt for mountain sheep. Coyote killed one male mountain sheep. He planned to take the neck bone and try it in the girl's vulva. He brought the meat home but he hid the neck bone away from the house. They had boiled meat for supper that night. Then they went to bed. He tried the same trick as he had the night before and the girl's vulva snapped at him. Coyote got mad and went outside and got that piece of bone he had hidden and tried that on her. The vulva chewed up the bone. Coyote moved to his own bed. Then morning came. They had boiled meat for breakfast again. After breakfast they told Coyote to go hunting again. Coyote killed a three-year-old male mountain sheep. He hid the neck bone. He tried his tricks again that night and the girl told him not to do that. Coyote got up and got the piece of bone and tried that on the girl. The vulva couldn't chew that up, it was too hard. This time he fixed her, pulled all the teeth out, all of them. Then he had intercourse with her. Next morning when the girl got up she was pregnant.

Coyote went hunting again that day. After Coyote left, the old woman asked her daughter what Coyote had done and the girl told her. Then the old woman wanted to try Coyote that night. So Coyote did the same thing to the old woman that night and fixed her up. He tried the old woman that night. He made a lot of noise when he broke the teeth on the bone and the daughter said, "Poor mother." The old woman was glad to get rid of the teeth. [Interpreter says that Coyote was a dentist.]

Next morning both women were pregnant. The day before, the girl had been pregnant and when Coyote came home he looked all over for the baby. He couldn't find what the girl had done with the baby. The old woman was making a big basket. Coyote didn't know what it was for. They sent Coyote out again that day. This day they were both pregnant. That evening when Coyote came back his wives were not pregnant and he looked all over for the babies and could not find them. Coyote didn't know why the old woman was making the basket. The old woman was working on the basket all day every day. Every night when Coyote came home he looked for his children but could not find them. Coyote went out hunting every day. Every morning the two women were pregnant when they got up. Coyote didn't know what the basket was for. The old woman didn't want Coyote to know what they were doing with the babies. They got up pregnant every morning. Coyote stayed there a long time, maybe a year. The old woman made a big basket. Coyote didn't know they had put the babies in the big basket. They were good babies. They did not cry. The old woman finally finished the basket. She put a big cover of willows on top of it so Coyote could not open it.

Then they sent Coyote home. He carried the big basket on his back. He came over the same trail he and the girl had taken on the way to the island. When Coyote carried the basket it wasn't heavy. While he traveled it kept getting heavier and heavier. He kept on carrying it. Coyote got so tired he opened the basket to see what was in it. (The big basket is still there on the other side of Ely. There is a spring coming out of the basket now. The basket has turned to rock.) When Coyote opened the basket lots of children came out. Coyote gave them names. He called one bunch Ute and Gosiute. He told the Utes to be Utes and talk a different language from the Gosiutes. He called another bunch Paiute. He called all the tribes of this land by name.

Coyote sang his doctor's song when he doctored Mole: "Morning is coming. It is getting lighter and lighter. The river is flowing. I am going to eat the mole."

—COMMODORE
(Lily Pete, translator)

Owl's Widow

There was once an owl and his wife. They had a baby son. It was their custom to stay out of the house when a baby was born (like we do) so they wouldn't catch disease. Owl went out hunting and told his wife to go back and fix the meat. He told her to have rabbit without feet. He went out to hunt rabbits again. His wife looked over all the rabbits he had killed. Owl let his wife eat only the lean meat. She got mad because he wouldn't let her have any fat. So she put a sharp bone at the door so he would step on it. This happened in winter and the snow hid the bone. Owl came home at night. He stepped on the bone and got sick. He told his wife to look at his feet. She did and kept pushing the bone in his foot. She wanted him to die. He got worse and worse. He couldn't go out any more to hunt. He couldn't walk. Then he died. Before he died he told his wife that after his death she was to go and marry his cousins, Badger and Skunk. She didn't want to marry Badger, and Owl said Skunk was nasty and not to marry him. He said for her not to marry Coyote. He told her to marry Chicken Hawk.

When Owl died, his widow went to see Skunk. Skunk's mother was an old woman and she was crying when the widow got there. Skunk heard his mother crying and asked her what was wrong.

Owl's wife had told the old woman the bad news about Owl. Skunk kept on asking his mother what was wrong. His mother told him she wasn't going to live long, that was why she was crying. She didn't want him to know that Owl's wife had been there. Skunk kept on sniffing the ground and he knew by the smell that Owl's wife had been there. Skunk looked for her tracks, but Skunk's mother had brushed away the tracks with sagebrush so he couldn't find them. Skunk kept on looking and found tracks far from the house and he came back and told his mother that she was lying. Then he followed the tracks and caught up with Owl's widow.

Skunk told her to pick his lice for him. She threw them on the mountainside. She turned them into mountain sheep. She told him to go and get them, so he went after the sheep. He killed some and said that Owl's widow could make a dress from the skins. He also killed two for Owl's little baby. While he was resting, Owl's widow and little boy ran away. They hid under some rosebushes. She wished that the ice would form on the river. Then they ran over the ice. Skunk wouldn't go over the ice. Then Skunk got mad and used his scent on them. He told his scent to go across the ice and kill them. His scent turned to fog. Owl's widow told her little boy that they were going back to his father's cave, but the fog caught up with them and killed them.

Very far from where the fog killed them, Badger was living. He told his children to go outside and see if anything was wrong. The youngest boy saw Owl's widow and boy. He was a doctor like his father. Badger had told his children to go out twice and look. He didn't have a wife. Badger was a doctor and went over and doctored Owl's widow and the boy. He went under the ground and dug to where they were lying. He doctored the mother first, then he doctored the boy, too. The scent of Skunk had got into their bodies and turned to blood. He brought them both to life and then he wanted to marry Owl's widow.

She didn't want to marry him. Badger told her to go to the house of Chicken Hawk but not to go near the mountains. It was the home of Red Ant. But she wouldn't take his word and went to the mountains. She heard people. She made a hole in the mountain and she saw a lot of red people there. She urinated there by the mountain. She went on and found Chicken Hawk's mother. There was a big colony of people there, Coyote and the rest. They went out hunting rabbits every day. Coyote was the chief.

Coyote was the first one to come home that day. Coyote's children told him that their aunt (Owl's widow) had come that day. Coyote told his children to go and tell her that he wanted some cold water. Owl's widow wouldn't let him have any water. Coyote thought that maybe she wanted him to come over himself. He took a rabbit and went over to get some water to drink. Chicken Hawk's mother didn't like it because Owl's widow was going to marry Chicken Hawk, but Coyote wanted to marry her before Chicken Hawk came home. The old woman told him that his children had been carrying water all day and she knew that he had plenty at his house.

Chicken Hawk came home late with just one rabbit. When he came home his mother nursed him at her breast. After he was fed he played with the little Owl. The old woman told Owl's widow to make a fire and roast some rabbits. She made just a little fire because there was just one rabbit. The old woman told her to roast some rabbits. She went over to get some rabbits from Chicken Hawk's mother because she saw a lot of them there even if Chicken Hawk had just killed one. After she saw all those rabbits she built a big fire and roasted them. The old woman told Owl's widow to take the rabbits out of the fire. She whispered to her and told her to take them out slowly. She told her that the little boy, Chicken Hawk, was funny. When she was taking the rabbits out, Chicken Hawk took one and flew away with it.

Little Chicken Hawk lived in a hole in the rocks. The old woman told Owl's widow that they wouldn't sleep well that night, for Coyote was going to be there. The old woman put Owl's widow in a pine-nut basket so Coyote wouldn't get her. Coyote came to the house that night. They got up in the morning and the men went out hunting again. Coyote came home early again with lots of rabbits. The old woman told Owl's widow to go get wood and haul it on her back. When she went out to get the wood she looked for Chicken Hawk's house instead and she found it. Owl's widow climbed up to his house and found a roasted rabbit in his rabbit-fur blanket. He had said his house was too small, so she made it a little bigger so she could stay with him. She took some wood home to the old woman's house.

Little Hawk came home again that night. Owl's widow went up to Chicken Hawk's place that night. The old woman told her to put her hand over Chicken Hawk's mouth when she went in so he wouldn't make a lot of noise. But she forgot to put her hand over his mouth and he flew away. Coyote got jealous and he shot with bow and arrows at Chicken Hawk's house. The old woman was afraid he might kill her son. She knew that Owl's widow had scared her son. Then morning came. Coyote saw Chicken Hawk sitting at his door and was throwing hints at (teasing?) him. Chicken Hawk got mad and didn't want to go hunting that day. But he went out hunting later. Chicken Hawk went to Coyote and told him to stick his bow in the ground. Chicken Hawk used his wings and broke the bow to pieces. His wings were sharp.

In those days there was just one big mountain. Chicken Hawk went and tore the mountain down with his wings and scattered it. He made lots of mountains out of the one big one. Coyote and the rest of the people watched him do that. Coyote told Chicken Hawk to stop doing that. So Chicken Hawk got mad at Coyote and came toward him. Coyote got scared and started digging so he could hide. The lizards and the bull snake and all the rest of the reptiles were people and were hunting with Coyote that day. Horned Toad was there, too. Chicken Hawk cut Coyote in half and hit Horned Toad—that is why he is flat now. Only Coyote died. Chicken Hawk brought the reptiles to life. All the rest of the people told Chicken Hawk to raise Coyote but he didn't want to. They kept on arguing because the others wanted Coyote to be their chief again but Hawk didn't want him to live. But finally he raised him again. Because Hawk busted the big mountain, that is why there are mountains all over now.

Owl's widow is Chickadee, a little gray bird with a black head. She is the one who owned the pine nuts and chased the thieves. She lives in the mountains and eats pine nuts.

—COMMODORE
(Lily Pete, translator)

Coyote and Bear

Coyote was traveling toward the west, on a lonely trail. He met a black man, Bear. They came close to each other. They were both looking for food. Coyote was sitting on the ground watching Bear. Bear did not see him. Coyote asked Bear if he wasn't afraid to travel on that road. Bear asked Coyote the same question. Coyote

asked Bear to vomit so he could see how many people he had
eaten. Coyote told him to shut his eyes and vomit it out. As soon as
Bear vomited, Coyote ate some of it. Then it was Coyote's turn to
vomit. Coyote vomited and vomited fresh meat. He vomited more
than Bear. They weren't afraid to travel on that road, for they were
both cannibals.

Bear asked Coyote where he was going. Coyote answered and
said he was going on that road where Bear was traveling. Coyote
told Bear to go up the road, up the hill to a place called (when you
shoot an arrow from a bow). He told Bear that he would meet a
man there but the man would not hurt him. So Bear kept on that
road and when he got there, there was somebody waiting to shoot
him. It was Coyote. He had gone around and got there first and
he shot Bear. Then he skinned Bear. He took the fur. He said that
he had often heard his father tell stories about roasting Bear and he
was going to try it.

Then Coyote lay in the shade. It was a hot summer day. He
went to sleep. When he woke up he heard voices. There were a lot
of flies. Coyote thought it was the flies who were making the noise.
After a while he heard the same voice again. There was a creek on
one side of the place where he was lying. He went over then and
listened. He found a lot of people there. He stood there watching
them. The people asked him what he was doing. Those people took
out their eyes and threw them up and then when they shook the
tree the eyes came back. Coyote told them he had been doing the
same thing while he was on his way. They asked him to go with
them up the stream and come back again. They knew he was Coyote. They had Indian carrots (*yampa*) to eat. They ate them a little
piece at a time. They wished that Coyote's eyes would not come
back when he threw them up in a tree. These people were some
kind of birds.

This is how Coyote got blind. He threw up his eyes and they
didn't come back. Coyote tried to catch the people but he was
blind. He heard voices and chased them around but it was only
bluebottle flies. There was a stream and Coyote was on one side of
it. Two girls were on the other side of the river. The girls asked
him what kind of man he was and told him to come over on their
side of the stream and kill buffalo for them. They knew by his actions that Coyote was blind. Coyote did not answer them so they
repeated their request. Coyote was standing there by the bank of

the river. While he was standing there he asked them what kind of girls they were. They answered by asking what kind of man he was. He didn't answer. The girls asked him again. He asked them the same question. They told him their big brother called them "girls." "Girls" is also the name of a tribe. They asked Coyote what tribe he belonged to. He said his big brother called him "young man." He forgot all about his roast of Bear. Coyote couldn't see the girls but he smelled them. They told him to cross the river. He couldn't see where he was going. He knew the river was wide. They told him that a little farther up there was a narrow place where he could cross. He nearly drowned when he tried it.

The girls rounded up the buffalo for him to kill. He couldn't see them at first when they told him that the buffalo were there. Then he got on the other side of them where the wind carried the scent of the buffalo to him. They told him to sit there and when the buffalo got near to shoot them. They drove the buffalo to him. He couldn't see them, he just shot anywhere. He shot one. He chased them and stumbled over the one he killed and that is how he found it. He couldn't find his arrows by sight, but he smelled them. The girls came to him. They asked him if he were blind, asked him why he couldn't see his arrows. He said, "I'm just counting my arrows. I'm not blind." They told him they would pick up his arrows for him. Coyote said he was going to hunt for the buffalo he killed. He found it. The girls asked him why he didn't take his arrow out of the buffalo. He told the girls to take it out. When they gave the arrow to him they told him they were going to make a willow hut.

The girls told Coyote to take the hide off the buffalo. After they finished making the hut they came back to him. They said he was blind, that he couldn't do a good job of skinning the buffalo. They said he cut it in the wrong place. He asked the girls if they were the same height. He said that he thought one of them was short, that was why he cut one side of the hide bigger than the other. They said they were both the same height. They told him they would carry the meat and that he should go to the hut they built. So he went to the hut and walked around in it. He couldn't find the door of the hut so he made another door. They asked him why he had made another door. He asked them why they didn't know anything. He said there were a lot of warriors around. They believed him. He wanted two doors so they could escape by either side. The girls made a fire. It was their custom to eat the stomach of the buffalo with sagebrush. Coyote ate it. They didn't cook it for him, just gave it to him raw.

They had their house there. They went to bed that night. Coyote had intercourse with them. They were virgins before they met Coyote.

Morning came. Noon came. They smelled something rotten. Coyote told them he had killed a mountain sheep there a long time ago. Coyote told the girls to pick his lice. So they picked his lice. Coyote went to sleep and they picked his lice. He had a big piece of rag over his eyes to hide the fact that his eyes were gone. They pulled that rag off and looked in his eyes and there were lots of maggots in the eye sockets. The older girl told the younger girl to put Coyote's feet on the buffalo's leg and told her to go get an anthill and put his head on that. They ran away from him. They didn't like the worms in his eyes.

After a while Coyote woke up. He said he felt lots of lice in his head. He kicked the buffalo leg and he bumped his head on a piece of log. Coyote got mad and went after the girls. He forgot his bow and arrows and came back again. Coyote followed the girls by smelling their tracks. He kept running, he couldn't find them. They went over the desert. They saw him coming as they crossed the desert.

The youngest girl had a rattle. She threw the rattle into a canyon. Coyote heard it and followed it and fell into the canyon. He broke his leg bone. He couldn't get up. The girls left him there. These girls were from a big tribe. When the girls reached home they didn't say anything about all that had happened.

After a long time they told their people about how Coyote broke his leg and ate his own marrow. Coyote's brother-in-law heard about it. The brother-in-law got up early and came after Coyote. He looked at his leg and then he took him home. Coyote's sister cooked for him. The brother-in-law had been playing Hand Game and had lost all his goods. The brother-in-law knew that Coyote was a good player. Coyote knew all kinds of games. The brother-in-law told Coyote to go play for him. Coyote had another wife at that time. Coyote won all the Hand Games. He played all day. Coyote was very lucky. Coyote won everything the people had. He played all kinds of games and every time he was lucky. The brother-in-law wanted to get a pair of eyes for Coyote. He made a slingshot and hung it up to dry. The brother-in-law wanted Coyote to go to sleep. The brother-in-law opened his eyes and killed all the worms with a slingshot. He took out the worms with a little stick. He took them out of both of Coyote's eyes. He saddled his horse and went out to the mountains. He killed a male mountain sheep and took out the eyes. He killed a three-year-old mountain sheep and took out its eyes. Then he came home. He tried to put the mountain sheep eyes in Coyote's eye sockets but they were too big. Then he put the eyes of the three-year-old mountain sheep into Coyote's eye sockets and they fit. Then he closed Coyote's eyes. Coyote was still sleeping. Then the brother-in-law covered Coyote's eyes with the same piece of rag that had been on there. Coyote got up. He asked for water to wash his face. He found that he could see. That is how Coyote got his sight back again.

After he found his sight they played football with Coyote. Coyote won. Coyote kept on kicking the ball.

—COMMODORE
(Lily Pete, translator)

Cottontail Shoots the Sun

A long time ago the sun was not far from the earth as it is now. It was hot then. It burned everything in those days. Cottontail was mad and he went over one morning with his bow and arrows to kill the sun. Every morning when the sun came up he said, "What are you doing, Cottontail?" Next morning Cottontail dug a hole and hid in it so the sun would not see him. When the sun came out the water boiled. The sun did not see Cottontail one morning when he came out. Cottontail was hiding and Cottontail shot him. His arrow did not hurt the sun, because it burned up before it got there. So Cottontail tried again to shoot the sun. He took a stone from his stomach and he killed the sun with that. Then the earth got on fire and everything started to burn. Cottontail asked all kinds of wood whether they burned or not. He asked Rock if it burned. They all said yes. So Cottontail kept on running.

He came to a bush and asked it if it burned and it said, "Just my top burns, my roots don't burn." So Cottontail dug a hole under that bush and hid in there. The fire burned the back of the Cottontail and smothered him to death. Then he came to life again. Cottontail wished for a hailstorm and the hailstorm came and put out the fire. Cottontail's eyes had burned, and he didn't have any eyes when he came to life again. So he took hailstones and put them in his sockets for eyes.

Then Cottontail went on his way and came back toward the west. When he was returning he killed a Woodchuck by smothering it with smoke. The Woodchuck girls were making fun of Cottontail so he killed them.

He was coming back to his aunts' place. He had two aunts. He had his crow feather there. He told his aunts that if the sun killed him, the crow feather would fall from the tree and that would be a sign that he was dead. When he reached his aunts' house he told them to make a fire, he was cold. They started a fire. They said they were afraid to go get wood. Wood was hard to get in those days. Every time they went after wood, it hit those two old women on the head, so they were afraid to go for it. When Cottontail's aunts told him this, he hit the wood with the same thing with which he had killed the sun. It was a piece out of his guts.

Then he told his aunts he wanted water to drink. They said Water was mean to them. Every time they went for Water it chased them and they were frightened to go get Water. So Cottontail hit Water with his magic weapon and fixed it. Everything was hard to get in those days.

Then Cottontail said he wanted something to eat. They ground up some seeds and gave him food. He kept on asking for more. This was all after he had killed the sun. He ate all the food up. He told them to go get some more seeds. They were afraid to go get seeds. They had some seeds stored in the brush and somebody stole them. There was a big rock where they had stored the seeds. Cottontail went to see what was wrong. When they got there Cottontail told them not to look at him, he was going to do something. He rolled the big rock away from there. He was the strongest person in the world.

—Commodore
(Lily Pete, translator)

Bat (1)

Bat had a house like this one, a good log cabin. He went out hunting every day. He brought back nothing but fat. Bat had two wives.

They went out every day to get seeds to eat. These wives were sisters. They always saved the fat for breakfast. The fat he brought them was really ice and it melted every night. Bat made them believe that this ice he brought back was fat, but it was nothing but ice and melted every night. The girls had a bag full of seeds. Every morning half of it was gone. In the morning when Bat went out hunting, the girls followed him to see what he did. Bat always took the same trail. They found him. Bat had been stealing their seeds and making them eat ice. Bat roasted some kind of root and took out some fiber from it. He told his wives this was deer sinew. The girls saw him fixing this. Then the girls ran home. He came back later on. The girls hid. Bat thought they were still out picking seeds, so he stole some of the seeds and ground them up. He sat in the same place and sat in the same way that the girls sat. He boiled the seeds and ate them. Then he went out again. The girls went home. They followed Bat and watched him. They heard him hollering that he was working hard, that the ice was hard. He never came home in the daytime, only at night. He was shamed because he only had a little ice to bring. When he came home they threw dirt in his face. It was stormy. Bat said, "Oh, fawn rain, springtime rain" (the time the deer have their fawns). Bat told his wife that his old grandfather had told him that.

So Bat's wives ran away from him. They didn't like that ice Bat gave them to eat. They ran away while Bat was out. Bat came home that night and called to his wives. He was calling them, telling them to put the fire out. He said, "Somebody killed the deer before I got there." Bat couldn't find the girls. He kept talking to himself. He asked himself where the girls had gone. "Maybe they are in our night bedroom. Maybe they are in our evening bedroom. Maybe they are in our day bedroom. Maybe they are in our noon bedroom." He couldn't find them in any of the rooms. He found their tracks going to the place where he had been picking ice. He found their tracks going on toward the mountains and he followed them. He found where they had slept that night. He kept on going and found them lying dead. Somebody had killed them. The left side of their bodies was torn. He cried. The girls had told him that he was mean to them. Then Bat talked to his dead wives. He said, "Owa tara-tara," to them when he cried. That's the way he cries. He found a big track near their bodies. He followed that track. He went over the mountain. He saw a man who made the big track on

the desert. He was very big, like a pine tree. It was Grasshopper.
   Little Bat said he was going to kill this big Grasshopper. Bat
ran after him, tried to catch him, and fell down. Bat couldn't find
him. Grasshopper had vanished. Bat looked all over and then gave
up. He went back. He looked around and saw the giant again,
shooting with his bow and arrow in every direction. Bat went back
to kill him but again Grasshopper disappeared. Bat fell down, he
fainted. Then Bat came to after a long time. He looked all over
when he got up but he couldn't find Grasshopper. Then he looked
and he saw a little Grasshopper. He thought it couldn't be the same
as the big one so he let it go. He did not kill it. He went back and
then he saw the big Grasshopper again. Bat got mad and went to
him again. He said he would never let Grasshopper live because he
had killed his wives. So he went after him. Bat fell down again.
When he came to he found the little Grasshopper there. He picked
up the little Grasshopper and looked at it. Sure enough, there was
blood on its hind legs. So Bat tramped him to death. Then he went
back. When he got on a hilltop he looked back and saw Grasshopper
lying on the desert, dead. He went to his two wives and he cried,
"Tara-tara." He talked and cried. He asked why they had run away
from him. If they hadn't run away they wouldn't be dead now. He
couldn't bring them to life again so he turned them into leaves of
cedar. This story tells why Grasshopper has red legs.

—COMMODORE
(Lily Pete, translator)

Coyote and His White Relatives

Once Coyote and his brother Wolf lived together. There lived a
white man and his wife close to their house. The white man and his
wife had nothing to eat, they were starving. They were the aunt
and uncle of Wolf and Coyote. The white people had just one
rooster and no hens. The white man asked his rooster if he knew
anything. The rooster crowed. The white man saw his rooster rolling in the dust. Then the rooster crowed again. The old man found
a loaf of bread where the rooster had rolled. Every day the rooster
made bread for them this way. Coyote had dinner with them every
day. Coyote visited them every day. They had a bed in their house.

Coyote saw their purse on the bed. Coyote stole it. His brother Wolf told him not to do things like that. Wolf saw Coyote take the purse. Wolf got mad at Coyote. They looked all over for the purse. It had money in it. Coyote was still there. They asked if Coyote had taken it and he said, "No." Coyote told them that he would not do a thing like that to his aunt and uncle. Coyote helped them look for the purse. They knew Coyote took it. Coyote shook his head, said he didn't take it. They went to their neighbor and borrowed a barrel of whiskey. They made Coyote drink it. Coyote drank the whiskey and pretended to be drunk. He staggered around. Coyote was not really drunk, he just did this to fool them. They kept on asking if he took the purse and he said, "No." Wolf had seen him take it. Wolf was very angry at Coyote. Then he went home. Wolf told Coyote he had seen him take that purse. Wolf told Coyote to give back the purse. Coyote went back to the old people's place and pretended to look all over for the purse. He had it in his hand. He put it back on the bed. Then he said he found the purse on the bed.

The white people had grain there. Rooster made the wheat. Rooster helped irrigate the grain. He scratched. Coyote got real mad. He asked his brother, "What is that?"

Wolf had a pistol. Coyote kept asking what it was. He told his brother to put two bullets in it for him. He said he was going to shoot the log. So Wolf put in two bullets for him. Wolf showed him how to use it. Wolf told him not to take it to their aunt's place. Coyote used it. Then he came back and asked him for some more bullets. Wolf refused, but Coyote kept on asking. This time Wolf put in three bullets for him. Coyote used all of them. He came back and asked for more bullets. Wolf put in some more. Wolf told him not to take the gun to their uncle's place. They might be scared of it. His brother Wolf saw Coyote going to the uncle's place with the pistol. He went in the house. He shot his aunt with it and killed her. Then he killed his uncle, too. Wolf got mad at him. Wolf saw him kill the old people. Coyote came home and told Wolf he had killed the white people because they had blamed him for taking their money. Wolf told Coyote to take them into the house. "Don't try to do anything with them." Coyote didn't want to take them into the house. Wolf made him do it. Coyote took out his uncle's stomach, cut it off. He forgot to take the pieces with him, he left them there. He was going to use them for killing mountain sheep. After he took them into the house, he just threw them down. He tried to pick up those pieces of stomach he had cut off, but they jumped away. Every time he tried they jumped away. Wolf saw him doing that and he laughed. Coyote told that piece of stomach to go get his people to come fight with him. He wanted to have war with them. So the pieces ran off.

Wolf heard Coyote say this. Then Coyote went back to Wolf and Wolf scolded him. He said, "What are your ears for? Why can't you hear what I say?" Wolf was sorry about their aunt and uncle. Wolf knew their enemies were coming so he and Coyote went after some people to help them fight. Before he left, Wolf told him not to say anything about him, but Coyote told them about him. The first people sent him to another tribe. A lot of people from different tribes came to Wolf. There were enough there to fight the enemy. Wolf told Coyote to try out his seat on a horse. When he came back Coyote asked Wolf if he did all right and Wolf said, "No, try it again." Coyote sat on the horse backwards, facing the horse's tail. Then he tried different ways but Wolf didn't like it. Coyote was training himself. Each time he came back he asked Wolf if he were doing well, but Wolf didn't approve. Next time Coyote stood on the horse's back. Coyote was practicing. The war had not yet started. Coyote kept on trying. At nighttime they went to bed. Wolf told Coyote to look out for enemies. Coyote saw what he thought was lightning in the west. He told Wolf the lightning was coming closer.

The enemy came that night (the American soldiers). The war started. Just Wolf and Coyote were having war, the other people had gone away. It was these other people who were fighting Wolf and Coyote. Coyote couldn't kill any of them. He would go out attired in a different warbonnet each time. They recognized Coyote even though he wore different warbonnets. The other people said Wolf was the brave warrior, that he would kill all of them. Coyote didn't kill any of them, but he didn't get killed. Then Wolf's turn came. Wolf sent Coyote up the canyon and told him to pack up all their belongings. Then Coyote left. Wolf scared the enemies and drove them back. The war continued. Wolf killed thousands at a time with one arrow. Coyote got mad because he hadn't killed any. He grumbled. There were not many enemies left when Coyote looked back. Then Coyote wished that his brother would be killed and Wolf was shot in the leg. When Coyote had gone on a little farther, he looked back again. They were coming after his brother. Coyote cried. He stood and cried and cried. While he was watching they caught his brother Wolf and killed him. They took his hide off.

Coyote made his home there. He cried every day. He pitied himself. While he was living there he made bows and arrows. He made lots of arrows. After he finished them he went after the enemy. He found the place where they had camped the night before and he hung up one arrow there. He kept on tracking. Every time he found where they had camped, he put one arrow there. He kept going after them. While he was going, he kept thinking of two old women that he saw. He caught up with them. He came around and met them, so that it looked as though he were coming from the opposite direction. He hid in the bushes on their trail. These old women told him that the enemies of Wolf and Coyote were their sons and that they had killed Wolf. They told him Coyote was still up in the mountains crying himself to death.

These old women told him they thought he was Coyote and they were scared of him. He said that the Coyote didn't travel around, that he was a coward. He asked them where they were going. The old women told him that they had a dance by themselves and they were coming from it on their way back to camp. They told him that their grandchildren came and got them. Coyote asked them what they did every night. The old women said they made a separate fire for them away from the other people. They danced around Wolf's hide every night. The women said that toward morning the people came and got them (these two old women) and made them dance. They told him that the people felt their (the old women's) heads every night. They were afraid Coyote might get in there some night. Then after they felt their heads, they made them dance. Coyote threw one old woman down and tramped on her and then he did the same thing to the other woman. He killed them by tramping them to death.

Coyote planned to take the bones out of the women and to hide himself in the skin. Coyote got in the skin of one old woman. Coyote put his extra penis inside the skin of the other old woman. Then they walked along. They started going. Coyote sent the penis ahead, he came behind. The penis walked faster than the old woman had. Coyote told him not to do that. They carried the old women's packs on their backs and they looked like the two old women. They got up on a hilltop and danced. The grandchildren came after them. The children felt them all over. Then the children took them home. Penis walked faster and Coyote would poke him with his walking stick. They made a separate fire, away from the other people, and gave them some boiled meat to eat.

The old women slept then. The mothers of the little girls took their children to the old women's place to sleep while they were dancing. They danced all night long. Coyote wished that the little girls would sleep a deep sleep. He tried his tricks on the little girls and killed all of them. Toward morning the people came to get the old women. They took them to the center of the crowd of people. Coyote nudged his penis partner and told him to dance slowly. They danced, these two pretended old women. Coyote planned while he was dancing. The people thought it was Coyote in the old woman's skin. Coyote ripped open the skin. He planned to jump over them. He jumped over them and he took Wolf's hide with him. He told the people to dance under their grandmother's skin, which he threw at them. They chased him. He fought with them. Coyote killed most of them. Then they lost him. Coyote escaped. They found nothing but his tracks.

They looked for him all over. They were still hunting him. Coyote called to them and told them they were blind. They went after him but lost him again. He changed himself into an old torch of cedar bark like the Indians used to make. The people looked for Coyote but couldn't find him. Then Coyote called again, "You must be blind," and started running. While he was running he changed himself into a rock. This time they recognized him. They knew the rock was Coyote. Then Coyote started running again. He ran behind the rosebushes. He kept running. He went over the mountain. He escaped. When he got to the mountain peak, he called to the people and told them to go back. He said he was going back to his place. So the enemy went back home. That was the last they saw Coyote. Coyote kept going his way.

Before Coyote had set out to get Wolf's skin, he had told Magpie not to eat Wolf's flesh that he left behind, but when Coyote returned, Wolf's flesh was gone. Coyote was mad. He found it, cleaned the flesh, and covered it with the skin he had brought home. Coyote went out every day to look at him. Coyote got Wolf's feathers that he used to wear. When Coyote had Wolf's feathers in his hand, he went blind. (Coyote went blind because he had torn Crow to pieces, as told earlier.) Coyote made a torch and looked for woodpecker's feathers. He put woodpecker's feathers on his arrow and shot it up to the sky and that is how he found his sight again.

Then he went and looked at his brother again. Every time he went to see his brother, he got after Magpie (his son) and scolded him. He looked over all Wolf's clothing and found his black paint. Then he lost his sight again. Again he made a torch and looked for more woodpecker feathers. He shot up an arrow with the woodpecker's feathers on it and got his sight again. Then he went and looked at Wolf again but Wolf was still dead. He tried to open one bundle of Wolf's. It was the darkness, the night, that Wolf had tied in there. Coyote opened it and again became blind. Coyote made a torch but couldn't find anything, it was too dark. After a long time he found his sight again (I don't know how).

Every morning early he would listen for his brother. Wolf used to howl every morning. When Coyote found his sight he went to look at Wolf but nothing was there. So Coyote went to look for his brother. After a long time he saw a girl. He thought he saw some-one sitting by the fire. Coyote had his clay pot with him. He knew it was somebody. Coyote was going up to the house. When he was near the house he hid his pot under a bush. Coyote found his brother Wolf there at the house. Wolf had lots of meat, mountain sheep meat. Coyote told Wolf about his adventures, how he had gotten his hide back from the enemy. Wolf told him to go back and get his pot and boil some meat and eat it. Coyote got mad at Wolf because his brother had seen him hide his pot. [Much laughter.] Then Coyote boiled some meat and ate it. In the morning Wolf told him to go his own way, that he wouldn't see him any more. That is how Coyote lost his brother.

—COMMODORE
(Lily Pete, translator)

Coyote Wins the White Man's Goods

There was going to be a race. Coyote bet with the people and won everything they had. He raced a footrace with two brothers. They went about six and a half miles and had to race there and back. They ran ahead of Coyote. He was behind. Coyote told them to run faster, he could pass them. Coyote got ahead of them. Coyote got to the end first. They raced back and Coyote was ahead. Coyote's brother's wife told her son that it looked like his uncle was ahead and coming first. The other people thought it was one of the brothers who was ahead. They made fun of Coyote. Coyote kept on running. The people knew then it was Coyote. When he got close to them he jumped over the pile of goods they had wagered. The two brothers came in way after Coyote. They told their people that Coyote flew, that he had wings.

Then they were going to play another game with him. There was a white man with a mule who was living with the people. After he won, Coyote lived out on the plains. The white man said he was going to cheat Coyote and win the goods that Coyote had won. The people told the white man he couldn't get the better of Coyote. The white man went out where Coyote lived and said, "Let's play games." Coyote didn't pay any attention to him. After a long time Coyote came to him. When Coyote came the white man said, "Let's play." Coyote's tricks weren't there. He had left them on the other side of the mountains. The white man said to Coyote, "How are you going to get them?" The white man told Coyote to borrow his burro and go get his tricks. Coyote said, "Yes, I'll do that." So Coyote got on the burro's back.

When Coyote got on the burro, the burro wouldn't start. It came back again. Then Coyote came back and asked for the white man's hat. Coyote said the burro knew it was Coyote on his back. That was why he wouldn't walk. Coyote asked for the white man's clothing. The white man took his shirt off and gave it to Coyote. Coyote got on the burro again after he put on the shirt. Again the burro refused to go. Coyote told the man to take his pants off. Then Coyote started again and this time the burro stopped again. He wouldn't go. Then Coyote came back to the white man again. Coyote told him to take his shoes off. Then Coyote got on the burro and the burro came back. Coyote asked for the white man's spurs. This time Coyote started again. He started, Coyote used the spurs on the burro. When he was a little way away Coyote called back to the white man and told him that he couldn't cheat him. Coyote went off with the burro and all the white man's things.

The white man was naked. Coyote fooled the white man. He had said he would be back by noon. Coyote told the white man to wait there for him. The white man stayed there under the hot sun. When Coyote didn't return, the white man went home naked.

When the people saw him they said he looked like an old faded piece of wood. The white man was ashamed. He put his hand over his penis when he came near them. The people told him he couldn't fool Coyote, that he had lost his burro and goods. The white man had a cabin there and he went there and put on some other clothes. The white man told the people that Coyote said he would be back at noon, but Coyote didn't come back. The people said he would never see his burro again. The white man went to visit Coyote on another burro next morning. He waited there but Coyote didn't come. So he came back again. The white man got fooled. Then the white man gave up.

—COMMODORE
(Lily Pete, translator)

Rolling Rock

A long time ago there were lots of people. Coyote was living there. At that time Rock owned all the blankets. He always spread them out on the ground. One day Coyote decided to go out and see what kind of blankets Rock had. He found Rock and saw lots of blankets. They were not rabbit-skin blankets, but colored ones like the white man's. He tried them on to see how he would look in them. He tried them all and said, "They don't look good on me." He picked up a red one and thought that one looked good on him. Coyote kept looking at himself after he put on that blanket. Coyote took the red blanket, he stole it. He folded it up and hid it under his arm and went away.

Coyote climbed up a hill. He looked back and saw Rock still there. It was a big round rock. Coyote climbed a little farther up and looked back and Rock was still there. When Coyote looked back the third time he saw Rock moving toward him. Coyote ran up the hill. Coyote said, "Whoever saw a rock roll uphill?" He thought Rock couldn't roll uphill, so he went up the hill. Then Rock climbed. Coyote ran sideways. "Whoever heard of a rock rolling sideways?" But Rock came right after him. Coyote climbed over the mountain. He ran through the timber. He said, "Whoever saw a rock roll through timber?" Coyote didn't want to give up the blanket. Coyote heard Rock rolling after him. Then Coyote went over the desert. "Whoever heard of a rock rolling over the desert?" Rock kept right after him. Coyote got scared. Then Coyote ran through thick mud. "Whoever heard of a rock rolling through thick mud?" Coyote got scared, so he ran over the water, he crossed the river. Rock ran right through the water. Coyote kept running. Coyote went up another hill. He said, "Whoever heard of a rock running uphill?" But Rock ran right after him.

Then Coyote knew he couldn't run away from Rock. Coyote was tired. Coyote asked Black Bear to kill Rock for him. He told Bear that Bear was stronger than Rock. Bear tried his best but Rock ran right over Bear and killed him. Coyote kept on running. When he was running he met a big snake. Coyote asked him for help but Rock ran right over Snake and killed him. Coyote kept on running. Coyote didn't want to give up the blanket. Coyote asked Eagle for help. Rock killed Eagle. Coyote kept on running. Coyote asked Chicken Hawk for help. Chicken Hawk answered him. He knew Coyote had taken the blanket. "You should not have taken that blanket." Rock killed Chicken Hawk. Coyote kept on running. Coyote kept on asking for help. Coyote was very tired now. Coyote asked Night Hawk for help. Night Hawk was lying on Rock, resting. Coyote said he wasn't strong enough to crush Rock. So Night Hawk crushed Rock to pieces. After the Night Hawk crushed Rock, Coyote lay down to rest and he vomited green water. That is why we have horse blankets today, because Coyote stole them from Rock.

—Commodore
(Lily Pete, translator)

Crow

Once Crow lived with some other people. He went out hunting. He hunted a killdeer. He saw that bird coming and he shot it and hid it under the branches of the cedar tree. His favorite word was, "Hu-u-u-u-u." Every time he said something, he said, "Hu-u-u-u-u." He told his people to go and get the meat. So they went over and made a fire and looked for the meat and couldn't find it. The people thought he had meant some kind of a cow. Then they found his arrow sticking in this little bird. They heard his voice on the other side of the hill. He came to them and said, "Hu-u-u-u-u, where is my piece of meat?" He told them to look for some more. They told him they couldn't find it. He told them he was at war with the people on the other side of the hill. When they went back home they talked about Crow and said that he was a liar. Crow told them not to go to that war. He said, "Hu-u-u-u-u, you will blame me for it if people are killed." He said he was going to wage the war himself. They told him he was a liar.

—COMMODORE
(Lily Pete, translator)

Coyote and Crow (1)

Coyote and Crow were living together. Coyote was uncle to the Crow. They were starving. They didn't have anything to eat. Crow dreamed one night. Crow went out one night. He believed his dream. He had dreamed about the buffalo. He found a dead cow and he went to the cow and ate the fat. Coyote was starving. He kept up a big fire. He kept looking for his nephew, Crow. Crow slept in the tree. He came back with the fat from the cow. He put it by the fire when he came back. Coyote was starving, he couldn't go to sleep he was so hungry. Coyote put some of the fat on the hot coals and then ate it. He saw Crow still sleeping in the tree. Coyote felt a little better after he ate the fat.

They had their home there. After they had eaten all the meat, Crow dreamed the same dream. So he went out again and brought home some meat for Coyote to eat. Coyote didn't know where Crow had gotten the meat.

One night Coyote didn't go to sleep. He wanted to know where Crow got the meat. When Crow went out after the meat some people caught him. One of his feathers had come off and fallen at the place where Crow had taken the cow they had killed. That is how they knew the thief was Crow. They got mad at Crow. The people killed lots of cows and left one man on guard there with his bow and arrow, ready to kill Crow. When they saw Crow stealing, they killed him. The guard saw Crow crawling into the cow. He came out again. He had eaten all the flesh out and just left the skin there. Then the guard killed Crow. After they killed Crow they had all the meat they wanted. Coyote didn't know Crow had been killed. Coyote got very thin.

—COMMODORE
(Lily Pete, translator)

Spider Plays Hand Game

Once there lived a spider. He played Hand Game with people. He
played Hand Game with Jackrabbit and Cottontail and the smallest
rabbits. They were all humans at that time. The rabbits won feathers from Spider. They beat him all the time and won everything he
had. They played Hand Game at night only. They slept during the
day. After the sun went down they got up. One day Wildcat came
to visit. On his way there he killed Cottontail who used to play
Hand Game. Wildcat found Spider lying by the fire. While he was
sleeping, Wildcat roasted the rabbit and he put the hind end of it at
Spider's mouth. Spider picked it up and smelled it. Wildcat said to
Spider, "What do you think rabbits are? They are something to eat.
They are not people like Wildcat and Spider. When they come tonight I will hide in back of you, in your blanket." He said he would
blow their hands in different directions so they couldn't win. "Tell
them you have a stomachache, that you have to go out every once
in a while." Wildcat told Spider to set out a trap for them.

So they came and made bets. Spider won. Wildcat had said to
tell them he had a stomachache and had to go out once in a while.
He set the traps. The old rabbits got wise. They didn't want to bet
the feathers they had previously won from Spider. Spider said, "If I
had been like you, you wouldn't have that feather." They wanted to
keep those feathers. They said they were going to quit playing.
They got up and got ready to go home. The big Jackrabbit was the
first one to go out and get caught in the trap. Then they all got
caught in the trap. Wildcat and Spider killed them. The rabbits' ears
are the feathers they won from Spider.

—Commodore
(Lily Pete, translator)

Coyote Plays Hand Game

Coyote once lived with some people. He played Hand Game with
them and he lost every time. One day Cottontail came to him and
asked if he had been playing Hand Game. Coyote answered and
said yes, he had won everything the people had. Cottontail told him
to tell the people that it was his (Coyote's) turn to win. Coyote did
the same thing that Wildcat had done when Spider played with the

rabbits. Cottontail told Coyote not to say anything. At midnight Coyote sang. [Song here; not translated.] Cottontail had said not to mention his name but Coyote did. Coyote kept on winning. The people got wise. They knew he was up to something. They told him to quit playing with them. Then Coyote sang his song for them. It was Coyote's Hand Game song. Coyote told them to keep on betting, that it was his turn to win. So they got mad and left.

—COMMODORE
(Lily Pete, translator)

Bat (2)

Bat and his big brother were camping with Coyote. One day they went after deer. Little Bat killed lots of deer. He sent Coyote to get them. Coyote could not find them because there were so many it looked like a mountain. Coyote couldn't find it, kept on running 'round the mountain of deer. Coyote thought that the pile of deer was a mountain. After a while Coyote found the road to the deer and said he couldn't carry the deer. They were too heavy for him. He went back to bed again. Big brother Bat went after the game. He went and got the meat. He killed one deer for each family.

They moved away after they got through eating that meat. (They didn't have any wine at that time. They played Hand Game.) Little Bat did not go with Coyote and Big Bat. He went on about a day later and followed them. Little Bat played Hand Game by himself. Little Bat couldn't jump over the river. He tried his best to jump over. He had Indian tobacco and he spilled it on the ground. Little Bat got mad and then he smoked all his tobacco and it turned into a cloud. Coyote got scared when he saw the cloud.

Little Bat kept on going and found Coyote's daughters getting something to eat. He married the oldest daughter. Then he married all the rest of the daughters (just temporarily). He told his wife to watch him go hunting. He went to the mountain peak. His wives told him to come back. The oldest daughter wanted Little Bat for herself. She didn't want the others to have him. Little Bat found a herd of mountain sheep and he killed all of them with one arrow. He divided the meat among his people. He gave his father-in-law, Coyote, two mountain sheep. There were a lot of people there to help eat the meat. Coyote was very thirsty. He went to look for muddy water. He found the muddy water. Coyote found pieces of meat in the water. He kept on going up the river and found some people. They were playing. Little Bat had the biggest mountain sheep and his brother the second biggest. Little Bat made Coyote ashamed by carrying the big mountain sheep. The people gave Coyote one mountain sheep and he couldn't carry it. Little Bat came and carried the mountain sheep and Coyote, too. When they got home they had supper. Bat knew it was going to be cloudy that day but Coyote wouldn't believe him. Little Bat knew their enemies were coming and the enemies killed Little Bat. Then the war started and the enemies killed everyone except Coyote.

Coyote caught all the arrows that were shot at him. He was having a war with the people. They didn't really kill Little Bat, for he came to life again and made fun of Coyote making war. The Snake girls were those who were having war with Coyote. They killed Coyote. The girls were looking for the chief, Little Bat. They couldn't find him but they found a little baby and it was Little Bat who had changed himself into a baby. They were playing with the little baby and they said they were going to raise him and have him for a husband when he grew up. Then the baby started to talk. The oldest sister took the baby. They knew the baby was Little Bat when he started talking. The oldest sister told the youngest sister to kill the baby. The youngest sister killed the oldest sister instead of the baby. She didn't want to kill the baby. The baby was hard to kill. The youngest sister jumped like a frog and the baby could not catch her. The two girls had killed a lot of people. Little Bat chased the girl home and caught her and killed her.

He went to his grandfather Snake's place and showed him his bracelet. Little Bat had something to eat. His grandfather had a big rock to grind roots on. The grandfather was a doctor. The grandfather kicked the rock and he knew that Little Bat was the chief. Little Bat scared the old man away and used the rock for grinding seeds. The old man got mad and tried to kill Little Bat but did not succeed. Little Bat threw the rock up and it hit Snake on the head and killed Snake and his daughter.

Then Little Bat went back to his people again. He found his people on the ground all dead. He raised his brother up with his magic wand. Then he raised them all up from the dead except the Coyote. Little Bat did not like Coyote. The other people told him to revive Coyote, too. He gave his magic wand to his brother and told him to revive Coyote. Coyote was wormy. These were the first people. They all went home after Bat raised them up.

—COMMODORE
(Lily Pete, translator)

Cannibal Giant

Once there lived an old woman and her granddaughter. They went out every day to gather pitch from pine trees. One day the Cannibal Giant found them. He chased them around. He can run fast. He chased them around a big tree. The grandmother and her granddaughter thought it was fun to have the giant chase them. They laughed. Soon they got tired. Then he caught them. He flicked his fingers at their nipples. Their breasts swelled up. Then he killed them and took them home. He ate their bodies, all except their breasts, which he cut off and hung up to dry. The grandfather went out to look for his wife and granddaughter when they didn't come home. He found the giant's tracks and followed them to his cave where he found the giant asleep. He had his bow and arrows with him but he could not kill the giant. So he shot at his penis and that is how he killed the giant. The giant is like a rock.

—MAMIE BONAMONT
(Lily Pete, translator)

Bear and Fawns

Once there lived a mother Deer and mother Bear. They each had two children. They went out to dig wild carrots every day. Once they planned to stay out one night. In the evening Bear came home alone and told the fawns that their mother was going to stay away another night. The fawns got scared. During supper the fawns came over and listened outside the Bear house. Mother Bear told her children not to tell the fawns that she had killed Deer and brought home the meat. The fawns were listening and heard the baby bear say how good the deer flesh tasted. The fawns were scared.

Next morning Bear went out again. She told the fawns their

mother would be back that day. When Bear left, the children played together at smoking each other in the cave. When the fawns started crying, the little bears let them out of the cave. Then the cubs went in but when they cried, the fawns left them in there and they smothered to death. Then the fawns painted the bears' faces with paint and stood them up by the rock. Bear came home and saw them. She said, "You're just wasting our paint." The children were dead. Bear got mad. She looked for the fawns but they had run away to their grandfather Crane. They told Crane to stretch his leg across the river so they could use it for a bridge. They crossed the river on their grandfather's leg. Bear chased them. The fawns had told Crane that Bear killed their mother and was chasing them. Bear asked Crane for a bridge. When she was halfway across, he shook her off and she drowned. So Bear floated down the river and died. Crane told the fawns to live on the mountains and eat grass. That is why there are deer on the mountain.

—LILY PETE
Arthur Johnson

Coyote and Crow (2)

Crow used to be a different color. Coyote first painted Crow white. Then he painted him gray, but that didn't look good either. Then he called him back. He painted Crow black and Crow flew away and the sun glinted off his black feathers and Coyote said, "He looks good now. That is the way he's going to be."

—ARTHUR JOHNSON

Eagle and Crow

Eagle and Crow were sitting on a hill watching the sheep grazing down below. Eagle picked out a fat lamb, pounced on him, and carried him off in his talons. Crow admired that and he wanted to do better than Eagle. So he flew way up but he didn't look like Eagle. Crow pounced on a big buck but he could not budge him.

—ARTHUR JOHNSON

Coyote and Mouse

Mouse fixed up some meat but when he looked around his meat had disappeared. He did not see who stole it. He said, "Next time I'll get him." Next time he pretended to be asleep but he was watching. Coyote licked the meat and said, "It's good, it must be fat." Mouse's mother went to Coyote and said, "My son is sick. You come doctor him." Coyote agreed to go. Coyote danced around the patient. Coyote had a stone and the old lady said, "Don't hit me." Coyote said, "I'm just trying my best to cure. I'm not going to hurt you." Coyote got down and when he touched Mouse with his weapon he broke the skin and he bent down to suck, but instead of curing he sucked all the fat out of Mouse. Mouse was dying. Coyote killed Mouse and his mother and ate them up.

(Coyote has his own song and his own way of speaking. Lots of animals have songs and peculiar ways of speaking. When they are doctors in a story, that is when they sing and why they talk differently.)

—Arthur Johnson

Two Brothers

Two young men were going after moose. They went along. One was an ornery fellow, the other one minded his own business, he was good. The younger brother was a braggart. The father had said, "You boys cook all your meals. Be sure to go to bed at a certain time and get up at a certain time while you're on your journey or something will get you."

They went along and met something. The older brother said, "Don't bother those things," but the younger brother insisted on killing them. He came back and said, "Oh, that was nothing. I killed them easily."

They went along and met some other animals. The older brother said, "Don't bother them, you'll get us into trouble." The younger brother said, "You said that before and I killed them easily." So he did it again.

They came to a place where there were signs of someone having dragged game along. The younger brother said, "I'm going to track that down." He met a hard-looking man and killed him.

One evening they sat around where they were going to camp. They heard somebody come along dragging something. A hard-faced man came up to them and sat down and said, "How's the meat?" He sat down and took some. The older brother had told the younger brother to go to bed early, but the younger brother would not obey. The stranger sat by the fire and said nothing. He ate the meat and then moved closer to the younger brother. He finished off one pile of meat, then another, then another. He tried to catch the younger brother by his testicles, and the younger brother called for help to his older brother. The older brother said, "My brother is getting into trouble tonight. I hope it teaches him a lesson." The stranger carried off the younger brother by his testicles and he screamed for help. Next morning the older brother tracked him and rescued him.

They came to a lake where they saw a moose. The older brother said, "Wait here and I'll chase him to you." The older brother chased the moose to him but the younger brother got scared and ran away. The younger brother came back and said, "What happened? I got scared." The older brother said, "Here, you've been boasting of all the things you killed and now you get scared." So he chased the moose to him again and again but the younger brother got scared and ran off.

—ARTHUR JOHNSON

Coyote Races With Frog

There was a little hill, peaked. Coyote was very boastful. He said to Frog, "Let's race. I bet I can beat you." So Coyote bet his buckskin hide, rabbit blanket, bow and arrow, all he had. You know how fast Frog jumps. Frog said, "All right. I'll race you." So they picked the place where they were going to start the race and picked out the course. Frog got lots of other frogs and stationed them a jump length apart along the course. Frog said, "Ready?" Coyote said, "I'm ready," and away they went. Frog leaped to a bush and the next frog leaped ahead and pretty soon Coyote was left far behind. There was a little wash—a canyon—and Coyote crossed that and looked back to see where Frog was. He thought, "I beat Frog easily." But Frog caught up, passed him, and Coyote couldn't catch up with Frog. He ran until his tongue was hanging out but he couldn't catch up with Frog and he lost the race and all the goods he bet.

Frog saw him some place later on and said, "Do you know we beat you?" And then Frog told him what they had done about the relay. When Coyote heard about the trick he sure got mad but he couldn't do anything.

—ARTHUR JOHNSON

Coyote and the Bear Cubs

Old Man Coyote was visiting around. He was walking along and met some bear cubs. One cub was swinging on a sapling. Coyote said, "I'm going to fix those bears." The bears said, "Jump on, we're having fun." So Coyote climbed on and had fun. Then he told all the bears to get on and he pulled the sapling way down to the ground and it flew up so high that all the bears fell off and were killed.

—ARTHUR JOHNSON

Origin Tale

An old woman and her daughter lived way across some water. The old woman sent her daughter after Wolf, to make some people. The girl met Coyote first and asked him where Wolf lived. He said, "In that house over there." When the girl went on, Coyote quickly ran around and got in the house where he had said Wolf lived. The girl came and asked him if he were Wolf, and Coyote said, "Yes." So he went off to her home with her. On the way he kept wanting to have intercourse but she would not let him. She crossed the water to the island where she and her mother lived. Coyote could not swim and he ran back and forth on the shore, wondering how to get across. The old woman said, "That isn't Wolf, that is Coyote. What did you bring him for?" Then she said, "Oh well, he'll do. He's a man."

So the old woman threw some ashes on the water and that made a path on which Coyote crossed. Coyote wanted to have intercourse with the two women, but they had *vagina dentata*, which prevented him. He got the bone of a mountain sheep and put that in and the teeth broke off on that. Then he had intercourse with the women every night. They got pregnant. The old woman made a basketry water jug, which grew bigger every day. Coyote heard murmuring in it. The old woman said he was to take the jug, go back to his own country, and then open it. On the way Coyote got curious and opened the jug too soon. All the good-looking, smart people came out and by the time he got the cover back on there were only a few poor, miserable people. These are the Gosiute and he put them down in Deep Creek and Skull Valley where they stayed.

—ARTHUR JOHNSON

Creation of the Deep Creek Mountains

It was Hawk who made the Deep Creek Mountains. Hawk was angry. It must have been because someone was fooling around with his wife. He flew up high, then dashed himself against the mountain (Mt. Wheeler) and broke it all up. It made all these mountains around here.

—ARTHUR JOHNSON

Coyote and Wildcat Disfigure Each Other

Old Man Coyote was going along. He found Wildcat sleeping. He wondered what he would do with him. He said, "I'm going to play a good trick on my younger brother. I'll fix him up." Coyote pushed his nose in, made his paws short, and made him look like he is now. Wildcat got up, went to defecate, and noticed how he looked. He said, "I know who did this and I'll fix him up." Coyote had said, "From now on you'll be known as Tukkupittseh and you'll live where you do now." Coyote laughed when he saw how Wildcat looked.

Coyote lay down to sleep. Wildcat found him and said, "I'll fix him up." He made his nose long and his body long. Coyote got up and went to defecate and noticed how he looked. He said, "Oh boy, this will be good. If there is water in a deep narrow hole, I will be able to drink it up." Wildcat said, "You'll be known as Coyote here-

Collecting pinenuts. Northeastern Nevada Museum, Elko.

after. You will howl around in the mountains and other places and will be Coyote."

—ARTHUR JOHNSON

Council on Seasons

A small bird was arguing with Coyote about how many months of winter there would be. Coyote said, "There will be as many months as I have hairs in my coat." Bird said, "That is too many. You would have to gather too many seeds in the fall. You could not get enough to last all through such a long winter as that. You will be thin and poor in the spring. Let's have twelve months in the year and each season will have as many months as I have toes. (He had three toes.) Then there will be enough food to last through the winter and it won't be so hard on the people." Coyote insisted on having as many months of winter as there were hairs in his coat. Bird flew away.

—ARTHUR JOHNSON

Theft of Pine Nuts

The people here wanted pine nuts. They had them way west in California. So they went after them. The people there were having the
Pine Nut Dance. Coyote, the chief, said, "We will go and get pine
nuts." The Rocky Mountain Jay got the pine nuts. They started off
with them and the pine-nut people pursued them. They caught up
with the thieves and searched them one by one but couldn't find the
nuts. The Rocky Mountain Jay had gotten the pine nuts and they
caught him. He had a sore rotten leg and he had hidden the pine
nuts in his rotten leg. They caught him and looked him over and
said, "This fellow is just about dead. Throw him away." So they
threw him away and he ran all right, he was not lame now. That is
why we have pine nuts here now.

—Arthur Johnson

Giant Cannibal Bird

A little boy lived with his grandmother. He went out trapping all the
time. He kept catching more and more difficult game. Finally he
caught a big bird and came back and told his grandmother. Then he
went back and the bird went after him. It wasn't caught in the trap
at all, it was just sitting there. The bird carried the boy off to an
island. There was an old woman there whose legs were broken, so
she could not get away. She showed the boy how the bird had broken her legs. The bird brought human flesh every day as food for
himself and the young birds.

The old woman told the boy that there were lots of bows and
arrows there and said, "If you can kill the bird you can get away
before he breaks your legs." So the boy first killed the two young
birds. The old woman told the boy that when the bird bent over to
drink, you could see his rectum, all red and wrinkled. "That's when
you can shoot him. Then after the bird is dead, you can make a boat
out of his feathers and get away." So the boy shot arrows into the
bird's rectum and killed him. The old woman made a boat out of the
bird's feathers and the boy sailed away.

Coyote saw a light floating around on the lake and he told
Mouse to go see what it was. "It may be my nephew out there. He
got carried away by that big bird." So Mouse went under the water

and came up by the boat and found it was Coyote's nephew in the boat. Mouse guided him home.

Coyote had fixed the boy up. He told him where he was to sleep each night. "If you do as I tell you, the cannibal won't bother you. Where you sleep the first night, there will be ghosts. They will be having intercourse, man with man or woman with woman, but don't laugh and you will be all right. No matter what the ghosts do, don't laugh."

There was also a very rough place where the boy had to cross. It was hard on the feet. The boy had to cross it before he got home.

The boy climbed up a tree to sleep, and cut off the limbs as he climbed. It made the tree slick. The ghosts smelled something to eat and tried to climb the tree, but just before they got to the boy they all fell off.

—Arthur Johnson

Coyote and the Trappers

It was all foggy in the wintertime. The people were having a rabbit drive. They drove the rabbits into traps. The people wished that Coyote would catch his own dog in his trap. So they drove his dog into the trap. Coyote was pleased at having caught the first game and he took it out of the trap and packed it on his back. Then the people all laughed at him and said, "Coyote caught his own dog in the trap." There is a bunch of stars you can see that are Coyote and the trappers.

—Arthur Johnson

Wolf and Coyote

Old Man Coyote and Wolf, his brother, lived together. There was a big war going on. Wolf said to Coyote, "Let's see you practice. The enemy is coming. You will have to protect our things." Coyote got on a big horse and did stunts. Wolf said, "That isn't the way. You can't do like that when you have to fight." So Coyote went out and slid under his horse's belly and did much better this time.

The enemy came and Coyote went out and the enemy could not hit him. The first time he went out he had on one costume, then he came back and went out again in a different costume. He did this again and again. Then Wolf said, "You stay here and let me go out." He went out on a white horse, all prettily decorated. Wolf told Coyote not to look at him because if he looked, Wolf would be killed. Wolf had one vulnerable spot. Wolf went out and performed great feats of horsemanship. Coyote wanted to see what his brother was doing out there. He wanted to see. So Coyote peeked out and just as he looked, they killed his brother.

The enemy skinned Wolf and took his hide away. Coyote looked out and saw all of his brother's body left there except the hide. So Coyote decided to follow them. He met two women who were menstruating. He asked them what they did and they said that they danced every night. He asked them how they behaved and they told him that they danced around Wolf's skin. So Coyote killed the two women and put his penis in the skin of one and he got in the skin of the other. Then Coyote and his penis did just as the two women did. They danced around Wolf's hide. Then Coyote stole Wolf's hide and ran away. He kept the hide wet. Every day Coyote looked to see if Wolf was coming to life. One morning he heard his brother howling. Coyote went to the spot where he thought the howling was coming from, but it kept sounding farther and farther away. Wolf went away. This is how Coyote lost his brother.

—Arthur Johnson

[Coyote Marries His Daughters (2).

Arthur Johnson says he knows this tale: "Our bad traits like incest and relatives marrying all come from Coyote. It is the way he did. Things happen in the human world according to the way Coyote did." —Anne Smith]

Western Shoshone Tales

1939

Coyote and Mouse

Coyote and Mouse lived together. Winter was coming. They had a hut all fixed up for winter. One night Coyote said, "I think we are getting hungry. We ought to get some rabbits. We'll go chase rabbits tomorrow. There is nothing else we have to do. We have to call for snow."

Night came and Coyote said, "I'll call for snow." He sang this song all night. [Song.] In the middle of the night he sent Mouse out to see if there was enough snow yet. Mouse went out. He was very light, he went out and stayed on top of the snow. He returned and Coyote said, "How is it?" and Mouse said, "Oh, not very deep yet. It isn't even up to my ankles." So Coyote sang some more. Toward morning he sent Mouse out again to see. Mouse went out and looked around. He was so light he didn't sink down in the snow, so he came back and said, "No, there is not much." So Coyote sang some more and it kept on snowing. Morning came and the snow was so thick you could hardly see. So Coyote thought he would go out himself. He said to Mouse, "I think you are telling lies." When Coyote got out he sank right down in the snow and he got buried in it. He couldn't get out for a while. Then when he got out he was angry. He took a sagebrush and he looked for Mouse. He was going to kill him, but Mouse had hidden. Coyote looked all day. It snowed all day.

At evening Coyote gave up hope of finding Mouse. At night it was clear and Mouse sneaked out. Before he left he tied a sagebrush torch to his tail and he ran out and got away. Coyote did not notice him until he was far off. When Coyote noticed him he started hollering, "Come back, my friend. You will freeze to death." Coyote hollered and hollered, but Mouse didn't listen, he just went on. Coyote gave up hollering at him.

Mouse traveled until he was way across the plain to another mountain. When he got up in the mountains he looked for shelter. He was going to a big cave, a rock corral. He found a bunch of mountain sheep there, standing around. So Mouse sat there. He was cold, all huddled up. He made a little chattering noise—*i ji i* (cold). He kept saying that. One of the mountain sheep said, "What is that making that noise?" Then they noticed this little thing that was making that noise. So one mountain sheep said, "Come over here and get warm inside my ear." But Mouse kept on making the same noise. Another said, "Come get under my arm and get warm." They kept coaxing him to come and get warm. Every one offered him shelter in any part of their bodies, but Mouse just kept on saying, "I ji i." Then one mountain sheep said, "Well, then, come inside of me," and Mouse accepted and went inside the mouth of the mountain sheep. By doing that he killed all those mountain sheep. By his magic power he took all the meat way up to the cliff. After he did that he made a big fire so Coyote would see the fire across the plain. Mouse knew Coyote was always hungry.

After the snow settled down Coyote said, "I believe that is my friend Mouse that has that fire going all the time. I better go visit him." So it took Coyote many days to clear a path through the snow across the plain. One day he got there. He found where Mouse always made fire. He looked up in the cliff and there was Mouse. Coyote called, "My friend, are you there?" Mouse stirred, looked down, and saw Coyote standing there. When he saw him he said, "Are you hungry?" Coyote replied, "Yes, I am hungry. I see you are eating some meat."

Certain parts of the meat Mouse didn't eat. He put it to one side and used it to defecate on. Mouse said, "Yes, I've got lots of meat since I left you—mountain sheep. If you are hungry, stand right close to the cliff and I'll send you down some meat."

So he took the piece he had used to defecate on and threw it down on Coyote. But the meat missed Coyote. So Coyote got meat and was happy. He didn't know how to carry it. He got his knife and cut it up and ate a lot of it. Then he took the meat and carried it off.

—Anna Premo
Owyhee, Nevada

Cannibal Bird (1)

Two hunters went from their home to another mountain to hunt deer. They stayed overnight on the mountain. Next morning when they got up, one of the men told his friend, "I had a bad dream last night. I dreamed that a great big monster with big wings something like Eagle came over and tackled us and took us away." His friend listened and said, "Do you believe it?"

"Well, I don't know—I can't get over it."

"Well, never mind your dream. We'll go hunt."

It wasn't a very good hunting day. A cloud came up and it looked stormy. They were in the woods and they heard a big terrific rumbling sound. So they ran under the timber and stood there. The man who had dreamed was so nervous he couldn't stand still. The rumbling noise came nearer and nearer. Finally it came, it crashed through the timber and landed on these two young men. Then it seemed as though it clawed the man who had dreamed. It fixed its claws into his ribs. The other man was also carried away, between the toes of Bird.

The man between the toes was alive. The man who had been clawed died while they were traveling. The live man didn't know where he was being taken. They traveled a long time.

Finally, Bird landed. It seemed to be on an island. There they were, one man dead, one alive. This was Bird's home. There was an old woman there, Bird's mother. Bird was there, then he went away for a while. While he was gone the old woman talked to the man. "Where are you men from?" He told her where they came from. Then the old woman said, "I am getting tired of my son because he is always murdering people. He will be back soon to eat his victim. What I want you to do when he comes back is this." She took out some obsidian rock from her buckskin bag. It was in flat pieces. She told the man to break them up. "When my son brings home a victim he picks it open at the stomach, there is clotted blood there. He drinks the blood, dips his head, then lifts his head up. When he has his head lifted up I want you to throw this bunch of flints into the blood. By doing that, you might kill him."

Bird came back after a while. He went to work on the body. He picked the stomach open, picked at the flesh, then he began on the blood. Then the young man took a handful of obsidian he had broken up and when Bird lifted his head to swallow, he threw the flint in and stirred it in so Bird would not notice it. Then he sat there and waited. Bird kept on dipping his beak in the blood and lifting his head. He got slower and slower. He would tilt his head back and it would be a long, long time before he put his head back. Then finally he flew up and went out of sight in the sky. The old woman and the young man watched. After a while they saw a black speck up there and it was coming down. Then it landed on the island. The island almost went down into the water when Bird landed on it, he was so heavy.

It was night now. The old woman and the young man ate and then went to bed. Early the next morning the old woman got up and went to work. She went over there and cut her son's wings off. She got the young man to drag one of the wings away from the body, then he dragged the other. She made him lay them right beside each other. She told him to weave the feathers to each other and make a boat out of it. That took him several days to do. She told him to make it waterproof so it would stand a long journey.

After he finished that she got busy and got wood, lots of wood. She broke the wood into small pieces and piled them on the boat. This took her several days, to get lots of wood. After she finished, she had lots of buckskin and she started making moccasins, lots of pairs of moccasins. Then she made buckskin pants and buckskin jackets. This took many days to do. After she finished there, she made caps. Then she prepared seeds, ground them up for his food—large piles of seeds. This took many days. Then, when everything was done she told the young man what they were for.

"Now you are going back to your own country from where my son took you. You are going to go through very strange country. Your home is far away and there are many dangerous people between here and your country. That is why I have spent all these days preparing for your journey. These caps, pants, shirts—you will take each one off after you pass these people. This is the reason I got lots of wood on the boat. You have to have a fire every night until you get on shore. There is a place you will come to when you get ashore where people come out all night. They seem to kind of slide off the hills. When you get there, sleep on top of a hill. If you sleep on the side of a hill they will slide over you and kill you."

She told him of all the strange wicked people he would meet on his way home. She told him what he must do in each case.

Finally, he sailed off in the feather boat. She wished for the wind to blow in the direction in which she wanted him to go. So he sailed night and day. It took him seven nights and seven days to get to shore where the old woman had told him to leave the boat. Then he went on afoot. Before he left the boat, the old woman had said he was to put on all his suits and to carry his spare moccasins over his shoulder. The food he was to carry in a buckskin bag.

He walked till it grew night. This was the place the old woman said the strange people who ran at night lived. This was where he was to sleep on top of a hill. Finally he found a hill and got on top of it. All night he heard those strange people. It sounded as though they were sleighing. They made lots of noise. Next morning when he got up he saw that those other hills looked as though an earthquake had struck them—all piled here and there.

The old woman had said that after he passed this strange country he was to take off a suit. He did.

He walked all day. When night was near he had reached a land where there were lots of rattlesnakes. She had given him a whole buckskin for each leg, to wrap it in so that when the snakes struck at him they wouldn't touch his flesh. He got to this land before night came. Snakes were everywhere, striking at him. It took him all night to go through this country. Toward morning the snakes got fewer and when daylight came he saw no more snakes. He felt relieved.

He walked on and on. There were many miles he had to go. He came to a place where the old lady had told him to sleep in a hollow tree trunk. She said there were strange people who lived there and got their victims by poking their sticks in all the hollow places and when they felt something with their sticks, they killed them. He tried to sleep in a hollow trunk. Many monsters came. They had strange voices. Many poked their sticks in his tree, but didn't quite touch him. By morning he did not hear them any more. He saw no tracks of them.

He walked on and on. The old woman had told him there was a place where the *tso'apittse* lived—stone giants with pitchy hands and a basket on their backs. They run all the time. When they meet someone they scalp him and put him in their basket to take home and eat. The old woman had told him there was lots of timber there, but the giants didn't climb trees because they were so heavy. She said that if they noticed him in the tree they would stay all night and day and wait for him to come down. He got in a tall tree. He heard them grunting around, saying, "We see a track, we see a track." He heard them saying that all night, running here and there making an awful sound with their feet. They didn't notice him in his tree and he sure was glad. When broad daylight came, the young man came down from his tree. The giants were gone.

The old woman had told him he would come to a place where there were lots of the genital parts of women. These parts ran all over at night. If they saw anyone the labia would just clamp on all over the body everywhere, and smother the person to death. The old woman told him he must get there before night came and make himself a tunnel, a hole underground, and cover the mouth of it with sagebrush to disguise it. She said he would hear those genitals making a clapping, slapping sound. He made his tunnel and got in. He heard the vulvae slapping all night.

After each danger he passed, though, he had to take off one suit. So the old woman had told him. She had told him there was a place he would come to where, if the people found anyone sleeping, they would tickle him to death. There were women who went around all night looking for people and tickled them to death. The old woman told him to find a deep cave and to hide in it until morning came. He found a cave and stayed there all night.

The old woman had told him that the next place he would come to he would have to wait all night. Owls lived there, and when the owl opened his eyes a flash of broad daylight would come. She told him he must run every time an owl blinked his eyes, and get through that country fast.

She had told him, "After you get through that country you will get to the land of frogs. There won't be any place to sleep—you will have to walk all night. The land of the frogs is very slimy. Then when you get through frog land, you will come to a country where you can sleep all day." So he passed through frog land.

The next land was more like his own country. The old woman had said the people there would be strange, wouldn't speak his own language, but they would not harm him. The name of these people is Nenemusi. (Anything that is strange, peculiar, funny, is called this.) After he passed through frog country he came to country something like his own. But it did not feel safe. There were many thickets and he saw strange things. He didn't feel that he could trust himself to sleep on the ground. The first night he spent up in a tree. He didn't feel safe on the ground. He heard something in the thickets. He thought he heard the giants whom he had met a way back. Next morning he went on. That night he saw tracks of some people. He spent the night in a cave. Next morning he saw some more tracks. He thought he was coming to where people lived. Finally he heard voices among the cedar trees. He went closer and closer. He met someone. It looked like a human except that he did not have any mouth. It made him look very strange. This mouthless person motioned him to follow, so the young man followed him. He went to his home and there were many people there, all of them without mouths.

When evening came, more of the mouthless people came. They had been hunting and brought home game. He wondered how they could eat it. After a while the hunters each had deer. They seemed to be having a good time. He watched to see what they did with the meat. They piled up all the fat in one place. They had a big fire there. They gathered around the big fire. Each person took big pieces of fat, threw them on the fire and leaned over to inhale the scent of burning fat. He had a big flint knife. He cut off a piece of meat and put it on a bed of coals. The mouthless people watched him cook it, turn it, eat it. They watched him and said, "Mmmmmmmmmmm." He felt very bad, sorry for them. He stayed with them all night. They were good to him. He couldn't sleep. He thought all night. He was sorry for these nice people with no mouths. He decided he would try and cut their mouths open in the morning.

Next morning came. They built a big fire, threw fat on the fire, and inhaled the smoke again. So, the young man motioned to one man and made motions that he was going to cut his mouth open. The man came willingly. He cut his mouth open and there were some teeth. He was surprised. The man was so glad, his mouth was all bleeding, but he wanted to eat right away. Then all the people wanted mouths and they cut each other. Some cut too wide, some not wide enough. They were so glad to have mouths.

He stayed there with them for a while. They went hunting again. Now they brought lots of game, everything. Formerly they brought mostly just fat. The young man went hunting with them. They were very happy. Now they had mouths, they talked, and he could understand some of the things they said.

While he was there one of them died. They didn't seem to know what to do. They seemed sorry, but they didn't know what to do. He felt very sorry and he cried. Then one of them said, "How shall we cry?" So then one of them made up a cry. So they tried to cry like him, they imitated him.

A day came when he said he wanted to leave. They didn't want him to leave. One old man brought a girl to him and said, "If you stay here you can have this girl." But he said he wanted to go home to his own country.

So he went on. He came to his own country. He came to the spot where he and his friend had been carried off by the bird. He came to the spot where his wickiup used to be but no one was there. He went on to another wickiup and learned there that his parents had died, his family were all dead. So he stayed with the people in this wickiup; they were related to him.

—ANNA PREMO
Owyhee, Nevada

Coyote Marries His Daughters

It was springtime. Coyote had six girls and one little boy. Coyote told his family, his mother-in-law, his wife, six daughters, and the little boy, "Spring is coming. Everyone is feeling good. Let's have a dance. We will start in the morning when the sun comes up."

Morning came. They were all outside. Coyote said, "I will be the singer. I will stand in the middle. You people dance around in a circle." (In a round dance, the Shoshone do not have a singer in the middle.) So they all got ready. Coyote sang, "Po ap, po ap," (wind come, bring wind). Coyote wanted wind. Coyote said, "When I sing, you just close your eyes. I will close mine, too." So he sang a long time. [Song here: wind come, bring wind.] The wind came, gently at first, then it came real strong. The women wore just a little apron in front in those days. The wind blew their aprons up and Coyote could see their vulvae. Coyote saw two, his mother-in-law's and his youngest daughter's, who had big vulvae.

He had made a plan before he started this dance. Later on he went hunting. He came back and told his family there were some enemies coming to war against them. He said, "I am scared. There are no men here, just you women and my little son." He started making arrows. One day after he had made a lot of arrows he told them the warriors were going to meet him behind a hill and he would fight them single-handed. He said, "While I am fighting with those people, I will let out my war whoop all the time I am alive and you will know I am still alive and fighting. When you no longer hear me I want you two to come get me." He pointed to his mother-in-law and his youngest daughter.

He went to war. The next morning they heard his war whoop and they knew Coyote was fighting. It lasted all day. Night came. Toward morning they no longer heard his war whoop. After the sun came up Coyote's wife said, "Go do as your father said. Go look for him and bring him back. Bring back what is left of him." So the mother-in-law and the youngest daughter went out. They found Coyote lying there. There was an arrow sticking in one leg and another in his loin. The daughter said, "I think we better pull them out." Coyote cried and said, "Oooh, you pull my spirit out with it. Don't do it." They had to carry him. The daughter took him first. She carried him and he acted silly. He kept sliding down and trying to have intercourse. She said, "If you don't quit that I'm going to drop you." So before they got to the creek she dropped him and went home. Then the old mother-in-law packed him. She packed him even though he did the same thing to her. There was semen running all down her legs. She took him home. When they got home the rest of the family looked at him and wanted to pull out the arrows. Coyote said, "Don't, if you pull them out I'll die right away."

There was no war, no enemy. Coyote had planned all this just to get at these two women.

So Coyote lay around pretending to be sick. He didn't hurt. The little boy had to go out and trap squirrels for them to eat. One day, Coyote said to his wife, "I believe I am going to die. These arrows are killing me. When I am dying I want you people to get ready to move. When I die, pile up lots of sagebrush, put me on the pile. Don't forget to put my rabbit net with me. (He always carried that net.) Don't forget to put my bow and arrow with me. Send our children away first. Tell them not to look back. Then set that sagebrush pile on fire and run away. Don't look back." He told his wife, "Now we have lots of daughters. There will be no one to look after them. You will move away from here and go to a strange land. There is a certain valley where you can go. There are lots of rabbits there for the boy to hunt. Men will come who will want to marry one of the girls. Don't pick a man with a high voice, pick a man with a deep husky voice. Some day you will have a son-in-law."

So the family moved away. But the boy still thought his father was alive. They kept on going till they got to the valley. Next morning the boy trapped squirrels and the girls got seeds. They did that all summer. One day a man came to their wickiup. He had lots of black hair, in braids. The mother said, "He has a husky voice." She said to the two oldest girls, "Take this man to your wickiup. Before your father died, he said you should marry a man with a husky voice. I guess this is the man for you." So the two girls took the man to sleep with them. All that night the rest of the family heard a thumping noise. They wondered what it was.

Next morning the mother told the boy to take his brother-in-law hunting with him. "Show him where to hunt." So the two went hunting together. They ran a cottontail under a little rock. The boy went on one side of the rock and Coyote was on the other. The boy looked under the rock and saw Coyote with his mouth open and he recognized his teeth. The boy ran home and told his mother, "I knew that man was my father. He is." The mother wouldn't believe him. Coyote came home after a while and things went on as before.

[Mrs. Premo said this is the end of the story as her uncle told it, but she knows the rest of the tale, as follows.]

"If that man is your father, there will be an extra penis under his pillow." They found the extra penis.

(Then follows the tale of the baking of the penis and the flight to the stars. There is a certain plant that grows underground. It has a root about six inches long. They dig up the root and bake it, peel off the black outer skin and eat it. *Tukumpi wea* means "sky penis." This is what the Shoshone call Coyote's extra penis.)

—Anna Premo
Owyhee, Nevada

Coyote Eats His Own Penis

Coyote always has lots of daughters, six daughters and one little son. Finally his family got quite scattered. He would come home and he wouldn't find his family at home. Sometimes he would find his wife only. Sometimes he would find only his little son. This son

is the youngest child. He got to missing his family. One time when
he came home, there was no one there. But the ashes in the fireplace were still hot. He noticed something baking in the ashes. He
said, "I wonder what this is. Maybe something good they baked for
me before they went away." He got it out of the ashes and cleaned
it off with sagebrush. He started to cut it with his flint knife. It was
about as long as his hand. He started eating it, then he heard a lot of
girls laughing at him. They said, "You dirty Coyote, you are eating
your own penis."

"What are you doing up there, you girls?"

"Well, we got up here because we got tired of living with a
dirty old man like you."

The Pleiades are Coyote's daughters.

—Anna Premo
Owyhee, Nevada

Porcupine Tricks Coyote

Porcupine was walking beside a river. He saw a bunch of elk there.
He killed one of these elk. He had just one arrow and when the elk
fell, he didn't know what to do with it. He had lost his knife. He
walked slowly along by some willows. Then he began to sing. He
sang, "What can I use to butcher my elk with." First he whistled it,
then he sang it out loud. Finally, Coyote came along and heard the
singing, about how someone had killed an elk and had no knife to
butcher it with. Then Coyote heard the song real loud and he ran
over. He found Porcupine and said, "What are you singing about?"
Porcupine said, "I'm not singing." Coyote said, "Yes, you were, I
heard every word you said."

"What did I say?"

"Oh, you sang, 'What can I butcher my elk with?' " Porcupine
said, "Oh, no, I sang, 'What can I cut my willows with?' " Coyote
replied, "No, you're telling me a lie. I heard every word you said."

Soon they came out from the willows. Coyote was restless. He
knew there was something around there. He ran around quickly.
Finally, he saw the elk. Coyote said, "Just as I thought. Here is the
elk lying here. How did you kill it?" Porcupine said, "I just had one
arrow and I shot at the elk and didn't miss it." Coyote said, "What
are you going to do with it now?" Porcupine said, "I'm going to

butcher it and eat it." Coyote said, "Oh, I know you have no knife. I tell you what we will do. Let's have a race. We'll start way over there and we'll run and whoever jumps over the elk can have it. You run first."

Porcupine didn't want to. He knew he would be beaten. But he walked slowly to the place Coyote had told him to stand. Coyote watched the time. Then Porcupine ran as fast as he could, coming closer and closer to the elk, then he jumped and landed on the elk's stomach. Coyote said, "That was easy." Then it was Coyote's turn. He didn't try very hard, he knew the elk was already his. He trotted along easily, jumped and landed on the other side. Poor Porcupine looked so beaten he didn't know what to do. Coyote took out a great big flint knife about seven inches long. He began to skin the elk. He told Porcupine, "Now, don't you touch it." Porcupine sat there and watched him skin the elk. Then Coyote cut off the two hindquarters. He got a bunch of willows and laid the meat on them. Then he came to the inside. He took all the insides out and laid them down. There is inside fat, the leaf fat, thin, around the intestines. You sort of peel it off there. Coyote peeled it off, then he cut out the stomach fat. He broke the intestines and they spilled on the stomach fat. Then he said to Porcupine, "Take this dirty fat down to the creek and wash it off. Then take these insides and wash them, too. Bring them back when you finish."

So Porcupine took the fat and the insides down to the creek. He washed the intestines and then he started washing the fat. It was a big job. Porcupine got hungry. He thought, "I guess it won't hurt for me to eat some of this." So he sat and he washed, and he ate some of the leaf fat, and he washed and he ate. He didn't realize what a long time he was there until he heard Coyote holler. Then when he took the stuff back to Coyote, there was only a little fat left. Coyote said, "What happened to the fat?" Porcupine said, "The water bugs ate it up while I was washing." Coyote said, "Oh, you lie. I'm going down to ask them." So Coyote ran down and asked the water bugs and they told him Porcupine had eaten the fat while he was washing. So Coyote said, "I'll go back and fix him."

When Coyote came back, Porcupine was sitting by the elk meat. Coyote said, "I know you lied. The water bugs told me you ate while you washed." So he started in tramping on poor little Porcupine. He all but tramped him to death. When he thought he had killed him, Coyote thought he would get his wife and children to pack the meat home. Coyote sat by the elk meat and defecated there, on two sides of it. He told the feces, "Watch that Porcupine and if he moves, you holler to me." Coyote left and the feces called, "Porcupine is moving." Then Coyote came back again and kicked and kicked Porcupine. This time he thought he had killed him. So he went off after his wife and children. Porcupine was alive but he didn't attempt to move. He lay still until Coyote got so far away he couldn't hear when the feces called out that Porcupine was moving. Then Porcupine got up and began singing. [Song here.] He sang, "Fir tree that grows by the water, grow here." The feces kept hollering. Porcupine got mad and hit the feces and scattered them till there was no more hollering. The fir tree grew. Then Porcupine wished the meat would go up to the top of the tree, and the meat went up there. Just as the last piece was going up, Porcupine heard Coyote and his family coming. They were all shouting. The children were so happy their father had killed a big elk and they had something to eat.

So Porcupine rushed for the fir tree and climbed up to where the meat was before Coyote and his family arrived. Coyote and all his daughters and his only son and his wife and his mother-in-law came. They all looked around for the meat. Coyote said, "What happened? This fir tree wasn't here. Maybe it was another place. Maybe I was mistaken." The little boy said, "No, you're not mistaken. Look, here is the stuff from the insides."

"I must be mistaken. This can't be the place." Then one of the girls looked up at the fir tree and said, "I see some meat up there." So Coyote looked and looked and finally he saw little Yi nits's eyes gleaming up there. Coyote said, "What are you doing up there?" Porcupine replied, "I brought up my elk that I killed. I'm living up here now." Coyote said, "You lie. You took the elk that I killed and took it up there. You know I can't climb. Give us some of that meat. It belongs to me anyhow." Porcupine replied, "No, it doesn't belong to you but I'll give you some anyhow. Tell your wife to put the baby way over there some place. The rest of you get under the tree." Porcupine took the ribs not split and said, "Stand there and hold up your hands to catch it." Porcupine was wishing that the front quarter of the elk would fall on the Coyote family and smash them to death. Porcupine called, "Are you all ready?"

"Yes!" So Porcupine pushed the front quarter down on the Coyote family and it smashed all the Coyote family except the baby.

Then Porcupine listened to see if they were dead. There was no noise so he knew they were dead.

A long time afterward—he waited to be sure they were dead—Porcupine went down and got the little baby. He dragged the baby and its basket up the tree. So they lived up there in the tree house, Porcupine and the little coyote baby. He fed the baby so much that it grew very fast. Soon the baby was too old to stay in its basket cradle. Then Porcupine taught the baby to use one limb when he wanted to defecate. The little coyote always went there to defecate. One day Porcupine noticed the meat supply was getting low. So Porcupine thought about that little coyote boy he was raising and about the meat supply getting low. So Porcupine went to the limb where the coyote defecated and cut the limb almost through, so it would be all right until someone went on it. Next time the little coyote went over, just as he was defecating, the limb broke and he fell to the ground and was killed. This is how the Porcupine killed all the Coyote family. Then Porcupine ate the rest of the meat and went down from the fir tree and went away.

—Anna Premo
Owyhee, Nevada

Tso'apittse (1)

Tso'apittse is a rocky giant with pitchy hands. When children are naughty their parents tell them the giant will come down from the mountain: "Zo a wi zo ho ho ho."

A young man and his wife went up in the mountains. He wanted to hunt deer. He had traveled up to that place before he was married and he knew the country better than his young wife did. She didn't know all the superstitions of this place. When they were to camp that night, her husband told her, "This is a place where we used to camp. There is a good spring near here where you can get water. There is something about that spring. It is a very pretty spring, wide and round. If you go there be careful, because this is Tso'apittse's spring. It is where the giant and his family get their water. When you get your water, don't look in the spring. Don't let your face be reflected in the water." She believed him. He said, "Don't stay at the spring, don't sit down, be quick about getting your water."

Anna Premo (lower right), 1890. Courtesy Beverly Crum.

He went hunting every day and she had to stay at camp alone. Every day she went for water and did just as her husband told her. Then one day she got to thinking, "I wonder what is wrong, why I can't stay by the water." She thought about how her hair needed washing. Why not wash her hair in the spring? So she went down. First she made a brush out of low sagebrush, she was going to wash her hair. She got to the spring, filled her jug, set it down, and started undoing her hair. She started washing her hair. She sat down to do this. When she finished, she leaned over and looked into the water. She could see her face very clear and she sat and admired herself. Then she began to brush her hair, using the water as a mirror. This was the first time she had seen herself and she thought how pretty she was, how beautiful her hair was. Then finally, she braided her hair and was ready to go home. To her surprise she couldn't get up. She was glued to the ground. Evening came, the sun was almost down. She kept trying to get up, but couldn't.

Meantime, the giant's children, who lived in the mountain, looked at the spring. One ran to her mother and said, "There is something in our spring. I saw something moving there." The mother went out and looked and saw it. Then Tso'apittse came home and they told him. He was happy. He warmed up his pitchy basket (he had pitchy hands, too) and put it on his back and ran to the spring. The girl heard his heavy footsteps and his breathing, "Wi wi wi." When he was near, the earth shook. The girl tried to get up but couldn't. Tso'apittse got to the spring. He kept hitting her on the breast with a flat club till her breasts all swelled up. Then he hit her head with his hands and scalped her. He killed her and slung her into his pitchy basket and took her home. His children came to meet him and were so glad he had brought something to eat.

The husband knew something must be wrong when he came to camp, for there was no fire there. It was too dark for him to track anything that night so he stayed there. He was very miserable. Next morning he got up very early. He was so nervous he couldn't sleep. He made a big fire and stood by it until the sun came up. When it was light he went down to the spring. He saw tracks where Tso'apittse had stood. He knew where the Tso'apittse family lived but he knew he could do nothing if he went there. So he went back to his parents' house to see if his father could help him. He told his father what had happened. So he and his father started making lots of arrows. So when he went back to the place he had lots of arrows. His father said, "You can't hit these *tso'apittses,* their bodies are made of rock. Their only vulnerable place is the anus. You go at night. Don't go in the daytime, for Tso'apittse is not home in the daytime. At night Tso'apittse will be lying down. Hanging above him will be your wife's breast. His legs will be crossed and he will be kicking at your wife's breast. When his anus is exposed, shoot at it."

So the young man went to his wickiup in the mountains and got ready to go see Tso'apittse at night. He went there. The *tso'apittse* family lived in a great cave. The young man looked in. It was dark outside. His father had told him to try not to make any tracks or Tso'apittse could track him and kill him, too. The young man was afraid to do anything that night. He looked around to see what he could do the next night.

The next night he went back there. He took some of his arrows with him. He got very close. He shot but his arrow didn't hit the anus. It tickled the giant and he grabbed it and it broke. The young man kept shooting but he couldn't hit the anus and kill him. So he went back to his wickiup. Next night he took more arrows and went back. He saw Tso'apittse kicking at his wife's breast hanging up there and it made him so mad. The third day he had looked over his arrows very carefully. One arrow had a longer point than the others, about four inches long. He thought his father must have put it in. It was an obsidian point. He went back that evening. He thought he would get him tonight. He shot a couple of ordinary arrows at Tso'apittse. Tso'apittse said, "Some straws are tickling me." Then the young man took the arrow with the obsidian point and shot and it hit Tso'apittse's anus. Tso'apittse said, "Ooooh," and squirmed around. His children didn't know what was the matter. The young man watched Tso'apittse squirm and die.

—Anna Premo
Owyhee, Nevada

Bat (1)

Bat lived way down in the bottom of the canyon. He would go up on top and travel around at night. He found two girls one night. He fell in love with one of them. He tried to whisk her down to the canyon where he lived in a magic way with his wings. He couldn't do it, she was too heavy. So, he told her what a fine hunter he was. At first he had not spoken at all, just tried to whisk her away. He told her there were lots of elk and mountain sheep in his country. She would never go hungry in his country, neither would her sister and their mother. The old mother found out that one of her girls was in love with someone. Bat never went to their house, he met the girls a way off. The mother noticed one of her girls was always going off to meet someone. The other sister told her about the girl's lover.

Then the mother asked the girl. She said the man she met told her about lots of fine things, buckskin dresses, how good his country was, how much meat they had there.

The girls' father was dead. The old lady thought the man sounded fine. She asked the girls where this man lived, but she said he never told her. "He just said I should bring my mother and sister and we would never go hungry."

The old mother said, "Bring him to me some day," and the girl said she would. So one day she told Bat her mother wanted to see him to make arrangements so they could move to his country. Bat said okay, but he would not go in the daytime. "I'll go see your mother tonight. Tell her to put out the fire before I get there." The girl said, "All right, I'll do that." She was so in love with him that she believed everything he said.

So Bat came. They had put the fire out and he talked to the old woman in the dark. He told her just the same things he had said to the girl. When Bat went, the mother said, "We have nothing to stay here for. The young man's country has lots of meat. Tomorrow evening we will move." The girl said, "We better wait till I see him again." So she met Bat and told him.

Bat was upset. "Here I've made all these false promises." He was living by the river, it was icy, and he had no meat. So the girl's family moved and got there at night. Bat met them at the river and took them to his place. He told his wife to go out in the daytime and gather seeds for their food. So she and her sister and mother went out for seeds. The old lady had a hard time getting out of the river bottom, the bank was rocky. She had to crawl and got her knees all bloody. This old lady was a little horned toad.

They lived that way for a long time. The girls were not easily discouraged. They were hard-working women. Bat told them he went hunting every night. He would come back at night and say he had killed a deer but it was too heavy so he brought just the fat. He told them to eat all the fat and not leave any of it overnight or it would be wormy and make them sick. So they always ate all the fat he brought. They weren't hungry for what he brought, for they lived on what they gathered. This went on for a long time. Bat never came home in the daytime. They never saw his face. Then they got to talking about him. "I wonder what he does every day. Where does he go?" The girls wandered all over in the daytime but they didn't find anything. Then they searched at night with a torch of sagebrush bark. They went down in the deepest canyon. They heard a noise down there, like thumping or chopping. They looked to see what it was. It was a deep canyon and their torch did not give much light. They could not get down and get back before Bat was due home. So they went home and planned to go with a bigger torch the next night. So they told their mother they had heard someone. She made a big torch out of the bark of the mahogany tree. It is better for a torch than sagebrush. She told the girls, "I'll make a torch and you go see who you can find down there."

The girls followed the river down the canyon through all its windings. They listened and heard the same sounds. They came to the place where the noise was. They saw someone pounding at the ice. It was Bat, this was the fat he brought home to his family to eat. They didn't let Bat see them but ran home and told their mother. She was very angry. They had had no meat since they came and they were angry that Bat just brought them ice.

Bat didn't show them his face because he was ashamed of it. He had such tiny little eyes and he was afraid they would not like his looks.

—ANNA PREMO
Owyhee, Nevada

Coyote Races

Coyote, his brother, Wolf, and Magpie were to run a race. Wolf told Coyote, "I want you to run a race with the five Mountain Sheep brothers. By doing that, if you win, we will have plenty to eat for a while. There will be plenty of witnesses." They did not think that mountain sheep were very fast runners. Wolf said, "Just as soon as you outrun the five brothers, I will be there to cut their throats."

Wolf had a certain place for them to start, at the crest of the mountain. The witnesses were to be at the right places all along there. After they got to the starting place, people got to saying that the mountain sheep were good runners. Then they saw Coyote, looking fine and fresh. They started. Coyote did not have a hard time outrunning them. Before they were halfway they were panting. Coyote got to the end of the course with such ease. He was so pleased with himself, he went around doubled over. Lots of people saw him.

Shoshone fandango, 1909. Northeastern Nevada Museum, Elko.

Wolf was very glad. He cut the throats of the mountain sheep and prepared a big feast. The people all ate. Coyote was very proud.

After this, Coyote was very sure of himself. Wolf said, "There is one thing more, I want you to race with Magpie. It will start way up on that mountaintop over there. Three magpies will race you." Coyote did not want to do this. He said, "What do you want to do, kill me? The Magpies are mighty birds. If I lose they will eat me up." Wolf said, "There would be lots of spectators. All the people will be watching on both sides of the course."

So the day of the race came. The Magpies got there before Coyote did. Then Coyote came, stepping from rock to rock (it was his superstition made him do this). One of the spectators sounded the alarm for them to start. All the spectators on both sides of the course made a lot of noise. Wolf was at the end of the course with a knife in his hand. Wolf had said to Coyote, "If you win, we will get all the pretty feathers of the Magpies. I want the feathers for my head. The wings I want for my buckskin suit." So Wolf was waiting to butcher the Magpies when Coyote outran them.

When Coyote started he was on the ground and he tore along. The Magpies put their wings against their bodies and just flew. It was downhill and they went very fast. When Coyote got to the bottom, there were the Magpies waiting for him. He didn't know what to do. He tried to hide from them. The Magpies said, "All right, here we are, ready to butcher you." Coyote said, "Don't butcher me right away. Let me go bathe in the cool creek before I die." So they let him. Coyote ran to the creek and tried to get under the water. (In the water there was lots of frog-blanket, green things that grow under running water.) The Magpies' quick eyes found Coyote hiding under this green stuff. So they went under the water and dragged him out. They killed him. So Wolf didn't get his Magpie feathers.

—Anna Premo
Owyhee, Nevada

Cannibal Brother

There were five elk brothers. The oldest had a wife. He wasn't very satisfied. He liked to wander here and there. He used to go out in the mountains. One time he killed a deer. He didn't come home. He stayed in the mountains till he ate all the meat. One day he cut his hand. He slept that night on the mountain. In his dreams he thought he ate something that tasted very good. The next morning when he woke up, his dream seemed very real. He kept thinking about it. The next night he went to bed. He dreamed the same dream. He did not know what the good thing was that he dreamed about. Then he dreamed there was a cut on his hand and that he was sucking it. When he woke up he found he was sucking his hand and that it was his blood that tasted so good. He couldn't forget it all day, how good his blood tasted. He kept licking at his hand till it was all dry. Next day he cut the calf of his leg and ate that. After he did that he realized that he could never go back to his home. "What shall I do now that I am ashamed to go back among my friends?" He even bit his tongue and ate it.

After a while, after a long time, he stayed in the mountains, eating himself. One of his brothers, the next oldest, came to look for him. He went to look for his older brother in the mountains. He called, "Where are you?" wherever he went. He wandered all over for a long time. Then there came an answer, "Here I am." He called, "Come here." "No, I can't come. A big stick ran through my body, that is why I can't come." So the brother came to the oldest brother. When he was a little way off, the oldest brother had a rope of deer hide that he threw at his younger brother and lassoed one of his feet. Then he pulled him over by him and he strangled his brother. He wanted to eat him. So he ate him.

Then the third brother got worried about the second who had gone to look for the first. "What is the matter? They go away and never come back." So he went hunting them and calling all through the mountains. One day while he was calling he heard a cry, "Here I am." Third brother said, "Where are you? Come to me." First brother said, "No, I can't. I'm not able to come to you. You come to me." So he went to him. Just like the second brother, the oldest brother lassoed him and pulled him to him, killed him and ate him.

A long time later the fourth brother wanted to go hunt for the three brothers who were lost. He was frightened yet he wanted to find out what had happened. Finally he made up his mind. He talked to the fifth brother and then he set off. He looked everywhere for his three brothers, but he couldn't find any of them. He called and then he heard, "Here I am."

"Come to me."

"No, I can't. There is a big stick run through my body. I can't move." So he was captured and eaten just like the others.

The last brother was the only one at home now. They talked about what could have happened to the other brothers. The people thought he better go look for them. So he took their advice and went up to the mountains. He thought about it a lot. He came to a place to cross a creek, a place to jump across. By accident, he stepped on a meadowlark. Hittoo, the Meadowlark, cried, "Oh, you broke my leg." So the elk came back and looked at Meadowlark's leg and, sure enough, it was broken. Then Elk said, "I'll fix your leg and make it whole if you will tell me what happened to my four brothers. I have lost my four brothers." So Meadowlark said, "Your first brother is a cannibal. He became a cannibal by eating his hand when he cut himself. First he sucked his own blood, then he ate his own flesh. He has eaten lots of his flesh off. Then his next brother went to hunt for him and he killed and ate him, too. The same thing happened to the third brother and then to the fourth. He ate them, and he will eat you, too, if he finds you."

So now Elk knew. He decided he would not go and hunt his brothers. He went home and told his people. He went to Coyote and asked what he should do. Coyote frowned about it. Then he remembered the widow of the first brother. Coyote called a council about this and they all talked about it. They decided they would move away. Coyote went privately to the widow of the cannibal and told her about her husband. He said, "We are going to move, all of us. You will go with us." "No," she said, "I am not going with you. You are not my man. I am going to stay here."

The next day the whole band of people moved away. They went down the river. The widow and her child stayed there. She lived there a long time with her child. One night she dreamed that her husband had come home. The next day she heard someone in the distance, singing. [Song here, in Bannock.] (The Bannock are speakers of Northern Paiute. With their drum the rhythm is different. When you sing, you sing in a different rhythm than the [Western] Shoshone do.) "What will those beautiful girls do when they know I have eaten all my brothers?" He sang this song over and over. It came nearer and nearer to the woman's wickiup. Finally she could hear it very plainly, close by. She was frightened now, not brave as she had been when Coyote wanted her to move with the people. She recognized her husband's voice. Finally he came into sight. He had something on his shoulder—bones all strung on the rope lasso he had used. She saw gaps in his body where he had eaten off his flesh. He threw the bones in front of her door and went in the wickiup. When he got in, he told his son to come to him. "Come sit on your father's knee." The boy was frightened, then he came. The father danced him up and down on his knee singing, "My little boy, I am going to eat you pretty soon." The mother thought about how foolish she had been not to move with the other people. Then she thought quickly, "I'll take my boy and run down to the creek." She stuck a horn spoon (like they used to stir seed gravies with) under her arm secretly. She thought how could she get that boy away from the cannibal. She said, "May I take the boy down to the creek and wash him up? He has soiled himself. I want to clean him up in honor of your homecoming." But the cannibal did not want to do this. He kept dancing the little boy on his knee, singing that dreadful song. Finally she got him to let her take the boy. "You be quick and bring him back. I've been lonesome for many years." So she took the little boy. She ran to the creek as fast as she could. When she got there she told the willow, "After we leave here I want you to cry like a baby and keep on crying like a baby all day."

Watching a handgame, Owyhee, ca. 1920. Courtesy Beverly Crum.

The willow agreed. She put the light horn spoon on the water and it became a boat. There were fast rapids in the river. She put her boy in the boat and got in and they sailed off. They went way down the river and landed in a valley. They got out and took the spoon with them. They went on afoot. She hoped to find her people some place there. So she did. They slept one night and next day she overtook her people and told them her story.

Crane was the head man of the bunch. He said to the woman, "Don't be afraid now. You are with your people. We will protect you if your husband comes. We will look for your husband every day. We will send spies out. We will do this to protect our people. When we find that he is around here, I will decide what to do."

There was just one crossing on that river. Crane thought they would trap the man there. "I'll put two spies at this place and one messenger. When they see him coming, the messenger can come to tell the people." The woman had described the man and they could recognize him by the way he had eaten the calves of his legs. They could see the bones sticking out.

A long time after, the messenger came saying a funny-looking man carrying bones on his shoulder was coming. He was singing and sang just what the wife had previously heard him sing, "What will the beautiful maidens do when they find I have eaten my brothers." So Crane took two of his councillors and went to the bank of the river by the crossing. He had them dig a little pit there, a shallow grave, a trench. He said, "I want you to bury me here and leave one foot sticking out of the ground, and the other foot doubled under." So they did what he said and buried him with one foot sticking out of the ground straight up in the air and the other doubled under. Then they went home. Crane stayed buried all that day and that night.

Next day the cannibal came across the river to the side where Crane was. The first thing he saw was a freshly dug grave. Then he noticed the leg sticking up there. Cannibals are always looking for anything like that. He went to the grave. He had eaten most of his own body and he was hungry. He began pulling on the leg sticking up in the air. Then the other leg, the right one, kicked him so hard he fell over dead.

—ANNA PREMO
Owyhee, Nevada

Man Taken Captive by Bear

There were no buffalo around here. The people from here used to go up to Montana to get buffalo. They had no horses, they had to walk. They hunted on the way for food. Before they set out in the morning they would decide on the place they were going to camp that night. One evening, one of the young men didn't show up. He had dreamed many times, and told them about it, that a mother bear had taken him. They always joked over it.

They had to move on. There was nothing they could do. They had it in their memories that they had lost a young man. They thought he might have met another tribe. So they went on their way to hunt buffalo. They stayed a long time. Finally they set out for home. They came by the valley where they had lost the young man. They stayed all night there. Next morning they moved on. While they were going, they were walking, they heard someone calling. They looked to see where the voice came from. They heard it several times. Then they saw someone running fast. Here he comes. It was the young man they had lost. They were so glad to see him. He was happy, too. They asked him where he had come from and why he was running so fast. He told them right away. "You know what happened to me when we were camped here? I was caught by a she bear. Where have I been all this time? Locked

up in a cave. She is after me right now. She will be here any time
and she will kill me." The people looked in the direction from which
he came and they saw the old bear. She was coming fast. Finally
she got there. The people lined up in two parallel lines, making a
road for her. The young man was at the other end. They had arrows all ready. The bear didn't notice the line of people. She saw
nothing but the young man at the end. When the bear went between the lines of people, all the men shot at her. Near the end, the
young man started running and the bear ran after him, but she died
before she got to him. They said they would butcher her and they
did. When they started taking her insides out, they found a human
infant inside her. So they wouldn't eat the bear. They just took the
hide and the claws. Then the young man told how the day he had
left to hunt and had not returned to camp, he was caught by the she
bear. She hugged him and took him home. He couldn't get away.
From then on he wasn't his own boss. Every time the bear went
away she locked him up in a cave. She kept him captive. Toward
spring, she got too sure of herself, she didn't lock him up. Then
came warm days and she would be out all day. Then one day he saw
dust in the valley and he ran away. He told details of how he and the
bear had slept together. That was how she had that little baby in
her uterus.

—Anna Premo
Owyhee, Nevada

[Mrs. Premo said this is a true story told by her grandmother.
They say that she-bears always take a young man to sleep with them.]

Coyote and the Wood Tick

Coyote was trotting along and he heard someone talking. He listened and got mad. He went back to the place where he heard it.
There was lots of grass there. He kicked the grass. "He is always
after his daughters. He has intercourse with his daughters." Coyote couldn't find anything in the grass. He would go on, but then he
would hear that voice calling him that bad name again. So he asked
his rectum—that was always his advisor. His rectum said, "You go
back there to that place and in the grass you'll find a little red thing
like a ladybug." So Coyote went back and he found that little red

thing and he kicked and kicked it and flattened it out. That is how the wood tick got flat. Then Coyote went on and he didn't hear any more name calling.

—ANNA PREMO
Owyhee, Nevada

Cannibal Giant

He had a house to which he would invite people. The first time they came, everything would be all right. Then, next time there would be a big feast and lots of people would come. He had a big thorny sickle that cuts for miles around and when the people were coming in great numbers he would swing his sickle and kill all the people. His hands stayed clean that way and the people died far off and the survivors didn't suspect him.

Then, one time a family came who had a wise little son. He hunted all the time, he was a good hunter. He found lots of skulls, skulls of the people who had been killed by the giant. He went home and told his parents about it. They went away and came back with some more people. Then they went to visit the giant. The little boy was with them. The boy met an old man there. He did not live with the giant but near there. The old man told him to warn his parents to leave because the man they came to visit was a cannibal. He never pitied anyone. He killed people for miles around. The boy said, "Oh, one time when I was out hunting I found lots of skulls. That must have been it."

The giant's name was Naahpaihtem Pambi, Six Heads.

—ANNA PREMO
Owyhee, Nevada

Orion's Belt (1)

A woman was always running off. She made tracks on the ground with her vulva. Her husband saw these deer tracks made by the vulva when he followed her. She ran and ran. She was afraid he would punish her. She asked power of Piake Piake (the caterpillar that changes into a sort of dragonfly—it has a black-and-white body

with transparent wings, but it is not a dragonfly.) The woman borrowed a wing from the insect and got up to the sky. She is part of
Orion's belt.

The woman was running away from men, she was scared of
them.

—ANNA PREMO
Owyhee, Nevada

[Mrs. Premo does not know who the other
two stars in the constellation are.]

Coyote and Fox

Fox was living alone. He hunted a lot and had plenty of meat.
Coyote was always hungry. Coyote came to Fox's house. Fox had
some eggs. Coyote asked him where he got them. Fox said, "Oh, I
go out and look for Sage Hen and ask her kindly if she will let me
have some eggs. She is my neighbor. She always gives them to
me. You have to be good to her if you want to get anything from
her." Coyote asked where she lived and Fox said, "She lives way
down in that valley, down in the sagebrush." Coyote said, "I'll go
see her some day." So he ate with Fox. Two or three days later
Coyote thought about Sage Hen and her eggs. He went down to
where she lived. Sage Hen had already hatched her young. Coyote
looked all around for eggs but couldn't find any. He could only find
the nest egg—there is always one egg that doesn't hatch. Coyote
found that one rotten egg. He was very mad. He killed all that
bunch of chicks and smeared them with the rotten egg so it looked
as though they had eaten that rotten egg and died.

—ANNA PREMO
Owyhee, Nevada

Coyote Wants to be Chief

People from all over the country—all kinds of animals, even Stink
Bug—gathered together in a valley for a council. Rumors were go-
ing around that a lot of them wanted to make Coyote the head man.
Meadowlark told Coyote that Coyote was going to be a great chief.

As he was going along, Coyote met Skunk, who told him the same thing, that Coyote was going to be the biggest chief there ever was. Then Coyote met Badger and he said the same thing. Every time Coyote heard this he got so swelled and he wished he would meet some more people who would tell him the same things.

Coyote wanted to find his brother. Wolf had been away for a long time. Coyote ran around that valley so fast, looking for Wolf, that he got all tired out.

The council was to start before the sun came up. Coyote didn't sleep the night before, he was so weary. In the middle of the night Coyote got sleepy. He still had a long way to go to get to the council. Coyote sat down to rest a little while in some timber. He didn't want to go to sleep but he was very weary. His eyes began to close. He picked up some little yellow flowers and propped his eyelids open with them. He fought sleep but he was so tired. Finally he fell asleep and didn't wake up till noon the next day. He got up and ran toward the valley. To his surprise he began meeting people. They were coming back from the council. He started asking, "What did you talk about? Who became a chief?" And they all told him, "Your brother did. He is the biggest man in the country now. He is the chief."

Coyote wanted to find his brother. Then Coyote found his brother and asked him if he were the biggest chief. Wolf said, "Yes." The people all wanted him to be the biggest chief.

—Anna Premo
Owyhee, Nevada

Weasel

Weasel was bad. He was a wicked man, killing everyone. Weasel and his little brother went along killing people. They came to the home of two old women and a daughter. The two old women were not home. Weasel had intercourse with the girl and pushed her dress inside her with his penis. Then he killed the girl and roasted her in the fire and left her there in the fire. Then they went on their journey.

The two old women saw the men going on their way and said, "Our son-in-law has been good to us. He must have killed a deer, butchered it, and roasted it in the ashes and left it there for us." So they took out what was in the fire and started eating. They didn't suspect anything until they got to the lower par' of the body where they found the apron inside the girl. Then they vomited and cried and cried. They didn't know how to get revenge. One of them said, "Let's take all of our pubic hair out and find the tracks of these men and plant the hair in their tracks, one by one. Then let's set fire to the hairs and tell the fire to burn, burn, burn until it catches up with those men and burns them up."

So they did that. The fire roared along and finally caught up with the Weasels. They ran and ran. The older Weasel tried to make a backfire but they could do nothing. The fire caught the younger brother first. He ran while he was on fire and cried, "Brother, I am burning all over!" Then the fire got to his head and he cried, "Brother, my spirit is leaving me!" Then he died. The fire caught the older brother then and killed him.

—Anna Premo
Owyhee, Nevada

Eagle Hunting

There is a hot spring in Elko. Everyone goes to bathe there. There is a cliff on one side. There used to be an eagle's nest there. One day when there were young eaglets almost ready to fly, there was a man and his wife there. They wanted the feathers. The woman was to hold the rope while the man lowered himself to the nest. He got down to the nest. One of the eagles flew up close to the wife and she reached after the eagle and let the rope go. The man fell into the boiling water.

—Anna Premo
Owyhee, Nevada

Water Babies (1)

The place where archaeological remains are is a spring called Paoh-maa, Water Baby. A long time ago a water baby lived there. Some Indian doctors still believe in them.

A long time ago women did all the work. When they went to

get the wood they would have to lay the baby down. Then the baby would cry and when she gave him the breast to nurse, it would swallow the breast, and then the whole mother. The water baby would swallow the baby while the mother was away and then swallow the whole mother.

Tom's stepfather says when he was a young man he and another man were out hunting. They killed three or four deer. At night they made a wickiup and a big fire. Then they heard someone crying. His friend got so scared he just shook. Tom's father had never heard a water baby before. When they got back his grandmother told him it was Porcupine they heard.

—ANNA PREMO
Owyhee, Nevada

Comments from Anna Premo

Sometimes when two or three old men are telling a tale, they can't agree and will argue over the right way to tell it. They also often argue about which moon it is. Tales are told on winter nights, usually by old men. They sing and dance in the appropriate places. Tales should not be told in summer or they will bring on an early winter.

They call Wolf and Coyote brothers (*nanapapi*). Coyote is called *itsappa*, both the animal and the myth character. *Isa* or *pia isa* means "Wolf," "Big Wolf." Mrs. Premo says there are no separate special names for myth characters.

When children are mean, parents will say, "We'll call Tso'apittse to come from the mountains and take your head in his pitchy hands and take you home for his children to eat you."

Tso'apittse means "ghost." A whirlwind is a ghost. People believe that you can see the face of a ghost in the whirlwind. A whirlwind can spin a child around and make it sick. Then the Indian doctor names the dead person in the whirlwind who tried to take the child away.

Mrs. Premo's aunt used arrow points for luck. She sewed them in a piece of buckskin, which she wore around her neck. It protected her from witchcraft or gamblers using things against her for luck.

When a girl got pregnant and wouldn't tell who the father was, the people called it Coyote's child.

Tom and Anna Premo (center), Owyhee, ca. 1920, with Presbyterian missionary. Courtesy Beverly Crum.

Once when they were haying and it was hot, an old woman said, "It's too bad that Cottontail and his brother were short or they could have thrown the sun higher and it wouldn't be so hot."

There are songs in most of these tales. Each character has a particular way of singing. Tso'apittse has a particular way of talking—he adds *wi m* on the ends of words. When he is running he says, "Wi wi wi wi," all the time.

Coyote has a particular way of talking; *pai pai* is added to the ends of words. Cottontail has no particular way of talking. They call him *tapu* but they also call him *tataputtsi,* a sort of nickname. Wolf has no particular way of talking.

Skeleton Ghost

A man was traveling east toward the Utes. He told them there was a spring there where they could not sleep. He said, "I did and it made me run away from all my folks." A couple of boys didn't believe it so they took a pack horse and traveled over there. They built a hut of sagebrush and went to bed. In the night they heard sounds of drums and cries of warfare in the distance. It was getting

closer and closer to them. The boys were scared and couldn't stand
it and they ran away and left the pack horse and everything and
went home.

They were telling about it at home. One man said, "Oh, there's
nothing to it. What's dead is dead." He was going to try it. He got
there and he piled up lots of wood for an all-night fire. When darkness came he sat listening. From below him he could hear the war
start and mournful cries. The sound kept getting nearer to him.
Close to him he could hear somebody say, "Phew," like it was
tired. The man looked out and finally he saw it come into the fire-
light. It was just a big skeleton. It came in and sat by the door. The
man said, "If you'd said you'd killed a mountain sheep, I'd lend you
my knife."

Skeleton: "Lend me your gun, then."

Man: "If you'd said you were going hunting, I'd hand you my
gun."

Skeleton: "Give me something to eat, then."

Man: "If you had a place to put the food, I'd feed you."

Skeleton: "All right, then, we'll have a fight."

Man: "If there were a war going on we'd fight. But there isn't,
so we won't fight."

But then they started for each other. They stood up and were
fighting. The Skeleton dragged the man and the man dragged him
back. When the fire died, the Skeleton got stronger, so the man
threw wood on the fire. In the dark the Skeleton would win, so the
man kept trying to keep the fire up. They fought till morning and
there was a great cloud of dust hanging where they were fighting.
The man was almost licked. At daylight the Skeleton said, "Oh, you
are very powerful, a wonderful warrior." This man was a war chief.
The Skeleton said, "Where you see a big tree, look and find my
bow and arrows cached there. I'll give them to you."

So he looked for the cache. After a while he saw a grove and he
looked in there. Inside was the same skeleton he had been fighting
with and a bow and arrows. He wondered if that was what he was
supposed to find. There was once a big battle there. It is always
that way at an old battleground.

This is a true story.

—HERBERT HOLLY
(Tom Premo, translator)
Owyhee, Nevada

Tso'apittse (2)

Tso'apittse started from his house to hunt for people. When he walked, the mountains shook. He sang, "I wonder if there are any Pine Nut Wood people here." He was walking in the forest to look for people to eat. As he came through the trees he saw a couple of fresh human tracks. The people were hunting cottontails. Tso'apittse said, "Ah, human cottontails have been here," and he looked to see which way the tracks went. He started at a trot to trail them. The people heard Tso'apittse coming and saying, "Whi, whi, whi, whi." That scared them. The only way they could get away was to climb up. So they started to climb up the hill and down the other side. When they got to the foot of the hill, there was an old woman camping there and they made for her house. The old woman said, "You keep on going. I'll use my club on him." She dreamed that she was a monster-fighter.

Tso'apittse was already coming down, still hot on the tracks. The old woman was in the back of the house. Tso'apittse sat down and said, "Hudu." Then he got up and the old woman jumped up too and they had a hand-to-hand fight. Tso'apittse had a conical basket for packing things in. It was lined with pitch. He threw people inside and they stuck and couldn't escape. He tried to put the old woman in but he failed. The old woman finally threw Tso'apittse on his behind. He got up and saw the print of his behind on the ground. He got up crying and went home because he wasn't allowed to have the print of his behind on the ground.

So afterward, Tso'apittse tried to make another hunt. He looked for more human tracks. As he went over the saddle of the mountain he came near a man who was traveling. The man stood still and froze with his arms outstretched like a tree. Tso'apittse walked right by him. Tso'apittse looked at the man then went on. He stopped again and looked. He was suspicious. He would go away and look back to see if it moved. The man was still there. Tso'apittse said, "What is it? A burnt stump?" He went back a way and looked again. He couldn't make up his mind what it was. Tso'apittse came right up close. The man just froze and didn't dare breathe. Tso'apittse said, "He has a penis and a nose." He tickled him but the man didn't move. Tso'apittse pushed him over and the man fell with his arms out and he didn't move. Tso'apittse went away and said, "Oh, it's just a burned stump." The man didn't get up until Tso'apittse was gone. Tso'apittse kept going on down to the valley.

Near a big pine a couple of boys ran into him. Tso'apittse said, "Young human cottontails." He chased them around the junipers panting, "Tsoa whi whi, tsoa whi whi." They kept on chasing around in the junipers. He said, "I'm going to have a feast." They kept on running and the two boys hid behind a tree. When Tso'apittse wasn't looking they ran to another tree. They got up to the summit and looked back and saw Tso'apittse still running around the tree saying, "Whi, whi, whi." After a while when they were a long way off he started trailing them again. They went down the other side of the mountain and came to an old man's house and said to the old man and his wife, "Tso'apittse is chasing us." The old man was a doctor and he sat down and started singing and said, "You'd better go along home." The old man was calling on all his spirit helpers. He was calling the last one when Tso'apittse came in at a trot. Tso'apittse had big red eyes and he popped them out to look fierce. Tso'apittse sat down and said, "Hudu." The old man's wife was hiding back of the house. The doctor had all his spirit helpers. Tso'apittse was looking back the way he had come. The doctor made some waving motions with his hands over Tso'apittse's head and took out Tso'apittse's spirit and threw it back up the trail. Tso'apittse saw his spirit going up the trail and he jumped up and chased it back up the mountain.

Around Eureka on the hillside is a big rock that looks like a person. They say that is Tso'apittse's body where he died chasing his spirit.

—HERBERT HOLLY
(Tom Premo, translator)
Owyhee, Nevada

Another Tso'apittse Tale

A man and his wife had one child. They kept telling him, "Don't cry or Tso'apittse will hear." He was an unruly child. Afterward they heard Tso'apittse coming. The mother and father went to the back of the house and hid. They were mad at the child. Tso'apittse came in and said, "Oh, my little granddaughter, here is some rat liver for you." He had some pitch and he warmed it in his hands and said,

"Tsoawet," (deathly) and put his hands on her head. When he pulled them away her scalp came off with them. He took her home with him.

(When Tso'apittse comes, the children are held there by some power and the parents get away alone.)

So Tso'apittse went hunting again to find the father of the little girl. He came upon him and chased him and finally caught him and put him in his basket. Tso'apittse was going through the pine trees. The man reached up and grabbed a limb, and Tso'apittse went on without knowing the man had gotten away, and went home. Tso'apittse got home to his children and said, "There is one human cottontail in my basket, go and look for it." They looked and said, "There's nothing there." Tso'apittse jumped up to see for himself. Then he started back to where he had caught the man. The man heard him coming and hid and watched him. A big blizzard came. The man started for Tso'apittse's house and cut a big pine club on the way. At the cave the man killed all Tso'apittse's children. Pretty soon he heard Tso'apittse coming and he blocked the door with trees and branches. Tso'apittse said, "What has grown in my door?" He shook it and could not get it out. Just as the trees were about to give, Tso'apittse gave up. He said, "It's cold." He tried again, but had to give up. He couldn't move. Toward morning the man heard Tso'apittse cease whining. He was frozen. The man leaped out and saw Tso'apittse lying down, frozen to death. So he went off without making a sound. He thought Tso'apittse might just be sleeping. The man was never bothered anymore so he thought he must have killed him.

—HERBERT HOLLY
(Tom Premo, translator)
Owyhee, Nevada

Theft of Pine Nuts (1)

They were playing Hand Game. One man was lying on his stomach watching the game and he inhaled the smell of pine nuts. He came near dying, it was so strong, and it brought blood in his throat. It seemed queer to the people and they said, "Ask him what is wrong. He doesn't do that unless something is wrong." They asked him and he said, "The smell comes from the north." They held a council and said, "Now we will go and investigate." These men were east of where Austin, Nevada, is now.

The first night they camped at Tu Sunguwe—hot springs are now there where they camped. Near Gold Circle is another hot springs where they camped next night. The last night they camped at a place now called Chinese Hat, the buttes near Owyhee. They didn't cook there. The chief stayed on a little butte. The others camped on a big one.

Next day they went to Juniper, where the first pine nuts were. When they got there it was fall and pine-nut season. They schemed to play Hand Game and to have some of the fellows look for the pine-nut kernel when everybody was playing. Mouse was to look for it because he can work well at night. Cottontail was to blow his flute to make people forget things and listen to him. Reports would come in to the chief (Raven) that they hadn't found it yet. In olden times they used to tie things for safe keeping on top of a slick pole. And that is where they found the pine nut. They wanted Flicker to knock it down. That night he buried his tongue in damp dirt to make it stretch longer. While Cottontail kept people amused and put them to sleep, Flicker knocked a hole in the pine-nut sack and they all poured down. In the bunch was one that was a seed. They took it and started back with the seed while everybody was still gambling.

An old woman was watching the pine-nut post. She tried to warn the people and say, "The pine nuts are stolen." But Cottontail patted her mouth with his hand so they couldn't understand. By the time she told the people, the thieves had a head start. The pursuers finally caught up and noticed that the pine nut kept changing hands and they could never grab the right one. In the bunch of people was Coyote. He would run ahead over the mountain and back again. He said, "Let me carry it because I'm fast and they can't catch me." But they did not want to give it to him because he was Coyote. The men who were pursuing the thieves caused a sheet of ice to form in front of them. Coyote would come to the edge and try to tear up the ice with his teeth. Chief Raven was standing at a little distance. People said, "Let the chief do it." But Coyote said, "What does he know? He is lost in the fog. Let me do it." But Raven started to sharpen his knife (his beak) and the other people were right on top of them already. Raven flew at the ice and cut it in two and they passed through. But the enemies went

through it right behind them. They finally had to give the pine nut to
Coyote because he was fast and he ran ahead, but he bit the end off
of it and blew it out to sow pine-nut trees. He said, "Now there will
be pine nuts growing here." So they took the rest of the nut away
from him so he wouldn't sow it all.

The enemies were right on top of them again, so Raven took
it. The enemies could always tell where he had hidden it—under his
wings or wherever it was. The chief of the enemy was chasing Raven, chief of the thieves. Everybody else fell behind. Raven wished
that his thigh would rot and then he hid the nut in the stump and
said, "If he kicks me, this leg will fly off." The enemy kicked him to
pieces and turned around facing his people who were coming up.
He took out his pipe and started to smoke. His friends came in one
by one and he said, "You fellows cut him and find the nut." They cut
him up but didn't find the nut. The enemy chief remembered then
that the rotten leg had flown off when he kicked Raven so he looked
for it but only saw tracks where it had run away. Off in the hills
there was lots of smoke where everybody was already roasting
pine nuts.

The people said, "What are you going to do?" He said, "I'm going over and invite myself to the pine-nut feast." The chief was
Crane. They gave him some pine-nut soup when he came. His
people went home but he was going to be friendly even if the others
had stolen from him. They gave him something mixed with the pine
nuts instead of the good stuff. He said, "I'm going home to Duck
Valley and eat water bugs." When he jumped off to fly home, an old
woman took a stick and hit him and knocked off his tail. That is why
he has to put his legs out behind him when he flies.

—JOHNNY DICK
(Tom Premo, translator)
Owyhee, Nevada

Bungling Host (1)

Jackrabbit had a camp and Coyote came and visited him. Jackrabbit
said, "What can I cook for us?" He had his bow and arrow on the
wall. He took it and shot under every sagebrush and when he came

Mary Hall in front of her house, ca. 1930. Courtesy Beverly Crum.

back he pulled out all the sagebrush and laid them on the coals of the fire. When he took them out of the ashes they were nice fat rabbits and they had a fine meal.

In return, Jackrabbit came and visited Coyote. Coyote remembered what Jackrabbit had done and said, "What will we have to eat?" He took his bow and arrow and shot all the sagebrush and pulled them up in the same way Jackrabbit had done and then he laid them on the fire. To his surprise, when he took them out of the fire they were smoking sagebrush stumps. Jackrabbit went home.

So Coyote went and visited Otter where he was camped near the creek. After visiting a while, Otter said, "What can I get for us to eat?" He took a short twig of willow, split it and dove into the water with it. When he came up, the twig had speared a lot of fish. So they boiled them and had a fine feast.

Otter came to visit Coyote. Coyote said, "What will I find for us to eat?" He took a willow twig as Otter had done and jumped into the water. But he started to drown. He filled up with water and he only got out by his magic. But when he got out he had no fish. Otter went home.

Coyote went to visit Beaver in his camp by the creek. Beaver said, "I don't know what we'll have to eat." But he heard his children playing on the bank, so he killed a couple of them and cooked them. He said, "Don't touch the bones with your teeth, but lay them aside right here." After they finished, Beaver threw the bones in the creek and soon Coyote heard the little beavers playing on the bank again.

Beaver returned Coyote's visit. Coyote said, "What can I get for us to eat?" But he heard his children playing outside. He went and killed them and boiled them for supper. Beaver wouldn't eat any because it smelled so bad while it was cooking. Coyote ate some and then threw the bones in the river. The bones sank to the bottom, much to his surprise.

Coyote went to visit Mountain Sheep. Mountain Sheep said, "Let's see what I can find for supper." He took his bow and arrow and went off. He shot his arrow straight up in the air. When the arrow turned to come down he turned around and put his rear end up and the arrow shot him in the anus. He put down a tray and twisted the arrow and pulled all his fat out. They had it for supper.

Mountain Sheep went to visit Coyote. Coyote said, "What will we have for supper?" But he remembered what Mountain Sheep had done. He shot his arrow up in the air and turned around so the arrow would hit him in the anus. He was scared and shook but the arrow hit him in the right place all right. He bawled and ran around. Whenever he touched the arrow he cried like a child. Finally he pulled it out but it was only a bloody arrow. Mountain Sheep had to go home hungry.

Coyote got disgusted and left the country so guests wouldn't bother him. On his way he found a nest of little sage chickens. He urinated on them, threw dirt on them and went on. The mother hen found what he had done and followed him. When he was coming along the river, she hid by the bank to scare him. When Coyote was opposite she started to fly up and scared Coyote so he fell into the water.

The reason sage chickens look speckled and dirty is because Coyote threw dirt on the chicks. Sage hens always fly out and scare people that hunt them the same way the mother hen did to Coyote.

Coyote got mad and got his bow all ready to shoot. He said, "If she tries that again I am going to shoot her." So he traveled along with his bow ready. Again Sage Hen scared him, so he dropped his weapons and fell in the water again.

He went on and soon he came upon a wildcat sleeping. It was daytime. Coyote pushed Wildcat's nose in and the tail, too. That is why Wildcat looks that way today. When Wildcat woke up he found his nose gone. He followed Coyote's tracks and soon found him asleep. He rolled Coyote's nose between his palms to make it sharp and then he pulled his tail out long. Coyote woke and saw the shadow of his nose, so he felt it and it was real long. When he got up he felt something behind him. It was his tail and it scared him.

—Johnny Dick
(Tom Premo, translator)
Owyhee, Nevada

Origin Tale (1)

Coyote was camped near a big river making rabbit nets. He was the only one there. No other being was around. As he was sitting there he noticed and felt a yellow glare was all around him. He sat there and saw the yellow light around him but he didn't turn around. He looked and his eyes lit upon a young woman without any clothes on. That light came from her flesh. She saw him, then she disappeared. He saw her going farther away and said, "I'm going to chase her." He was in such a hurry he got tangled in his net. Finally he got after her and caught up to her at the river. He said, "You carry me across the river." She took him on her back and started across. He kept sliding down. She said, "You behave yourself or I'll throw you in the river." Finally he got down to the place he wanted and got what he wanted quickly and she threw him off. He floated down the river to a bend where there were willows and got out on a bank. He got out and got to her home before she did. There was an old woman at the camp. She was in the ramada and he sneaked in the tent and rested. As he lay on his back he noticed arrows hung up on the walls as if they had all been taken from different men. But there were no men around and Coyote began to get suspicious. Meanwhile he heard a voice talking to the old woman. It was the daughter. She said, "I threw Coyote off in the river." The old woman said, "Sh-h-h, Coyote's inside." The old woman said to Coyote, "There is my daughter's bed opposite the door. You can sleep with her."

Night came and Coyote wanted intercourse. He started feeling and he felt something snap like a dog. He knew what it was so he went out and got a young, straight rose stem with lots of thorns and a stone pestle. In those days women had teeth in their vagina. Coyote stuck the stone pestle halfway in the girl's vagina and she snapped and broke her teeth. He cleaned out the teeth with the rose thorns. That was the original sin and sin was to continue.

After a while she told him to go get some water in a basket to wash the children. Coyote went to the spring. There was lots of mud and grass so he slid on it all day and forgot about the water. After a while he remembered and went back for the water. Before he had committed the sin there were no people. On the way to camp with the water he noticed people all over. They had multiplied and were going east. When he got there he noticed some children, dark, with big stomachs. They were too weak to travel. The others had all gone. The women had left the poor ones behind. But Coyote was not discouraged. He took water in his mouth and blew it on the children and made this prophecy, "Even if you are ugly and poor you will sometimes conquer." The white people were made over here and then went east. The Indians were Coyote's children and I believe Coyote's prophecy that they will always win and that the whites will be licked.

—JOHNNY DICK
(Tom Premo, translator)
Owyhee, Nevada

Coyote and Wolf

Coyote and his brother, Wolf, were camping together. Every time Wolf went hunting he brought home a deer. Coyote would go out but he couldn't kill anything. He kept asking Wolf, "Where do you find these deer all the time?" He kept nagging until Wolf finally told him. He said, "There is a certain hole where they all are. You open it up and let one out and then close it." Coyote went there and opened the hole, then hid in front of it to be in position to shoot, but the deer started coming out too fast for him. Finally they all got out and that is why there are deer all over now. Coyote said, "Deer are too easy to kill. It would be more fun if the deer could smell and dodge a hunter." So he grabbed a deer and punched holes in his nose, so after that all deer could smell. Coyote had a hard time getting near a deer, but he finally aimed at a big buck, but he missed and shot a fawn. He brought it home to Wolf and said, "Here is something tender for your teeth." Wolf had already seen the deer going out into the mountains and valleys but he didn't say a word. He was disgusted with Coyote.

Coyote stewed some of the meat and said, "Come on and eat," but Wolf was mad and wouldn't eat. Coyote ate so much that his bowels got loose and he had to defecate. He went out on the hillside and his feces rolled down the hill. Coyote turned around to see where his feces went and he noticed a bunch of enemies going down the valley. He came home and told his brother, "The enemy is coming." Wolf got up and smelled and sniffed. He told Coyote to go west and get some tall canes for arrows and to come back quickly. Coyote brought home a lot of canes. Wolf held up a cane as though it were an arrow and said, "Arrowhead and feathers form on it." Then he dropped a completed arrow. He did that for all the canes.

He put Coyote in the house and told him, "Remember, you stay in here and don't peek out. If you do you will cause me to be shot."

Wolf was going to do the fighting and Coyote was to stay hidden. The fight commenced. The fight was so interesting that Coyote couldn't stay in. He wanted to watch his brother fight. All he could see was the enemy. He jumped up and looked out the smoke hole. He saw the enemy being mowed down but he didn't see Wolf.

Finally he caught hold of a pole and held himself up and saw his brother. The minute he caught sight of him, Wolf fell dead. That was all. The enemy went on.

Coyote couldn't get out of the place until the next morning because Wolf had tied the place (house) up. He found Wolf's body but the enemy had taken his hide. Coyote started trailing the enemy and spent night after night on their trail. He finally came up near their camp. He came across one old woman getting wood. He asked her what they did with Wolf's hide. She said, "We hang up the hide and have a dance." He asked her which side of camp she lived on and she told him. He killed her and beat her to a powder and shook her bones out of her skin and then he put on her skin and picked up her bundle of wood and went to her camp.

He went the wrong way and some boys said, "Grandmother's lost, let's take her home." So they took her to her place and left her there. Coyote put down the wood. He saw Wolf's hide there and started crying. The boys asked why he was crying and Coyote said, "Build up that fire so it will burn better, the smoke is bothering my eyes." Then Coyote said, "Now I do hate this Coyote. As a song of triumph I'd like to sing over the hide tonight." Then Coyote said, "Tonight nobody stays home. Everybody is going to dance."

The young women took their babies to Coyote so the grandmother could care for them. The babies were quiet because Coyote cracked their heads in and laid them in a row so they wouldn't make any noise. Coyote was to sing and he wished the night to be as long as two nights and he would sing all night, twenty-four hours. Everybody was dancing except the real old women who were standing back and watching. They noticed Coyote's ankles and recognized him. The dance continued until morning. Coyote said, "Eat your breakfast, then go to sleep. I'm going to sleep awhile." So he lay down and pretended to go to sleep.

After they ate, the old women said that they were going to sleep. They always had the hide on a pole. Coyote slipped off the old woman's skin and jumped up the pole and got the hide. The old women tried to shout and warn the people but Coyote covered their mouths so nobody could understand. He got away and every night he buried the hide in fresh dirt. Wolf's hide would wake him in the morning and say, "Get out of bed." Coyote thought that his brother was resurrected, but each time only the hide was there.

Tom Premo and daughter Beverly Crum (right), Owyhee, ca. 1930. Courtesy Beverly Crum.

The last morning when Coyote woke up, he found his brother sitting there with the hide over him.

—JOHNNY DICK
(Tom Premo, translator)
Owyhee, Nevada

Eye Juggler

Coyote saw some little black-headed birds with black tails. They were playing. Coyote said, "What are you doing?" They said, "We toss our eyes up into the willows then shake the tree and our eyes fall back in place again." Coyote tried it but his eyes stuck on the twigs and he couldn't get them back. So Coyote had to make another sense, a sixth sense, which he put into his eye sockets and it led him around.

—JOHNNY DICK
(Tom Premo, translator)
Owyhee, Nevada

[Johnny Dick told "Eye Juggler" at the end of "Coyote and Eagle," then said it should come at the beginning.]

Coyote and Eagle

Coyote had a house. Two young women came to visit. They said, "We have come to marry a man called Blackie." This was Eagle. Coyote said, "My brothers always called me Eagle. You've probably heard of me." But the girls knew that Eagle had a house nearby and knew that he was a mighty hunter, always killing deer. They did not stop but went on to Eagle's place. Coyote got up a scheme. "I know where Eagle always comes when he is on his way home with a load of meat." Coyote was going to take his meat away. Coyote dug a big pit on the path and covered it with branches to trap Eagle. He had a forked stick to pin Eagle down when he fell in. Eagle was coming into sight. Eagle was trapped as Coyote planned and Coyote held him down with the stick. Coyote said, "Give me your meat." He took all his belongings and clothes, too. After he had all his belongings he killed Eagle, took his load and went on.

He went to Eagle's house and tried to make the women believe he was Eagle. They were going to let him rest. He laid his head on one woman's legs and the other put out her legs for his feet and took off his shoes. The older sister looked at his lice. He tried to resist but they held him. Without being asked he shook his head and said, "I have no red lice." He told on himself. The younger sister had already noticed that he had Coyote's feet.

Next day he went hunting again. While he was gone, the sisters fixed a board for his head and one for his feet instead of letting him use their laps. After he went to sleep when he returned, they put his head and feet on the boards. This gave them a chance to run away. They put ants on his head so he would feel them moving and think the older sister was scratching him. Coyote felt the ants and in his sleep he shook his head and said, "I have no red lice." He bumped his head on the board and woke up and missed the girls. He started to trail them. The girls noticed that Coyote was gaining on them. They tried to shake him but he was catching up. The older sister said, "Coyote hears your beads rattling and that is how he follows us. Throw them in the canyon." So the younger sister threw her beads into the deep canyon. Coyote couldn't see, but he followed the sound of the beads and fell into the canyon. After a while the girls peeped over the rim to see him and saw that he had broken his legs and was eating the marrow out of the bones. They said, "Oh, you nasty Coyote, you are eating your own marrow." He said, "If you only knew better you would know that this is mountain sheep marrow."

—JOHNNY DICK
(Tom Premo, interpreter)
Owyhee, Nevada

Rolling Rock (1)

Coyote was camping with his brother. His brother had a beautiful ring that Coyote wanted. He kept asking about the ring but his brother wouldn't tell him where it came from until one day he said, "Way over there on the rock there are a lot of them. You take one, but don't touch the others." Coyote went over but he was so greedy he filled all his fingers with rings until there was no room for more. He started to dance and held out his hands and watched the rings as he danced. Then he went away and as he went he looked back and noticed that the rock began to move and roll. After a while he looked again and noticed that the rock was rolling after him. He climbed and the rock climbed after him. He said, "It can't roll sideways." So he went to one side and still the rock followed him. It was almost on top of him when he reached the flats.

He saw a man there so he said, "Nephew Night Hawk, the rock is upon me." So he passed him and nephew was going to catch the rock. Night Hawk dived the way night hawks do after bugs and hit the rock and the rock smashed against Night Hawk and broke all to powder.

Night Hawk told Coyote, "Go straight now and don't bother anything and quit trying to do everything anybody is doing."

So Coyote went on and he met a bunch of birds that were singing. Some birds that live on pine nuts flew over. They were black with red breasts, and were about the size of flickers. The little birds would sing and the birds flying over would drop and the little birds would eat them. Coyote said, "What are you doing to make them fall?" The little birds answered, "We sing [song here] and pull out some pubic hairs and throw them up and the birds fall down."

So Coyote went on. He saw the big birds flying, so he sang and pulled out some hairs, but he was too anxious and pulled open his stomach and his guts fell out. He hurt himself badly and then went away.

He saw some chipmunks eating wild carrot roots. Coyote said, "How do you get them?" They answered, "We put our tails down in the ground and pull out the roots." So Coyote tried but only got little roots. He said, "How do you get such big roots?" They told him to push his tail in up to the butt of it. So he tried it but he couldn't get his tail out again. Every time he moved it went in deeper. He got so far in that just his nose was sticking out. He said, "Little brothers, the earth is swallowing me up." The chipmunks laughed and ran away.

After a while his brother, Wolf, came along and pulled him out. Wolf said, "Now behave yourself. There is a person coming through water on a raft with a load of rendered fat. You may eat once with him but no more." Coyote was sitting on the bank. He saw the person with the fat floating down on the water. The man told Coyote, "You can have one bite, no more." So Coyote took a bite and went on. He told the person, "There is another man below who likes to eat fat." So when the stranger floated on down the river, Coyote ran ahead and stopped down below. After a while the raft came by and the person said, "You can have one bite." Coyote opened his mouth and the person noticed that there was fat hanging between his teeth. So just as Coyote bit, the fat melted and Coyote bit into the air.

—JOHNNY DICK
(Tom Premo, interpreter)
Owyhee, Nevada

Cottontail and His Brother Shoot the Sun

Big Cottontail had a brother, Little Cottontail. They were angry at the lowness of the sun. It traveled too low, it was too hot. They started from their own country. They camped every night and dug a trench so they would be ready to shoot the sun when it came out in the morning. They did the same thing every night until they came to the end of the earth. It took them a long time to travel to the end of the earth. They got to the shore of an ocean.

The arrow would shoot about a hundred feet. There was a little rocky island there where the sun came out. They made a lot of holes in the ground to hide in. Big Cottontail made a very deep hole straight down and a curving trench along the surface. Little Cottontail made a shallow hole and trench, not deep like his brother's. They stayed in this place quite a while before they killed the sun, because when the sun came out, he turned his face away from them. When the sun got up he would sit for a while, then reach up and catch hold of something, pull himself up, jump and then he would be up in the sky and would travel.

They shot and shot at the sun but their arrows would burn up before they reached him. They ran out of arrows. They had nothing left except the torch of sagebrush that they carried. That is what they used to kill the sun. They shot him with this torch. As soon as they shot the sun, they ran down their holes. The last thing Big Cottontail heard was his brother screaming. It took quite a few days for the dead sun to cool off. The water boiled. It was very hot. Cottontail and his brother stayed in their holes. Big Cottontail wished for North Wind to blow. He wished the wind would bring snow. Just as Cottontail wished, the North Wind came, bringing rain and snow. It got cold. Then came Frost. Finally Big Cottontail came out of his deep hole. He thought something must be wrong with his brother, for he did not see or hear him. He was afraid he had burned to death. Just as he thought. He searched in the hole that Little Cottontail had made and he found him there, dead. He pulled him out from the trench and he revived him. After Little Cottontail came back to life, they went over to where the sun was. They got to butchering the sun and took out the gall. Then Big Cottontail told his brother, "Let's make a sun out of it." Then they made the moon out of the bladder. They made stars out of some other part of the body—maybe the eyes. As they were pushing the sun up they said, "You've been too hot all these days. Now you go way up high and don't be so hot anymore." They got everything done. They made everything perfect. Big Cottontail thought about going home. He said to his brother, "I think you better stay here. You can't be following me always. This will be a good country for you." So, Little Cottontail stayed there and Big Cottontail started home alone.

When Cottontail started home, he started killing people. When he was on his way he met a bunch of pine-nut birds. There were lots of them playing on a young cedar tree. They were swinging on a sapling, bending it down and letting it spring back. So he said, "Let me ride." And they let him get on and swing. Then he said, "It's your turn," and they all got on and he pulled the tree way down to the ground and let it spring back so hard that they were all thrown off and fell to the ground dead.

Then he went on his way. He heard Mourning Dove crying. He stopped to see Dove. He asked her, "What are you crying for?"

"Oh, I am lonesome, my son died. That is the reason I'm crying." Big Cottontail stayed all night with Dove. He didn't harm her. He mourned with her. Next morning he left.

He passed a rocky hill and he heard something there. Voices calling, "There goes old Cottontail. He's coming back from killing the sun." It was the groundhog calling out, making fun of him. This made Cottontail mad. It made him feel very bad to have people call like this to him. It reminded him of what a hard time he had on that journey to the end of the world and how hard it was to kill the sun. When people talked this way to him, it made him feel so bad it brought tears to his eyes. So at the bottom of this rocky hill Cottontail made a good hot fire and got lots of red-hot coals. Then he called to the rocky hill, "Move!" When the hill moved, lots of groundhogs appeared. He killed and roasted them and carried some along to eat on the way.

Then he went on his way. He met Coyote. He gave him a roasted groundhog and said, "I have something for you to eat." Coyote was so glad to get it. While he was eating it he said to Cottontail, "Where did you get the groundhog? It tastes so nice." Cottontail said, "I got it over at that rocky hill. That's a good place to get groundhogs." Then Cottontail told Coyote how he caught the groundhogs by calling the hill to move. So Coyote was very pleased and thought he would go over and try it.

After Cottontail left, Coyote went to the rocky hill and made a fire there. He was going to do what Cottontail had done. Then he called to the rock, "Give me groundhogs!" After he hollered that way, lots of groundhogs came out. He killed them all, then cleaned and roasted them. He ate some and he took some with him. While he was eating he thought about another rocky place where the groundhogs were bigger. So he thought he would go there as soon as he finished eating. So he went there to the other rocky place. He made a big fire and called to the rocky hill, "Give me groundhogs." He called so many times that lots of groundhogs came out—so many that they ran after him and chased him. So Coyote ran round and round the fire. They chased Coyote till he gave up and they caught him. He fell right into the bed of coals where he had planned to roast the groundhogs.

Cottontail went on his way. He came to a woman's wickiup. She was making a water jug of willows. Then Cottontail spoke to her, "What are you making, my sister? Is that a water jug?"

"Yes, it's a water jug."

Then Cottontail said, "Let's play a game of weaving each other in the jug. You let me get in and you weave, then I'll get out and you get in." So Cottontail got in the jug and the woman wove and then he said, "This is enough. Let me get out." Then the old woman got in. Cottontail started to weave. While he was first weaving he did good work. Then, after a while, he began to weave funny and he wove the jug closed so that it was just a round ball, all closed up. Then he used it for a ball. He bounced the old woman around in there until he killed her.

Then he went on his way. He came to a place where Hummingbird and an insect named Pi Ak lived. Cottontail talked to these two brothers. They were licking the wild honey that is on the willows sometimes. Cottontail said, "How do you get that sweet stuff to eat?" Hummingbird and his brother said, "We shoot at it with our bow and arrow. When we shoot at it, there is honey left on the point of our arrows and we lick that." Then Cottontail said, "Shoot at it now while I am watching you." The brothers said, "Oh, we are afraid to do it, because when we shoot at it, it chases us." Cottontail insisted, so they shot at it. But Cottontail himself shot at it and hit it. It came down from the sky and Cottontail shot at it. Often, when it came down from the sky, it burned the brothers when it hit them on the forehead. When Cottontail shot it, it all came down in a heap. Then after Cottontail shot it down, he asked them about their water and they said, "Oh, the water always chases us." Then he said, "What do you do for firewood?" and the boys said, "The wood always runs after us and chases us." Then Cottontail took his bow and arrow and shot the water. It made the water divide, come apart. He did the same thing to the sagebrush, and then the wood and water couldn't chase anybody anymore. These were the only people he met on his way that he did not kill. This was because when they saw him coming they had said, "Red Willow, our brother is coming," and Cottontail liked that name so he liked those brothers.

Then Cottontail went on his way. In the afternoon he heard lots of voices. Sounded as though people were hunting for something. Cottontail moved under an overhanging rock. They saw him there, they were hunting rabbits. They said to each other, "There's a rabbit there," but Cottontail ran out through a hole in the back of the rock and got away from them. After he ran away from there he walked till he came to a wickiup. There was one girl there. She was the sister of the boys who had chased him from under the rock. He went into the wickiup. When he got inside he painted red circles around his eyes. Then when the boys came in and saw him they got scared and went out again. One by one they came, were frightened and went out again. There were lots of boys. Outside they would say, "Oh, I'm not frightened, I'll go in," but when they went in they were frightened and came out again. Their sister was sorry for them and she said, "You better wash that point off your face. It frightens my brothers. They are getting cold outside and want to come in." So Cottontail washed his face and the boys came in.

Cottontail had taken an oblong rock and hung it at the door when he first came in. The girl had not seen him do it. Cottontail wanted the boys to hit their heads on this when they came in. When the boys came in, they bumped their heads on the rock and then they came in and began preparing the rabbits they had caught. They put them in the ashes to cook. They did not give the stranger any. So Cottontail took a piece of his rabbit-skin blanket and wished it would turn into a rabbit. It did and Cottontail put it in the ashes to roast. When he thought his rabbit was done, he shot an arrow at it and dragged it out with his arrow. This was fatter than any of the other rabbits. After they finished eating they went to bed. Cottontail didn't go to sleep. He stayed awake. Then he got up and blew his flute. He went outside and blew his flute, like a song. When he was sure they were all asleep he went inside and made sure and then he set the wickiup afire. Then he tried to take the girl out. She said, "Why do you want to rescue me? I want to stay with my brothers and burn up with them." So Cottontail left the girl there and she and her brothers all burned up.

Then Cottontail went on his way.

—ANNIE BEALER
(Anna Premo, translator)
Owyhee, Nevada

[Annie Bealer counts up here, how many adventures Cottontail has had. She takes a long time here trying to remember which episode comes next. It is very important to get it straight.]

[Mrs. Premo says once when they were haying and it was hot, an old woman said, "It's too bad that Cottontail and his brother were short or they could have thrown the sun higher, and it wouldn't be so hot." Cottontail's brother's name is Tsug. He is singed all over by the sun. He is smaller than Cottontail, has shorter ears, they are round, not pointed.]

Cannibal Bird (2)

Two young men went out hunting and a water bird took them away. These men were away out hunting. They camped at a certain place. One morning they were getting ready to go hunting and their

folks said, "You two be careful because there is something about
this country which makes it necessary. You have to be careful of
that water bird." One of the two young men didn't believe this. So
when they had gone, he said, joking, "I'd like to see that water
bird. I don't believe there is such a thing."

When they were in the timber, still together, they heard a
sound. It was a kind of roaring sound, but they did not see anything. The sound seemed to be coming from underneath the sun.
The sun was shining and when they looked, it was too bright for
them to see. When they heard this sound they were frightened and
wondered where they could hide. They thought about what their
folks had said and thought this might be that bird. They ran under a
big tree but the bird came right down, smashed the limbs of the
tree, and came down on them. The claws caught hold of the men
and the bird carried them off. He took them to his home. His
mother was there at his home. The old woman found that one of
the men was dead, the other alive. The old woman didn't eat human
beings, she lived on fish. The home of that bird was on an island.
He ate humans. After they got to the island, the bird didn't notice
that one of the men was still alive. The old woman hid the live man
with her big basket. The old woman said, "I am disgusted with my
son and the way he eats human flesh. I am tired of it."

After a while the bird flew back. He was ready to eat his victims. The old woman had to cut open the man for her son so that he
just had to dip his bill in and drink the blood. Before he came to eat
the blood and flesh, the old woman got out some obsidian and broke
it into pieces and threw them in the blood. So when the bird was
drinking the blood, his head would move slowly. His feathers all
ruffled up. He couldn't get his head down—it stuck up. Then he
started to leap up toward the sky. When he flew up, the old woman
told the man under the basket, "You watch him. If he is still alive he
will come down in a certain way. But if he is dying he will come
down in a different way." They lost sight of him up in the sky and
then they saw him again, wobbling back and forth as if he were dying. Finally he fell down toward the island. The old woman said,
"Watch him. If he is dead, he will just flop back and forth." So the
young man watched and said, "I think he is dead." The bird fell to
the ground.

Then the old woman went to work. She burned the joints of

the wings and took them off. She told the young man that she was going to make a boat. While she was making the boat, she said, "If the wind takes you this way there is nothing but water, but when the wind carries you the other way you will be going toward your own country." She got him ready and sent him off in the boat. She could see the boat just going round and round the island. He had a fire on the boat. The wind didn't come up. This went on for many days. The old woman got worried. Then she wished that the North Wind would blow. The wind came up during the night and next morning the boat was out of sight. Before the old woman put him on the boat, she said, "When you get to shore there will be two Water Boys there. The boys will give you advice as to what you are to do."

Finally, the young man got ashore. He met the two Water Boys. They are the Water Boys that travel around the world all night and meet each other at a certain place. When they meet, their heads bump together and they laugh. The boys had just met and they were happy and they used him as a ball, throwing him back and forth to each other. Every night when the boys were about to start off around the world, they would put the young man on a forked stick. There were many monsters that came out at night. Then they put him up high where nothing could reach him.

These monsters came out from the water at night. Then when the Water Boys came back in the morning, they would take the young man down and play with him, throw him back and forth like a ball. Every day the Water Boys made moccasins and buckskin suits for him. That is the way they spent their days. The young man stayed there a long time. Then the Water Boys talked to him. They told him of places where he would spend the night on the journey to his home. They told him that the first night he would be in a land where there were many lizards, water lizards. He must get lots of wood and make a circle of fire around the place where he would sleep. So when he camped the first night, he made a circle of fire and slept in the middle of it. The lizards came out, many of them. Toward dawn they almost got him. Then morning came and they vanished and he went on his way.

The Water Boys had told him that on the second night he should look for a place with a ditch that goes straight for a way then has a sharp curve in it. He got there before the sun came down and it took him a long time to find a suitable place to sleep. So he slept in the curved part of the trench. He spent a peaceful night there and went on the next morning.

On the third night the Water Boys had told him to camp early, make a fire and keep it going all night. They said the fire should be in a sandy place, that the lizards live in the sand. All that night he kept the fire going and the lizards came one right after the other. They stood and looked at him but didn't come close. The night wore on and they kept coming one right after the other. Then morning came and he was safe.

On the fourth night the Water Boys had said this night he would meet the *Tso'apittse* who lived there and that they would tickle him. They told him to stand all night by a dead tree. "Lots of *Tso'apittse* will come and tickle you." So he got there and did as the Water Boys had told him and stood by a dead tree. Tso'apittse came and felt him all over and said, "It looks like somebody, he has ears, mouth, head, everything." They would push at him but he never laughed. The Water Boys had told him that if he laughed he would die. Morning came finally and he was safe.

The Water Boys had told him to spend the fifth night in a cave that was irregular. The opening goes in and then comes a curve. He was to hunt for a cave like this. This was another place where Tso'apittse lived. If they found him outside they would carry him home and eat him. So he found the right cave and spent the night there. Tso'apittse stopped at the mouth of the cave and said, "Sounds like we hear someone breathing in there." They had a stick with a hook on it and they would poke it in and feel around and try to get hold of it. Then morning came and he was safe.

On the sixth night the Water Boys had told him he would come to a very deep, dark canyon. They had told him he must wear his buckskin suit there. They said the canyon was full of rattlesnakes and that every time an owl cried he must run fast. So he got there and night came and he traveled through many snakes. He couldn't hurry even when the owl did cry. He tried his best to hurry, but everywhere he stepped there were snakes. He had on lots of suits and leggings and gloves and by morning they were all worn out. He came near the end of the canyon and saw a narrow light opening where he could get out. Finally he got to the mouth of the canyon and came out into light again.

The Water Boys had said that after this journey he would be in his own country where he would meet no more dangers. So he walked on after he got out of the canyon. He saw smoke and he went toward it. He arrived and found people there. They had deer and they were cooking it but they didn't eat. They just inhaled the smell, for they had no mouths. They gave him meat to inhale but instead of that he ate it. They all watched him, they were surprised that he had a mouth and could eat. One of the people motioned to him that he wanted to have a mouth cut. So the young man started to cut a mouth on this man and he found that under the flesh there were teeth. The man found that he could laugh and could eat now. Then they all wanted mouths and began cutting each other themselves. They didn't wait till their mouths were healed before they ate—they ate while they were still all dripping blood.

This place was close to his own country and he got home.

—ANNIE BEALER
(Anna Premo, interpreter)
Owyhee, Nevada

Bat (2)

Bat is a hunter. He goes hunting all the time. Someone was jealous of him. One fellow was jealous of him. He took Bat to his home. He had a red-hot rock there and he made Bat put it in the palm of his hand and shut his hand on it. The man said, "If you do this, you will be a good hunter and kill lots of game." After that Bat went hunting, but he never did kill anything.

—ANNIE BEALER
(Anna Premo, interpreter)
Owyhee, Nevada

Chitawi

A man went south with some other men. While he was there he captured lots of oxen. Then he brought them back home with him. Lots of oxen. They made a corral and put them in. Then they started eating them up. Their people were living there. The few pieces that were left of the ox heads are over near Squaw Valley. When spring came they would move on to another place and drive what oxen were left along with them. They went two or three days' journey to another place.

Chitawi (the name of the man) had sons and daughters. There is a place, a sagebrush knoll, where he used to go up alone and beat his drum and sing.

They didn't stay there. They moved on toward Midas (about eighty miles from Owyhee). They didn't stop at that mountain but kept on traveling. They came by the mountain by Tuscarora (a ghost town now, used to be a mining town). They kept going till they came to another little mountain. There was a white cabin there and the people there found out about the oxen. The few white people there found out. Then the people on the Humboldt found out these Indians were catching oxen. Then the militia came after them and overtook them. The guns roared but the Indians got away, but they left the oxen behind them. The soldiers pursued them through the mountains, Midas, Tuscarora. The militia had some Indian scouts and they advised Chitawi's people that if they wanted to live, they better separate from Chitawi. Two scouts, one George Washington, one George Hyde, one Hideoha. These scouts told them they must separate, for the militia were watching them. Some of the people listened to the scouts and some didn't. Families left secretly, they were afraid of Chitawi. It was said that Chitawi started in young, as soon as he saw white people, he was on their tracks. He liked to eat their oxen. He had been mixed up in the killing of white immigrants. He didn't fear the militia or believe the Indian scouts. But the militia kept after them. They got over to Shoshone Mountain (not far from here) and the militia caught up with them there. There is lots of timber there. Chitawi was an old man of sixty then. He had his oldest son, a middle-aged man, with him. The militia caught up with them. They told the Indian scouts they were going to attack. They sent a spy ahead to see how to attack. The spy returned and told them just where the Indians were. The soldiers went to this place during the night. Early the next day the soldiers told the scout to tell the Indians that the soldiers were there, that they must surrender or fight. Instead of telling them to surrender, the scout shouted to his people to fight. The guns began to roar. Just one man escaped to tell this story. He ran and got way on the hill. The soldiers shot at him but didn't hit him. After a while, when the militia had killed a bunch of Indians like that, they gathered up their possessions, rabbit blankets, jugs, etc. When they were searching like that they found Chitawi, he was killed, his guts were spattered all over.

—ANNIE BEALER
(Anna Premo, interpreter)
Owyhee, Nevada

Rolling Rock (2)

A long time ago Rock used to chase people. In those days people used to get their wishes. If they wanted groundhogs, all they had to do was to call and they would come and then they cooked and ate them.

One time Coyote wished to go up in the hills. He wanted some groundhogs so he called for them. Instead of groundhogs coming, Rock came and fell on his tail and wouldn't let him go. It stayed there until Coyote died of starvation.

—JULIA PANGUISH
(Anna Premo, interpreter)
Owyhee, Nevada

Orion's Belt (2)

Orion's Belt is an arrow. There were lots of deer coming along. Coyote was hunting. He was a man. He ran into a bunch of deer. Then he shot at them with his bow and arrow. The three stars are Coyote's arrow.

[Mrs. Bealer says all the stars have names and stories about them.]

—JULIA PANGUISH
(Anna Premo, interpreter)
Owyhee, Nevada

The Flood

Once upon a time there was a man. He got mad and said, "Our land doesn't seem to smell good. Everything stinks. I think we better make another land." They slept that night and all through the night he sang and sang and sang. He wished for a great water. The great water came. It took everything away and cleaned up all the land. It washed the highest mountains everywhere.

The people went on top of the highest mountain and stayed there till the water went down. It went as this man wished it would. After the water died down, the land and everything was perfect again and clean.

—Julia Panguish
(Anna Premo, interpreter)
Owyhee, Nevada

Water Baby

When Julia was little they used to hear Paohmaa (water baby). When you hear the crying, it means someone is going to die. Owl is that way, too. When Owl comes around the house at night talking, that is a sign there is going to be a death.

When anyone is going to die, Bull Frog croaks around the house.

—Julia Panguish
(Anna Premo, interpreter)
Owyhee, Nevada

Rat and His Mother-In-Law

Once Rat spied his mother-in-law's vulva and then he thought, "I better do something to get her out some place." So he made a scheme. He said to his wife, "Take off your dress and give it to your mother. She and I are going hunting. She can butcher for me." So he went hunting with his mother-in-law and then they went to a fandango. She wore her daughter's dress. When they got to the dance, Rat sang for the round dance. There were lots of people there. Rat sang and his head went back and forth as he sang. Rat was having a good time, singing. Somebody poked him in the stomach, someone with horns, and left a scar there. Wood Rat still has that scar. Next day he and his mother-in-law left the dance. They went toward home. On the way they spent a night together. They had separate beds but Rat kept telling his mother-in-law, "There are lots of ghosts in this valley," and the old woman got afraid. She started moving closer to him and finally got into his bed. So Rat got at her. She got pregnant and later had a baby. When they got home she was ready to have the baby.

—JULIA PANGUISH
(Anna Premo, interpreter)
Owyhee, Nevada

Council on Seasons

Once Coyote and Wolf were going to make the calendar, make the months. Coyote said, "Let's have ten months of winter." He wanted ten months because he said, "Then we can get all the rabbit skins we want and have rabbit blankets." Wolf said, "No, we don't want such a long winter."

Wolf said, "Babies will be born by a woman flicking her thumb and finger." Coyote said, "No, it's better to lie between a woman's legs, let her have a baby as a result. Then when the baby comes, the woman can go off and have her baby in a separate house. It looks better that way. Then when the woman and baby have stayed out there and been washed clean, they will come back to the house and eat deer meat."

Wolf said, "When we make anything like clothes or shoes, we'll just press the skins together and the things will be made."

"Oh, no," said Coyote, "it is better to have to sew them and prick yourself and see blood come out. If the awl slips, it will prick the woman's leg."

—JULIA PANGUISH
(Anna Premo, interpreter)
Owyhee, Nevada

Bungling Host (2)

Elk and Coyote were together. They got talking. Elk said, "What can we eat? We could sit and eat and tell stories." Elk shot up at the sky with his arrow. When the arrow was coming down he stooped over and the arrow went into his anus. He twisted the arrow and caught his kidney fat and pulled it out. Then he and Coyote sat down and ate it. Next day Coyote wanted to do the same thing when Elk came to see him. He shot an arrow up, stooped over and got the arrow in his anus. He pulled out his kidney.

—JULIA PANGUISH
(Anna Premo, interpreter)
Owyhee, Nevada

Coyote Avenges Bear's Death

A long time ago there were Coyote and Bear. They were brothers. Bear was the oldest and Coyote was younger. They were getting ready for a fight. They made lots of bows and arrows, preparing for war. They made quivers of deer hide to pack their arrows in. They spent years getting these all ready. One day they saw a big cloud coming, way over in the distance. They thought this cloud was the enemy coming to do battle with them. It took years, not days or weeks, for that cloud to move toward them. So, Coyote and Bear kept on preparing for a big battle (just like the Germans). They stored away lots of food. Finally, that cloud of dust came closer. Then the Bear locked Coyote up in the house. Bear said, "You stay in the house and I'll do the fighting." Then the battle started. Bear fought them alone. Coyote stayed in the house. He tried to get up and see out, he was anxious. Meantime, Bear was killing people right and left outside. Coyote finally grabbed some sticks way up in the wickiup and pulled himself up. As he caught the main pole he looked out. Bear changed himself into various forms while he fought, such as rainbow, willows, a bunch of grass. Coyote looked out and saw Bear transforming himself. Coyote wished that they would shoot his brother in the calf of the leg. Then he wished that Bear would sit down with his back to the enemy. Then he wished the enemy would skin him. His wishes came true. Bear was shot in the leg, he sat down, he was skinned.

Then the enemy started off, taking Bear's hide with them. Afterward, Coyote felt sorry about this. He cried for his brother. Then he started making arrows. It took him a long time, years.

The enemy who took Bear's skin, when they camped at night, would dance around Bear's skin and play with it.

Coyote started off after the enemy. He took all his arrows with him. He hunted for the places where the enemy had camped at night. At each of their camping places, he left a quiverful of arrows.

Before Coyote started he defecated in the mouth of his brother's dead body.

Coyote got to a place where he saw the enemy had had a fire and he figured when they had been there. Then he found where they had wintered. He found many camps. "They were here last year." Then he came to a place where they had built willow shades. "This must be where they were last summer." Then he came to a place. "They were here just a few months ago." As he walked along he would cry. He cried so much that the salt from his tears crusted all around his eyes.

He got to a place where they had camped. He looked at the ashes and said, "They were here recently." He stuck his hand in and found the ashes still warm. He saw some bones lying around and he started eating them. Then he found another place where they camped and he said, "They were here yesterday." Then he wished. "I wish I would find an old woman. I wish that I could ask her all about everything, about her people, about my brother's skin, how her people lived, how they go to bed at night, what they do. I wish I would meet an old woman from their camp."

So his wish came true and he met an old woman. She was very tired and had fallen behind the rest of the party when they were traveling on. Then Coyote caught up with her and started talking to her. They sat down and told lots of stories. The old woman told Coyote, "My grandchildren (grown-up men) have been singing every night. They take Coyote's brother's hide every night and throw it over their shoulders and dance and sing with it." Then the old woman said, "What do you do for a living? My grandchildren hunt ducks and rabbits, that is how they live." Then Coyote said, "What do you do?" The old woman said, "When I am traveling, I gather lots of grass, rye grass. I pile it up and take it in my basket. It is for my grandchildren's beds. I take it to camp and lay it in little piles and they sleep on them for beds." She said, "When I get to camp with the grass and when they are ready, they come and feed me. They bring me ducks and I hold the feet up like this and I begin eating it. Every night my grandchildren dance, they never miss a night. All night they dance and then, toward morning, they come and wake me up and make me come over, put on the hide and sing and dance around." After Coyote had heard all this he said, "Is that all?"

"Yes, that's all." Then Coyote kicked her to death and said, "Now you lie here like this and now you talk." Then he shook her flesh out of her skin [laughter] and he put the outer skin on himself. He took her talking-stick and her burden basket. He tried to walk like an old woman and to make his face all wrinkled up. Then he set out on his way. He gathered piles of rye grass just as the old woman had done. When he got to camp he laid out the piles of rye grass just as the old woman had said she had done. When they brought him food, he held the duck foot up just as the old woman had done.

Toward morning they came and got the old woman, Coyote. [Laughter.] Then Coyote got out to the dance place and they threw the hide over his shoulders. She started in dancing, did a peppy step. One person noticed it and said, "It doesn't look like our grandmother, the step is too fast." Then he noticed Coyote's eyes. "Those don't look like our grandmother's eyes, they look like Coyote's eyes." Then Coyote whined, "Oh, don't talk about me like that. I'm not Coyote." (This said in a whiny voice.) Coyote tried to groan like an old woman who was tired, but a coyote's howl came out. [Laughter.]

It was just gray dawn. Coyote wished that everything would work out. Coyote wished for the old woman's skin to come off quickly in the twinkling of an eye. It did and fell to the ground and Coyote yelled, "Here is your grandmother's skin, you dance with this." So Coyote ran off with his brother's skin over him. They chased him, they shot at him with their bows and arrows. When Coyote reached those camps where he had left quivers (he was out of arrows), he found the quivers he had left there and he had more arrows to shoot. Then Coyote wished for a fog or cloud so they wouldn't see him. When the fog went away they would discover him again and chase him. Then the enemy lost Coyote.

When Coyote got home he found his brother's body was lying there with no skin on it, but it had a big moustache. [Laughter.] This was because Coyote had defecated there. Then Coyote spread the skin over the body and went to sleep beside the body. He thought toward morning he heard his brother say, "Make fire." Then he heard it again, "Make fire." He jumped up and made a fire. So Coyote and his brother were happy together.

After a while they went hunting. Older brother told younger brother about something he wanted him to do. Older brother said, "When you kill a deer, there is one thing I don't want you to forget to bring home—the *haikwii* (inside the intestines, but before you open it; it is not the liver but looks like it; it is not edible [spleen]). Coyote and his brother separated when they hunted. Coyote met a deer and chased it and killed it. He butchered the deer but he forgot to bring the *haikwii* home as older brother had asked him to do. He took the meat, went a little way and remembered the *haikwii* and went back. When he got to where it was he started to pick it up but it flew away, crying, "Haikwii, kwii, kwii."

When he got home he found his brother there. Coyote told what he had done and older brother said, "I told you not to forget that *haikwii*."

That winter they had lots of snow. It was a hard winter. They didn't have any wood. Older brother thought it was because Coyote had forgotten the *haikwii*. So older brother kept scolding Coyote about it. It snowed lots. Coyote made a fire someplace. His brother did not like him much any more. Coyote heated a round rock in the fire until it was red hot. He threw it. It rolled a long way through the snow and made a path to his house, a dry path. He followed the path home. His mother was home. He stayed there all night. It snowed all night after he got home.

Coyote had a younger brother, Mouse. Coyote told him, "I want to go hunting this morning. You go out and try the snow. Tell me how deep it is." So the boy went out and came back and said, "Oh, there's only a little bit of snow." So Coyote went out and he sank through the snow. Finally he managed to get out of the snow and came in the house. He was angry and he wanted to kill Mouse, but Mouse ran out and away. Coyote could see him a long way off, just a little black dot on the snow.

Mouse met people who didn't have any mouths. All they could say was, "M-m-m-m-m-m." They wanted to eat, but couldn't. They would make a fire, cook food, and just inhale it. They were *nenemusi.* Mouse took a piece of meat, cooked it on the coals, and then started eating it. The *nenemusi* started crying, "M-m-m-m-m." So Mouse took one of those people and cut a mouth for him. Then they all wanted mouths and started cutting them. They began to eat while the blood was still flowing from the cuts.

In a dead log there are great big black ants. They used to be the *nenemusi.*

Mouse stayed with the *nenemusi* awhile. One day they all went hunting. When they were out hunting they found a deer locked up in a willow jug. Meantime, they met Coyote. He was the one who took the cover off of the willow jug and the deer all ran out. They tried to run the deer down but they caught nothing. They shot at a fawn and wounded it, but it kept on going.

There was a wickiup there and the little wounded deer ran toward it. In the wickiup was young man Rattlesnake. Someone said to him, "You shoot at the deer, he won't see you because you are gray and close to the ground." So Snake went out toward where the deer was coming. As the deer came near, Snake bit him in the side and he died. Then Snake lay on top of the dead deer, for the people who had been chasing the deer were coming. When they got there, Coyote was at the head of them. Coyote said, "Get away— that is my deer and you are spoiling the skin." Then Coyote started skinning the deer. Snake could do nothing about it. Coyote took the deer.

—Julia Panguish
(Anna Premo, interpreter)
Owyhee, Nevada

Big Dipper

The Big Dipper is Coyote and his son-in-law, trapping. It is their rabbit net. Coyote and his son-in-law, after they got the rabbits out of the net, began to roast them. They made a big fire. Soon they heard lots of people coming. Then they saw them coming. These people were also getting rabbits in nets. Coyote and his son-in-law saw them but they didn't like them so they took their rabbits out of the fire in a hurry, put them in their bags and ran away before the others could see them. You can see the ashes of their fire—the little dusty stars. The Dipper is the trappers and their net. They

Jenny Owyhee, mother of Julia Panguish, ca. 1930. Northeastern Nevada Museum, Elko.

took their meat because they were ashamed or afraid of the people who were coming. The people were like magpies, blackbirds, crows, chicken hawks, snakes, frogs.

—Julia Panguish
(Anna Premo, interpreter)
Owyhee, Nevada

Man and Ugly Girl

Once there was a girl. She looked very pretty from behind. She had long, long hair. A young man admired her. He hadn't yet seen her face. A long time ago they had pottery to cook with. The young man hung around the wickiup where the long-haired girl was. Finally he said, "Our pot is boiling over. Look!" And then the girl turned around and he saw her face. It was very ugly—she was Porcupine. The young man ran away from her—she was so ugly.

—JULIA PANGUISH
(Anna Premo, interpreter)
Owyhee, Nevada

Coyote Gets Racehorses by a Trick

Coyote thought about visiting another bunch of people. He thought of some people he knew who had a good racehorse. He wondered how he could win it. He wanted to eat it. He wished for a black-and-white rabbit for his racehorse. He wished to find the rabbit and turn it into a racehorse. His wish came true and he had black-and-white racehorses. When he got close to the camp, he was riding one and leading another. The chief of the camp came to Coyote. Rumors went around that a man had arrived who wanted to race with their racehorse.

Next day they prepared for a race. They saw Coyote's two horses and they all admired them. When the race was to start, Coyote had to get a jockey from the camp. He wanted one of them to ride his horse. He found someone to ride his horse. Then Coyote told the jockey, "I don't want you to whip him while he is running. When the other horse catches up to you, just whistle at him and kick at him, don't whip him." When the race was halfway, Coyote's horse was ahead. Coyote's horse won. They led him all over, they wanted to race him again and they had another horse to put up against him. They thought that while the horse was tired they could beat him with a fresh horse.

The race started. Coyote had the same horse, same jockey. The other people had a different horse. Coyote's horse was far behind this time. In the middle of the course Coyote was wishing that the jockey would whistle. Then the jockey whistled and as soon as the horse heard it he went ahead like a shot and Coyote's horse won again.

Then the people wanted to buy Coyote's racehorse. One man offered him two horses for him. They planned another race. This time Coyote was going to race his second rabbit horse, the white one. The new race started. The jockey of Coyote's horse forgot and whistled right at the start and Coyote's horse just shot right ahead and won in a second. He ran away from the opposing horse. Then the people wanted to give Coyote two horses for the white horse. He traded it for two horses. Now he had four horses. (His white horse was a snowshoe rabbit.)

Coyote went home now with his four horses. While he was on his way Coyote ate those four horses.

Next morning the people at the camp went to look at their racehorses and they found two rabbits there—a black one and a white one.

—JULIA PANGUISH
(Anna Premo, interpreter)
Owyhee, Nevada

Wolf Replaces Coyote's Eyes

Wolf and his brother, Coyote, lived together. Coyote was out and he found two sisters. Coyote wanted to marry them right away. The girls wanted him to go out and hunt for them, get deer or something. They found a bunch of buffalo. Coyote had a weasel skin over his eyes. He started shooting at the buffalo. Coyote was a poor shot, he couldn't get any. Finally, by chance, he killed a poor little one. The girls made fun of him, "You can't shoot." He began skinning it. Coyote was very poor at skinning an animal and they made fun of him. Coyote said, "Oh, I've skinned more than one buffalo." They all finished skinning and butchering. So then Coyote wanted to have some fun. "Come here, let me put my head on the lap of one of you and my feet on the lap of the other." The girl who held his head, he asked her to hunt his lice for him. While she was picking his lice, she looked at his eyes. She lifted the lid and saw a bunch of worms in there. She thought, "This is why he couldn't kill any buffalo." Coyote had gone to sleep while she was hunting his lice. He was so sound asleep that the girls talked to each other, "I think we better try to run away. We don't want to live with a man who has worms in his eyes." So they planned, "Let's get that buffalo hide and put it under his head." Then she said to the other girl, "You go get a bunch of ants while I fix the hide under his head." She got the ants and put them in his hair. Then they fixed everything up and made lots of tracks around the house to confuse Coyote so he couldn't track them easily. Then they ran away from him. They ran as fast as they could. They came to the edge of a canyon with steep sides.

Coyote woke up and looked for his wives. He hunted and hunted for them but he couldn't see very well. Finally he got onto their tracks. The girls had scaled the walls of the canyon. Coyote was close behind them. They planned, "We'll go straight here, then we will make a sharp curve along the cliff." They wore necklaces around their necks that they always wore. So one girl took off her necklace and jingled it. When Coyote heard it he ran fast after them. He fell way down from the cliff. He fell down into the canyon. He broke his leg. The girls looked down from the top of the cliff and they laughed at him, made fun of him. Coyote looked up and said, "You girls mustn't laugh. Your husband is eating mountain-sheep marrow." He really was eating the marrow from his own broken leg.

From that canyon Coyote managed to get up and he went to his brother Wolf's house. When he got there he found that they were having target practice. Wolf was losing in this game. Wolf knew that Coyote was a good shooter and Wolf gave him his bow and arrow and said, "Now you win back what I have lost. I've lost lots." So Coyote started shooting. His sight was so poor that he didn't want to shoot, but Wolf insisted. Poor Coyote did his best. There were people standing around. He was bound to hit them, his sight was so poor. Then Wolf wondered, "What is the matter with my brother. He has always been a good shot." So Wolf said to Coyote, "You better lie down, rest, go to sleep."

At the beginning of the story you remember Coyote had a weasel-skin over his eyes. When Coyote lay down, Wolf looked under the skin and saw that Coyote's eyes were full of maggots and worms. When Wolf saw that he thought, "How can I take these maggots out? Maybe I better do it while he is asleep." So he thought about the buffalo. "Maybe I better go kill a buffalo and take his eyes and use them for Coyote." So Wolf went out and came back with buffalo eyes for Coyote. He fixed Coyote's eyes while he was asleep. He cleaned out the maggots and put in the buffalo eyes. Then Wolf took off the weasel skin and threw it away. When this was all done Coyote woke up. He looked around, he used his eyes, he looked everywhere. He felt good. Now he knew he had good

eyes. Wolf took him back to where they were still playing the target game. He wanted him to win back their losings. They played and Coyote hit the bull's-eye every time. He won back all his brother had lost. Then he won all the stuff from the other people and got all their goods. So Wolf and Coyote were very happy at getting back all Wolf's goods and getting all the other people's stuff.
Each went his own way.

—JULIA PANGUISH
(Anna Premo, interpreter)
Owyhee, Nevada

Owl's Widow

Poniattsih (Skunk) was in his winter hut. He was singing away, making moccasins. His mother was outside making a basket. Skunk had a brother, Owl, who had one child and a wife. Owl and his wife did not get along together. She put a bone where he stamped his feet and he stepped on it. Owl died from this wound. The widow took her child and went away. They traveled to where Owl's mother lived. While Skunk was singing in his winter hut, the widow and child visited outside with the mother. After they left, the mother cried and cried. Skunk came out and asked, "Mother, what are you crying about?" His mother didn't tell him about his brother's death. But Skunk caught a scent of the woman who had been there. "It smells like a young woman." Then he went and smelled his mother, "Oh, mother, you don't smell like that. You smell old." [Laughter.] Then after a while his mother said, "Your brother Owl's widow and daughter were here and told me Owl has died." Skunk was so mad because his mother hadn't told him before that he let go his stink right in his mother's face. Skunk tracked his sister-in-law and child. The woman saw him coming and she threw back some lice from her head. They turned into deer. Skunk caught up with the woman. He took off his fur blanket and threw it over the widow. Then he ran after the deer. The widow and daughter removed the blanket and spread it over a sagebrush and ran off. While Skunk was hunting, he came back to see if they were still there. He saw the blanket on the sagebrush and thought they were still there. Then he went back to the deer.

The widow and child came to a place with lots of ice and the woman said to the ice, "When Skunk comes, don't let him cross. Make everything all smooth so he will slip and fall." The widow and the girl crossed the ice safely. They ran and ran till they came to a thicket of thorny rosebushes. The woman said, "When Skunk comes, don't let him through. Hold him as long as you can."

Skunk came to the ice and had a hard time but he finally got across. Then he came to the rosebushes and he had a hard time. He got so mad that he let his filth out.

The widow and girl saw a big black cloud behind them. She said, "Hurry up, little daughter, rain is coming and we'll drown." Sometimes the child walked and sometimes her mother carried her. They ran fast. But the cloud caught up with them and it was Skunk's filth. It killed the woman. The child didn't die. The woman fell lying on her back and the child was lying beside her, nursing her.

Badger's sons saw them and found them. The little daughter was just barely moving, nursing her. Badger didn't believe much what his oldest son said, but he had great faith in the younger son. He told him to tell him what he saw. So the younger son went out and looked and came back and said, "Yes, I think there is someone lying over there." So Badger went out and looked and dug. He traveled underground and came up near the woman and went underground again and came up right beside the woman. Badger was a doctor. The woman's breasts were exposed and Badger put his penis between them and kept trying to copulate.* Then he doctored her and after a while she revived. Then Badger went back to his wickiup.

The widow and her daughter went on. They came to a great camp of people. Coyote was there. When the widow got to camp they went to a wickiup, which turned out to belong to Coyote's mother. The widow did not know it was the house of Coyote's mother. Then she found out that Chicken Hawk was the youngest son of this woman. Chicken Hawk was just coming home from hunting. He had one small rabbit. The old woman dressed it and put it in the ashes. The widow and girl were almost starved. They didn't think that one little rabbit was going to be enough. When the old woman went to turn that one little rabbit and took the ashes off it they saw it was just lots of rabbits. When they were done the old woman started to take out the meat. There were just lots of rabbits. They all had plenty to eat. Chicken Hawk took two and flew away. He didn't sleep at that wickiup, he just ate there.

The widow was restless. She left her child sleeping at the old woman's. She wanted to go see Chicken Hawk. When she got up there, Chicken Hawk was not expecting her and he got scared. He yelled out loud, Coyote heard it, took his bow and arrow and said, "Who is frightening my brother?" The old woman said, "Look out, you might shoot the little girl's mother." And Coyote got mad and said, "Why didn't you tell me so I could have her? Why do you want Chicken Hawk to have her?"

The widow spent the night with Chicken Hawk. Next morning Chicken Hawk found he was lousy. He scratched all over. He caught lice from the widow. The lice made him very mean. Next morning Coyote made a speech, "All the men will go out together to round up rabbits." Chicken Hawk went with them but he couldn't do anything because he was so lousy. He just sat around and scratched. Neither Coyote nor Chicken Hawk killed anything that day. Coyote killed his own dog and carried that home on his back. He didn't want to go back without anything.

[*Badger's penis is used by the Shoshone as a cure for rheumatism or other pain. You rub the sore spot with the penis. They used to eat badger fat, it is just like cod-liver oil. Badger was a shaman. —Anna Premo]

—JULIA PANGUISH
(Anna Premo, interpreter)
Owyhee, Nevada

Alligators

Buffalo were in the water. They preferred water to land. When people went to hunt buffalo they were pestered by alligators. One time an alligator tried to get the people but the people killed the alligator. They cut him open and found a fully clothed person in a feather bonnet in his stomach.

(*Babowaiji* is "alligator," or "water lizard.")

—JULIA PANGUISH
(Anna Premo, interpreter)
Owyhee, Nevada

Owl Kills Birds by Naming Them

Coyote had a camp over at Charleston Mountain. There were lots of people there. In the morning he started out to go south. He went to the place between Shoshoni and Tacoloa where there was water running on the flat. Owl was living there. Bluebird was there. Owl was sitting on a rock cliff. Owl would fly around and call Bluebird (by his name) who was down below. Owl said, "Bluebird," and Bluebird died. Another bird came along the next day. Owl flew off the cliff and called his name and he died just as Bluebird had. Next morning Bullet Hawk came along and sat on the little rock. Owl flew down and called, "Bullet Hawk." Bullet Hawk died. He did that every day and killed some bird by calling his name.

Finally there were only two people left in camp besides Coyote. They were talking about what to do. Coyote said, "I'll go over there and you fly over to watch me." So Coyote went over there and sat on the little rock and Big Hawk flew way up in the sky to watch what happened. Coyote said, "Owl, I'm sitting here, call me." Owl watched him and didn't say anything for a long while. Owl came flying to the little rock and started to mumble. Big Hawk flew right at him and cut his head off.

So Hawk and Coyote went back home.

—Tom Steward
Beatty, Nevada

Coyote and Turtle

Coyote and Turtle went out hunting and they went over the mountain together. They found some mountain sheep. They climbed around on a cliff to get above the sheep. Turtle wanted to see but Coyote said, "You've got a long neck, you'd better keep back or you'll be seen." Then Turtle killed the sheep. So they started to skin the sheep. Coyote didn't even have a rope to pack it with. But Turtle had a rabbit net to carry it in. Coyote said, "I've got no rope." So he went down the mountain to find a joshua tree to make a rope from the fibers. While he was gone Turtle put all the meat in his net and started to pack it all away. Coyote walked down to a joshua tree but the tree kept moving away. Coyote would run and the tree moved a little faster. Coyote tried to throw a rock at it but he couldn't hit it. Turtle was wishing the tree would move so Coyote wouldn't get back too soon. Turtle picked up the meat and started away with it.

Coyote never could catch the tree, so he finally came back to where the kill was made. Everything was gone. Turtle kept going, taking his meat home. Coyote followed him. Turtle had a cave in the mountains and he hid inside. Coyote came around and said, "Can't you let me have a little meat for a feast?" Turtle gave him the guts, that was all. Coyote got mad. In the morning Coyote asked his sons, "Did you ever dream of rain?" The littlest one said, "Yes, I've dreamed of a rainy country." Coyote said, "Do you sing for rain when you have a dream?" So the little boy started singing and soon it started raining hard and it washed rocks from the mountains. Coyote wanted to wash Turtle out but Turtle hung onto the top of the cave and the water ran under him, but it washed all his little kids out. In the morning Turtle went looking for his children and he found them strung along the wash almost down to the flats. He brought them all back.

Turtle asked his boys, "Have you ever dreamed of hot weather?" The littlest one said, "Yes, sometimes I dream of hot weather." Turtle said, "Well, let's sing." They sang all night. In the morning it got hot. About the middle of the morning it was hot as hell. Coyote could hardly stand it. He told his boys, "It's summer coming, you'd better get in the water." So they all jumped in the water to get cool. But the water was already boiling and it scalded them out of their skins and killed them.

—Tom Steward
Beatty, Nevada

Wolf and Coyote Battle with Bears

Coyote wanted to go up north. He said to his people, "We'll go up there and gamble with the people." Two or three days they walked to the north. They came to a big camp. In the night they were going to gamble and play Hand Game. Coyote won all night. He bet everything but always won. Then he said to his people, "Come on, we'll go back home now." He went back and went up the mountain and found two girls and took them home with him to Charleston Mountain. Wolf was with him. Coyote had intercourse all day and night. He never went out. Wolf was in the mountains hunting every day.

After a week Coyote saw some rain coming way off to the north. There was lightning all night. It was coming closer all the time. Coyote got up early in the morning and went out to urinate and two bears came after him, growling. The bears chased him about half a day but Coyote always kept ahead and dodged them. About noon Coyote began to give out and the bears caught him and tore him all up.

Wolf came out of the house and the bears came after him. Wolf couldn't run very long so the bears caught him and killed him, too. The bears smashed up everything and wrecked the house, then they took the two girls away. The girls were their sisters. So, Coyote and Wolf were dead.

After the winter was almost gone and March came, there were great storms and blizzards on top of the mountain. Every day the winds came farther down the mountain. Finally the wind came down to where Coyote and Wolf had been killed. It blew all the dirt away from the bones of Wolf and blew the bones out. The bones came to life. "Well, I had a good sleep," he said. He began to look for his brother's bones. He found them and dug them up with a stick.

Coyote said, "Leave me alone, I want to sleep." Wolf didn't say anything. Next day Wolf said, "Make some arrows." For about a week they made arrows. Wolf said, "Make a lunch." So Coyote ground some seeds and everything was ready. "Let's go," Wolf said. "We'll go see those bears." Three or four days they traveled north and they camped near the bears' camp. All night they danced and Coyote sang. In the morning they started out. Wolf told Coyote to go first. Coyote went up to the saddle in the mountains and ran back and forth, yelling. The youngest bear said, "Somebody is out there and is coming to gamble." The oldest bear sent the younger one out to meet him. The bear chased him all around but Coyote always dodged him and shot the bear many times so that he had arrows all over him. The bear died. So the older bear went out and chased Coyote, but he never touched him. Coyote would always jump to one side. After about an hour Coyote killed the bear.

Wolf came along to help him skin out the bears. Then they started back home. They didn't want the girls this time.

—Tom Steward
Beatty, Nevada

Devil-Wife

A man had a little camp and lived alone. The (female) devil came in the camp. She stayed with the man and married him. He never could see her in the daytime, she disappeared. By and by the man got tired of his devil-wife. One day he went away, he walked over the mountains, then across the flats, walking on rocks so that he would not make a track. The she-devil followed, circling around to try to cross his tracks. Three ranges of mountains away she found a track where he had stepped on soft ground.

At night the man built a big fire in a circle and slept in the middle. She found the fire and all night she sat outside and begged him to come out. "Come on, let's have intercourse." But he would not come out. The next day she disappeared and the man ran away. After a while he came to where another man was camped. He said, "Let me hide from that devil." So that night the devil circled around and found his tracks again. When she came up and called, the man shot an arrow away. It had a big bump on it. She said, "What's that on the arrow?"

"Oh, it's nothing," he said. She said, "Oh yes, it's something." He said, "It's just where it was broken and I tied it together again." But she didn't believe him and went to look for it. He sneaked out and ran away.

He went along where a little bird named Tcuwi was sitting and straightening arrows. Tcuwi hid the man in a mountain sheep bladder with a bunch of arrows. The she-devil came along and started to look for her husband but the bird said, "Don't touch that. My wife keeps her basket-making stuff in there and she'll give you hell." Tcuwi said, "Now, come on." He wanted to have intercourse with her. They went into the cave. She thought he had a big penis so she said, "All right." So they had intercourse and he said, "How do you like it?" "Pretty sweet," she said.

While they were in the cave the walls of the cave came together slowly, closer and closer. "What's that?" she asked. "Oh, that's nothing. It always does that while my wife and I have intercourse." He was lying. He didn't have a wife. Pretty soon the cave closed up tight and Tcuwi flew out leaving the devil-woman stuck in there. That is how they got rid of her.

—Tom Steward
Beatty, Nevada

Coyote and the Devil

Coyote had an old house. He built a fire inside in the night. He sang
all night. About daylight there was a devil walking around outside
and singing back at him. So Coyote shut up and listened. Soon the
house caught on fire. Coyote jumped out the door and started running. He jumped over a big pile of brush and the devil could not get
over and lost Coyote's trail.

—Tom Steward
Beatty, Nevada

Ghost

Once a man was following a trail up the hill. He was going way up
and he saw another man standing on the summit. He went up there
but there was no one there and no tracks or anything. He went a
little farther and camped in a little shelter. About midnight he heard
somebody hollering and coming closer and closer. The man built a
fire in the house. The noise came closer. The man held the door
closed with a pine log and held his knife ready. The person outside
said, "Come on out and fight." After a while the noise went away
and he never came back.

—Tom Steward
Beatty, Nevada

Race to Koso Springs

Coyote used to live over at Koso Hot Springs near Owens Valley.
He said, "Let's go down south and eat some sugar cane (tules). All
the little animals and lizards went along. Frog went along, Horned
Toad and Doodlebug and all the little people. The people down in
the tule country were fast flyers. They all went down there and
scattered through the tules and pulled the leaves off and ate the
sweet canes. Toward evening Coyote heard the enemies, the tule
people, whistling all around them. Coyote had all the little bugs and
lizards on his side. They were on the ground eating away. Coyote
heard all this whistling and he thought, "What's all that whistling?"
So he came out of the tules and he saw the tracks of his people run-

ning back. So he followed and finally he caught up with a little Beetle who was packing a lot of tules for arrows. Coyote said, "What are you packing all those for, we aren't going to live." Coyote asked, "Where are all the rest?" Beetle said, "They all passed me a long time ago." So Coyote went on ahead and caught up with Bullfrog sitting under a greasewood bush. Coyote asked, "Where are all the people?" Bullfrog said, "They are way ahead." Coyote said, "Why didn't you tell me you were all going?" Coyote started ahead and went on. Bullfrog would jump way over and urinate on him while he was passing over. Soon Coyote passed him again and Bullfrog did the same thing. This happened over and over.

Soon Coyote saw the dust far ahead, about twenty miles. So Coyote started running as fast as he could with his brother-in-law still jumping over him and urinating on him. Soon they were catching up with the rest of them. They were all racing for Koso Hot Springs. Coyote and Bullfrog caught up with them.

The tule people, the hawks, and other birds, had gone ahead long before to wait for them. The little people were running along with Coyote in the middle of the bunch. Bullfrog was still jumping over them and urinating on them and Coyote said, "What do you want to do that for? I'm getting tired of it."

They were nearing Koso Springs. Roadrunner was there and had a big fire going in a deep hole. Bullfrog made a big jump and landed right on the edge of the hole. Coyote came in second and the rest were coming up behind.

Coyote and Hawk made a bet in Koso Springs before they all started for the tules and the other little people never knew about it. They were going to race for the springs from the tules, and the side that lost was going to be burned by the other side.

Coyote and Bullfrog were going to roast all the hawks. So they put them all in the fire. Only one was left—Bear (the sun). The people said, "We'll let him go." But Coyote said, "You would not let me go if I was left." So he grabbed Bear and dragged him to the fire and held him down with a stick. While he was doing this, everybody ran for their houses. Coyote kept one eye on the door of his house so he'd know where to go. Then he threw Bear in and it all went dark. Coyote got lost and couldn't find the house. He was lost. The people were mad because Coyote had burned the sun and they wouldn't help him find the door.

All winter Coyote crawled around in the dark. He stumbled

Handgame players, Battle Mountain, ca. 1920. Courtesy Beverly Crum.

around in the snow and fell off mountains and got lost. He went way back in the mountains in California, on the other side of Mt. Whitney. He crawled around and felt of the mountain and he recognized it. "This is where I used to go and this trail I used to travel." He felt his way around and he knew where he used to go. He crawled along on his hands and knees feeling the trail with his hands. Finally he came back where they roasted the birds. "This is where I killed Bear and the house is over there. I'll feel my way over there. Here's the trail. Oh, yes, here's the door." The people inside heard him talking and Bullfrog said, "Let my brother-in-law come in. He's a smart man and maybe he will have something to say about the sun being dead." So they opened the door and he crawled in. He ate all the rest of the winter because he was poor and bony from crawling around so much. They told him where to lie down.

In the spring, Bullfrog tried to feed him some fresh greens. Coyote slapped his hand away and said, "What do you want to do that for?" He didn't know what he was doing. Finally, when they put some more up to his mouth and he tasted it, it was sweet. He asked for some more and they gave him some more—a whole armful, and he ate all spring to get fat on his bones. The owls and rats and mice that can see in the night went out and got all the food. Coyote ate half the year and then began to pick up a bit. He felt good and he said, "We ought to talk about this. Maybe another sun.

We can all holler and see which one of us can call the sun back." So, one at a time they yelled for the sun. The little bugs hollered in their turn and didn't do any good. Coyote hollered and it got darker yet. Duck hollered and it began to look like daybreak. Flicker hollered and it got bright, then Red-headed Woodpecker hollered and the sun came up.

Coyote was eating everything that was lying around. All the green stuff that was growing. He said, "I'd better make the flavor better," so he urinated all over them. That's why some of the plants around here are bitter and you can't eat them.

—Tom Steward
Beatty, Nevada

Coyote Learns to Fly (1)

Coyote had a camp. Wolf lived with Coyote. He wanted to get some willows. He came down and he was cutting willows. Soon Coyote heard some singing. There were lots of flies there and he couldn't hear the singing well because there were so many flies. They went up his anus. He took handfuls of them and ate them. He did this twice. Soon he killed the flies and then he heard the singing. Coyote sang, too. He said, "Soon I'll be a doctor." He had a stick and he began to dance. Coyote began to laugh. He threw away his stick. He said to the geese (the singers), "Where are you going?" They said they were going north to look for a pregnant woman. Coyote said, "I'll go with you." The geese came down near Coyote. Coyote went over to them and said, "Give me some wings so I can fly," and they said, "All right." Each bird gave him a feather and Coyote put them on his arms. The geese said, "You fly down to that little hill and you stop on top." Coyote flew to the little hill, came down and looked the way they told him not to look. He fell down and hit his head on a rock. It killed him. The geese went away.

Coyote slept awhile and then he woke up. He felt his head with his hands and he got his brains and ate them. He said, "That's pretty good gravy." He got up and he saw his shadow. He saw the hole in his head. He said, "I ate my own brains." Then he vomited.

He looked way up in the sky and saw the geese. He got up and ran. He caught up to them. He saw them way up there. They went over the mountains. He ran and ran to get to the mountain. He didn't catch them.

He met someone who had a camp there. There were a bunch of women killed by the geese. There was a pregnant woman at one end. Coyote looked over all the women and found the pregnant woman. He cut up the woman and took out the baby. He said, "This will be my sister." Then he washed the baby. He got some mud and made breasts and hips for himself. That night he made a hot-rock dirt bed for himself. He acted like a woman who had just given birth. He came back this way. He had the baby with him. He came a long way. The baby grew big and walked. Coyote said to the girl, "Wolf is your brother." The little girl was singing. They were near home. Coyote said to Wolf, "I have a woman with me. I left her up there and you go get her." Wolf said, "You're lying. That is your sister." Coyote got her and took her to Wolf's place.

Wolf hunted deer all the time and every time he took one home. One day he left the deer up there and told Coyote to go get him. Wolf said, "Don't fool with that girl." Coyote butchered the deer. The girl was there. Coyote threw blood at the girl and said, "You have blood, go look." The girl said, "No, I have nothing."

Coyote went home. Wolf came to him and said, "Didn't you hear what I said? What did you do to that girl?" Wolf said, "All right." They washed the girl in water. Wolf gave her a stick. He told her to go to the top of the hill and then throw that stick back over her shoulder. The girl ran and Coyote called, "Come back here." The girl kept on going. She went to the top of the hill. She threw the stick and it turned into a boy. The girl was ashamed. The boy said, "You are my mother, why are you ashamed?" The two of them went away together. They went a long way. They made a camp. The girl made two baskets. By now the boy was big. The girl said, "You go to your uncles, Coyote and Wolf. Take those baskets. One is for Coyote and one is for Wolf. You will meet a storm, rain. Stand up by a tree, under the trees. Don't sleep in a cave, sleep under the trees."

The boy went, a long way. It began to rain. He stood under the trees. Soon he got all wet. So he found a cave. "I want to sleep, I'm wet. I'm going in the cave." So he went in the cave.

Next morning when he woke up, he got up. He stood up. When he stood he hit the roof of the cave. He had mountain sheep

horns. He had turned into a mountain sheep. He went up there.
Each basket is one of his buttocks. He went up in the mountains.
When he saw a mountain sheep band, he joined them. It was a very
rocky place.

He saw the Sky Boys, they were singing. The oldest Sky Boy
saw Mountain Sheep. Then the younger Sky Boy saw Mountain
Sheep and said, "Here comes a big mountain sheep." The older
Sky Boy says, "Don't bother him, he is Coyote's nephew." The
younger Sky Boy says, "I want to kill him." The older one says,
"Don't touch him, he's a human." The younger one says, "No,
that's no human, he's a mountain sheep. I want to get him." "All
right, you get him and eat him."

So he went down and shot Mountain Sheep. Mountain Sheep
made a noise when he was hit, he said, "Ouch! Go ahead, butcher
me." But younger Sky Boy didn't butcher him. He said, "That
mountain sheep hollered. Pretty soon Coyote will come after us."
Mountain Sheep boy is dead now.

Coyote and Wolf were both asleep. Then morning came and
Wolf said, "Our nephew was coming this way and the Sky Boy
killed him." Coyote wept. Wolf said, "What are you going to do?"
Wolf had lots of sinew. He said to Coyote, "You pack this sinew.
You give it to Spider." Coyote said, "All right." He took the sinew
to Spider and said what Wolf told him to. Wolf said, "Spider will be
up there. Tell Spider to make a web out of this sinew." Spider said,
"All right." Coyote told Spider how Sky Boy had killed Mountain
Sheep, his nephew. Spider put the sinew in the fire, cooked it and
ate it. Coyote said, "What are you doing with that sinew? That's for
a web." Coyote took the sinew away from Spider and went back
home. Wolf said, "Why didn't you do what I told you? You heard me
tell you. I told you to give that sinew to Spider. Never mind what
Spider does with it. Take it back to Spider."

So Coyote took the sinew back to Spider. Spider put it in the
fire again and started to eat it. Soon he had eaten it all. Then it began to come out his anus. It was very long.

Gopher covered up all the springs so that there was only one
place where there was water. Spider put a web over the sky hole.
There was a little house by the only place where there was water.
Coyote and Gopher were there. There was no other water. The
Sky Boys went down to get water. They couldn't go back to the
sky because of the Spider's web. The two Sky Boys sang up in the

sky. [Song here.] They were thirsty. The older brother said, "Where will we get water? There isn't any water anywhere. You can't go back through the sky hole because Spider put a string there. Coyote will be at the only spring with Gopher." Coyote was making hot rocks, putting them in the fire. When the Sky Boys went down to drink, Coyote watched them. When they drank, the feathers on their heads wagged. When they went to drink again, Coyote threw the hot rocks at their heads and killed them.

—BILL DOC
Beatty, Nevada

Coyote Avenges Wolf's Death

Coyote and Wolf have a camp together. Each has a smokehouse. Wolf hunts for deer all the time. When he hunts, he always gives just one to Coyote. He tells Coyote to go drag in the deer. Coyote can't drag it. Wolf says, "What's the matter? He's not heavy. Throw it up into the smokehouse." That's what he does all the time. Coyote can't drag the deer. Wolf says, "The deer are up in the mountain. You go up there and get one deer. When you catch him, butcher it and bring it all back. Don't leave any of it up there."

Coyote goes up to the mountain. He finds the deer. He butchers one. Then he puts all the meat in the hide to pack it. He starts to go. He forgets one part of the kidney. He takes one and forgets the other. He goes a way, then remembers he forgot the other. He goes back for it. There it is. He reaches for it but when he gets close it jumps away. It goes just a little way. Coyote gets up close and again it flies away. Every time Coyote gets near it, it flies away. Coyote runs and chases it but the meat goes fast. The meat talks, "I'll tell my people." Then it goes away.

Coyote goes home. Wolf says, "What are you doing? I told you to bring back all the meat. Why didn't you do what I told you?" They go into their house. Then Wolf sings. [Song here.] He says, "Coyote, you go get some brush. There is a storm coming. There is lightning. Yes, the storm is coming. That isn't a storm, though, it's somebody coming to kill you." Coyote goes and gets brush. At daylight the enemy are close. Someone is coming. Coyote gets his bow and arrows ready. Coyote says, "I'm first." He goes outside—

there are lots of the enemy there. Coyote walks around. Coyote has a hat of *walapai* tails. He has a breech clout. Wolf says, "I'm going out. Coyote, you stay in the house, don't look out at me."

Wolf goes out. No one can hit him. Coyote is wondering what Wolf is doing. Coyote makes a peephole in the wall of the house. Wolf is outside. When Coyote looks at Wolf, the enemy kills him. Coyote cries. Then the enemy go away, but first they skin Wolf and take that hide with them.

Coyote looks through Wolf's goods. There is a bag tied up. Coyote unties it and opens it. Inside there is another, in that another, many bags. Way inside is a little tiny one. He opens that and then everything gets dark. Then Coyote wants to tie it up again, but he can't recapture the dark. It is dark, no sun, no light. This lasts a long time. Then Coyote gets some brush and peels it. He takes the bark and rolls it up for a torch. He wants to hunt jackrabbits. He lights his torch at the fire and goes out. But he can't see any jackrabbits. He hears them making a noise. He throws his torch at them. Then he chases the rabbit. He catches it. That's the way he has to hunt now that it is dark all the time. He goes home and takes the sinew from all the rabbits he has caught.

Then Coyote makes arrows. He uses all kinds of feathers on his arrows; mallard duck feathers, woodpecker, all kinds of birds, lots of different kinds. He wants to make the sun come down. He stands in the doorway. He shoots an arrow out. Some of the arrows bring a little daylight. The last arrow has mallard duck feathers on it. He shoots it and the sun comes out and there is light now. Now Coyote can see his shadow. Coyote makes lots of sinew-backed bows and arrows. He makes lots of arrows, he makes arrow points, lots of them. He puts them in a quiver. He wants to go after the people who killed Wolf.

He takes all the bows and arrows with him. He follows their tracks. He goes over a mountain. Coyote makes a mark on the ground (draws a straight line) and leaves a bow and arrows there. He keeps on going. Lots of different places he leaves bows and arrows. He sees where the enemy have camped. He said, "They left here this morning." He goes on and catches up with an old woman. He goes around so as to appear to be coming from a different direction when he meets her. They meet and talk.

Coyote says, "I'm scared." The old woman says, "Are you Coyote?"

"Oh no, I'm not Coyote. I came from this direction, not from where Coyote lives." So they talk. The old woman tells Coyote just what she does. She is a very old woman and she tells Coyote just what she does. Old woman says, every once in a while, "Are you Coyote?" He answers, "No, I'm not Coyote." Coyote kills the old woman. He beats her and pounds her. Then he shakes all the bones out of the skin. He puts on her skin and looks like an old woman. He takes her basket and carries it on his back and he walks like an old woman. He goes on. He comes to camp. He looks for the grandchildren of the old woman. They say, "Are you Coyote?" He says, "No, I'm not Coyote." He falls down just like an old woman does. Then he gets up. One of the boys says, "He walks pretty fast, I think he's Coyote." They have a long pole with Wolf's hide hung on it. At night they dance around this hide. Near there they make a fire and make camp. Coyote cries when he sees Wolf's hide. Coyote lies down.

The small children are left with the old woman for her to take care of them. They leave them with Coyote, thinking he is the old woman. Coyote kills all the children. When it is near daylight the boys all call Coyote. "Get up, Mother," they say. Coyote gets up. They say, "Are you Coyote?" Coyote falls down like an old woman and they are convinced. They give Coyote Wolf's hide and he sings and dances with it. [Song here.] Coyote sings like an old woman. Then Coyote jumps and runs off with Wolf's hide. He throws back the old woman's hide. The boy says, "You see, that was Coyote." Then they look for the children and find they are all dead. They say, "We'll get that Coyote." So they chase Coyote.

Coyote runs fast. He gets to a place where he left some bows and arrows. He shoots and shoots but he doesn't hit. Then his arrows are all gone. He breaks the bow and throws it away. Then he runs. He comes to another place where he left bows and arrows and he shoots quickly. When the arrows are all gone he breaks the bow and throws it away. The boy says, "Where is he getting all these bows and arrows from?" Coyote runs. Then his bows and arrows are all gone. Then he comes to some brush. He goes along one side of it, he is tired. The pursuers look for him in the brush but can't find him. Coyote has turned himself into an old Coyote turd. Then one of the boys says, "I think that turd there is Coyote." He picks up a rock to hit the turd with but when he picks up the rock, the turd gets up and runs off as Coyote. "Yes, that's him, that's Coyote!"

Coyote runs. He's all in. On the other side of some brush he turns into an old white bone. They look and can't find him. One boy says, "I think that bone is Coyote." When he goes to pick it up, Coyote runs away.

Coyote runs. He is very tired. He comes to the place where he drew that line. He crosses it and says, "That's all." The pursuers look but can't find him. "See that line?" they say. "Maybe that's Coyote." They get a rock and Coyote jumps up and runs away. He runs and runs. He gets on the other side of some brush. The pursuers come and look for him. They can't find him; there is nothing on the other side of the brush. They look and look. Then they see him walking way up. But he is walking right there, just a little way from them. The boys say, "We can't get him, he's too far off now. We're tired."

Coyote goes to a cave. It rains. He sleeps there all night. In the morning he gets up. He can't go on. The snow is too deep. There is a spider web in there. In the web is a string. Coyote finds this shell. He picks it up. He gets inside it. "I think I'll go in here. This is pretty good." He wants to go back to his camp. He puts that seed in the entrance to the cave. The wind blows and carries the shell along. He goes, Coyote, inside the shell. It goes right over the snow. He travels fast. He gets home, into the house, and stops. Coyote comes out of the shell. He goes to Wolf's body. He had grown some hair on his head while Coyote was away. He puts the hide on top of Wolf's body. Coyote sleeps there that night. Daylight comes. Coyote hears Wolf cry. Coyote hollers. "Come back here," he shouts. Coyote hears Wolf's voice a long way off. Then he hears him no longer. Coyote follows him. He goes, Wolf goes, and Coyote after him. They go a long way, near the ocean. Coyote catches up with Wolf near the ocean. Wolf says, "What did you come here for?" Coyote says, "I can't go back." Wolf wants to fight. He fights with Coyote.

—Bill Doc
Beatty, Nevada

Cannibal Bird (3)

Two men had a camp. One was a boy, a little bird, the other was Coyote. The boy made a figure-four trap. He got lice in his trap. He set his trap at night and in the morning he went to see what he had.

One day he caught a little mouse and took it home to Coyote. Next time he caught a chipmunk and took it home to Coyote, who killed it. Then he caught a wood rat and took him home to Coyote. The boy brought the game home alive and gave it to Coyote, who killed it. Then he caught a cottontail and took him out alive and took it to Coyote. Then he caught a jackrabbit and he took it back alive to Coyote. Each day he set his trap a little farther away. Then he caught a mountain sheep when he put his trap up in the mountains. He drove the sheep down the mountain to Coyote's house. Coyote killed and ate the mountain sheep.

The boy said he was going up to the top of the mountain next time. He stopped at one place, looked it over, set the trap. Coyote told him not to set the trap so far off, that he would get something dangerous. The boy did not believe Coyote and set his trap. Next morning he went to look at his trap. He stopped near the trap, there was a big bird in there. The boy saw the big bird there. He walked around and the bird watched him as he circled. The boy wanted to catch the bird and the bird wanted to catch the boy. The boy got close. He jumped at the bird and the bird caught the boy. The bird put the boy on his back and flew away. He took him, he flew away with him. They went a long way and came to the ocean. They flew west. The bird had a camp there. His mother lived there on an island in the water. The bird used to carry people off to this place. He would bring a man. The old woman had a stick. She would cut the leg of the victim, break his legs, and the big bird would eat the person.

The bird landed there with the boy. Bird said to the old woman, "Fix that boy for me to eat and bring him here." The old woman used to pound the meat for Bird.

In the morning Bird went out to hunt. He went home at night and took a victim with him. He had a house on the island. He broke the legs of his victims and put them in the smokehouse till he wanted them. Bird played with the boy. He put him in his mouth. He went down and came out the anus. Bird laughed and said, "My meat is cooling off, it was too hot." Every night when he came home he played with the boy, he put him in his mouth, let him come out his anus. Bird went to a certain pool of shallow water to drink. The old woman said to the boy, "Don't go up to that house, there's somebody up there who will kill you." But the boy went up to the house to look. The old woman didn't know the boy went there. A man at the house asked the boy what made Bird laugh so much every night. The boy said, "He plays with me, puts me in his mouth and I get out his anus." The man replied, "That's pretty good. You can kill him. When you are inside Bird, you cut his heart and kill that big bird." The boy said, "All right, I'll do it." The man gave him a stone knife. The boy tied the knife to a string and hung it around his neck to hide it from Bird. Soon Bird came home. He went to drink water, then he came back to play with the boy. He played with him, put him in his mouth. The boy got inside Bird, pulled out his knife, looked for the heart, and cut it. Then the boy came out the anus. Then Bird flew away up high, then he fell down dead.

The old woman wept. The woman then took feathers from the wing of Bird and made a boat of them for the boy. She said, "You go home now. You will go across the water. You will meet with someone there who will play with a bow and arrow. This will be Grasshopper. He's not a good man, you look out for him. There is another one, Water Boy, a boy, who plays on the water. He is a good man."

The boy went. He went a long way till he came to the end of the water. He saw Grasshopper playing with his bow and arrow. Grasshopper walked back and forth, back and forth. When he saw the boy he held out an arrow, he wanted the boy to catch hold of it so he could pull him toward him. But Water Boy pulled out the little boy, pulled him to shore. When he took him out, he wrapped him up, put him up on a high post, hung him up there. Then Grasshopper came, he saw the boy up there and said, "What you got up there; what is that? I want to shoot him." Water Boy said, "That's my stuff up there, don't shoot it, don't break it." Grasshopper went away. Then Water Boy took the boy down and said, "You go home now."

—BILL DOC
Beatty, Nevada

Tso'apittse (3)

People had a camp. There were a lot of women there. One woman had a baby, a baby boy. Tso'apittse came and said, "Give me that little boy, I want to hold him. You're my friend, I want to pet the baby." So the woman gave Tso'apittse the baby to hold. When she got it, she ran away with the baby. She stole the baby. Tso'apittse started for her camp.

The boy grew bigger. He ate dripping from his own nose, which he blew into a cup. He added water to it and made gravy of it. That is all he had to eat. He kept growing bigger. Tso'apittse kept pulling the boy's penis. It grows long. Then the boy is grown, and Tso'apittse marries him. Every time Tso'apittse comes home she wanted to have intercourse with him. She says, "Come now, take out your penis." The boy is a man now. He goes to hunt mountain sheep. One day while he is out he meets someone up there (on the mountain) who says to him, "Do you know you are living with Tso'apittse? That stuff you eat isn't real food, it's no good." This person gives him mountain sheep to eat. There is never any fire or light at Tso'apittse's house. This man the boy meets makes fire and light. He tells the boy to make a fire when he got home. The boy says, "How do you make a fire?"

The boy puts the mountain sheep meat up in a tall tree and cuts off the lower limbs so there is a long smooth trunk. He brings home only the mountain sheep heart, lungs, and liver. He comes home.

When he gets home he make a fire. It's dark now and Tso'apittse comes home. She looks at the fire and says, "What are you doing? Put out that fire." The boy gives the mountain sheep heart to Tso'apittse but she throws it away. Tso'apittse said, "You must have met somebody who told you to do this." Tso'apittse never eats the heart. She hits the ground with it all night. Tso'apittse doesn't want any fire or any light.

Daylight comes. The boy says, "I killed a sheep up there. You go get it and pack it." Tso'apittse goes to get the meat. The boy goes away in the opposite direction. Tso'apittse goes to where the meat is, but she can't reach it. She wants the wind to blow, she wants a South Wind. A big wind comes but it doesn't break the tree where the meat is as Tso'apittse wanted it to. The tree is too strong. Then Tso'apittse wishes for another wind, the West Wind. It comes. It breaks the tree and Tso'apittse gets the meat and then goes home. Tso'apittse goes fast, she runs. When she gets there, she finds the boy is gone. She tracks him.

As the boy goes, he meets a woman gathering seeds for food. The woman hides him in her gathering basket and covers it with a smaller one. Tso'apittse comes and says, "Where's my man?" The woman says, "I haven't seen him." Tso'apittse says, "Look, that

little basket is crooked." The woman says, "Look up that way."
When Tso'apittse looks, the boy gets out and runs away. The boy
goes up a mountain. When he is near the summit, Tso'apittse looks
up and sees him there on the mountain. The boy runs. He meets
a man hunting jackrabbits. It is Coyote who is hunting jackrabbits. Tso'apittse comes and says to Coyote, "Where is my
man?" Coyote is making an arrow, putting the foreshaft into the
butt. Tso'apittse says, "What's the matter with your arrow? It's
crooked." Coyote says, "Tso'apittse, you look the other way."
Then Tso'apittse looks the other way and Coyote takes the boy out
of the butt of the arrow and the boy runs away.

The boy runs to another hill. Tso'apittse sees him up near the
summit. Tso'apittse runs after him. The boy comes to a man's
camp. The man is a rock wren, a bird who lives in rocks on top of
the rocks. He is a small bird with a long nose. The bird hides the
boy. The bird is going to make an arrow. He cuts a stick, heats a
stone arrow-straightener to rub the stick on to make it straight. He
has a stone pestle and puts it between his legs so that it looks like a
penis. Soon Tso'apittse comes and says, "Where's my man?" The
bird says, "I haven't seen him." Then Tso'apittse looks at the bird,
sees what she thinks is his penis, and says, "I want that." The bird
says, "All right, I'll give it to you." This bird had a cave for a house.
He says, "Come, let's go into the cave." So he and Tso'apittse go
into the cave and he gives it to Tso'apittse. The cave begins to get
small and Tso'apittse says, "What is happening to the cave?" The
bird says, "When I have intercourse with my wife, the cave always
does this." Then the cave got smaller and smaller and the little bird
got out the tiny hole that was left. When he gets out, the entrance
shuts up tight.

The bird saw the boy's long penis and said, "That's no good,
let's cut it off." So he cut it off.

Tso'apittse became echo.

—BILL DOC
Beatty, Nevada

Bee Steals Food

There was a camp, there were lots of animals, all kinds. They were
hunting deer. Coyote was there. Coyote was hunting. They all

come back to camp. They hunt again. Then Bee came. The people had piled the meat on brush. Bee saw the deer meat and stole it and took it back home with him. Next morning they hunt again. Then they came back. Coyote put his meat up on brush. Then Bee came, saw the meat, and packed it away. In the morning they go hunting again. When the hunters came back Coyote put a big piece of meat on top of the brush. Then Bee came, saw the meat, sat down and looked at it and took it away. Next morning they go hunt again. Then Bee came. There was a big pile of meat on the brush. Coyote sits and thinks what to do. He thinks it is too heavy for Bee to pack. Then Bee comes and sees the meat and packs it away.

Next morning the animals go hunting again—Chicken Hawk, Hawk, Crow—and then come back. They put lots of meat, the whole hindquarters of a deer, up on the brush. Then they hide to watch who is stealing their meat. Then Bee comes. He sits down. Then Bee packs it away. Next morning Coyote and the others go hunting again. They come back to camp with deer. Coyote puts a whole half of a deer on the brush; he thinks it is too heavy for Bee. Then Bee comes, sees the meat, sits down a while, and packs away the meat. He is big and strong. Next morning Coyote and the others hunt again. They come back and bring one whole deer and put it on the brush pile. Then that Bee comes, sees the meat, sits down, looks, then packs away the whole deer. Next morning they hunt again and bring back two deer. They tie the two deer together and put them on the brush pile. Pretty soon comes Bee. He sits down up there, he sees the deer, then he packs them away, both of them.

Coyote was angry. Pretty soon Coyote talked. He says, "Somebody go behind, somebody follow him and watch him." Hawk goes and watches Bee. He reports that he thinks Bee has a house up there, his house is a big pile of dirt. There are little holes and a big hole in the top. That's the way he goes in. Coyote says, "So, he's got a camp down there. Let's go see him in the morning. All of us will go."

In the morning all of them went. They come to the house with a hole in top. "That's the way he goes down." Coyote says, "Make a fire." He puts fire in the hole where Bee goes down. When the fire is made, somebody blows smoke down the hole. Coyote says, "You don't blow hard enough. Look, I'll blow." So Coyote blows hard, he blows like hell. He blows quite a while, I think he blows all day. His wind is all gone. He dies right there. Somebody says, "Coyote, get up there." Coyote said, "I'm asleep." Pretty soon he says, "I'm well." He blows again. He blows again hard. Then he dies right there. He lies down. Pretty soon the animals make him wake up. "Why, I'm asleep!" He watches for a while, then thinks he will try again. So he blows again. Pretty soon he's all in and he dies right there. Then he gets up and says, "That's enough." He takes out the fire and digs in the house. Soon he finds the deer meat. "Yes, he took that deer meat, away up here. Maybe Bee has some children, maybe he has lots of them. Maybe they all die. The smoke kills them." Somebody says, "That's enough, come back." That Coyote wants to see Bee. He says, "I'll go in up there." Some animal told him, "Don't go in there. He's not dead. If you go down and see him I think he'll kill you. Maybe he'll kill all the animals." "Oh," says Coyote, "maybe he's dead. I'm going to see him." When some animal said, "Don't go there," Coyote doesn't believe him; he doesn't believe he will be killed.

So Coyote goes down there. He looks, he talks to himself, he says, "What is it, what is it?" He gets up close to Bee. That Bee gets up. He gets some kind of a big rock, as big as a forearm. He takes the rock and Coyote jumps outside. Bee jumps quick, too. Coyote stands up over there. Bee hits this way and misses Coyote. Then Bee hits first from one side and then the other and he hits Coyote. Bee knocks him down. Coyote dies right there. Then Bee goes and all the animals chase him. Bee is mad, all his children are dead. He catches one animal and hits and kills him right there. Then he catches and kills another. The animals all run away and Bee pursues them. He killed lots of them. There are left Eagle and Chicken Hawk, the other kind of chicken hawk. Now only four animals are left. Bee pursues. He catches Crow, hits him and kills him. Now there are three left. He catches and kills Eagle. Now only Hawk and Chicken Hawk are left. Hawk says to Chicken Hawk, "Let's go up that water. Maybe he can't catch us in that water." So they go, but Bee follows and catches and kills Chicken Hawk. Now Hawk is the only one left. Hawk talks to himself. He says, "Maybe if I go in the water you won't be able to catch me." He runs on, he runs like hell. Bee runs like hell, too. Then Hawk goes into the water, a big pond. He dives in and when he comes to the surface he looks behind him. Bee dives in the water, too. Bee continues to pursue Hawk. Hawk talks to himself, "I think I can't get out. Maybe he will kill me. Well, I'll go to my camp.". (He has a camp in the rock, way up high.) "Maybe I'll escape there. But perhaps, Bee, you'll kill me."

So Hawk goes to the rock wall and goes in there. Bee goes in, too. Hawk goes outside, looks behind and there is Bee behind him. Hawk says, "All right, I'll kill you." Then he circles slowly down. He pulls out feathers from both of his wings. Then he goes in the rock again. He has the feathers in his hand. He sticks the feathers upright in the door that leads out from the rock. Then Hawk gets out and looks back. Bee gets caught in the wall of feathers, which close up on him. Bee is dead. Hawk is all in. Pretty soon he lies down on the mountain top. He is tired. Then he flies away.

Hawk talks to himself, "I will go see my people." Away he goes. He goes back to where Bee pursued and killed the animals. When he finds the first one that was killed by Bee he takes a stick, flicks him with it, and makes him get up. He is alive again. They go together and find Eagle and revive him. Now there are three of them. Then they find Crow and revive him. Then they go on and find Chicken Hawk and revive him. Then they find and revive a lot of others. They find Coyote. Hawk says, "Oh, Coyote is not a good man. Let's not make him alive." Some people said, "Oh, make him get up. Sometimes he is a pretty good fellow, sometimes he is no good." So he is revived. Coyote says, "Oh, I'm sleepy." He thinks he was asleep, but he was dead.

—BILL DOC
Beatty, Nevada

Cannibal Gambler

The animals have a house. Lots of animals. All kinds of animals, Coyote, Crow, Eagle, Chicken Hawk, Pigeon Hawk, Hawk. Pigeon Hawk has a wife, a small bird with a black head who comes in snow. Pigeon Hawk's wife is Snowbird. Pigeon Hawk talks to Coyote, says, "Let's gamble." Coyote says, "I'm going to another place to gamble." Coyote usually has pretty good luck. So Coyote goes away. He doesn't come back any more. He doesn't come back at night nor next day. Then another man goes away to gamble and he doesn't come back. Then another one goes and he doesn't come back any more. Then Crow goes. He doesn't come back. Chicken

Hawk goes. They don't come back. They go and don't come back. There is someone who has a camp someplace. Then Eagle goes. Only two men are left in camp now, and one woman. Then Pigeon Hawk goes. He leaves his wife behind. His wife cries when he doesn't come back. His brother, Hawk, cries too. The only ones left in camp were Hawk and Pigeon Hawk's wife. The woman says to Hawk, "I'm going to your house." Hawk says, "No, I want to live alone." The woman says, "I'll give you food." Hawk says, "No, throw it away. I don't want your food." So the woman throws the food away.

In the morning the woman could not hear Hawk any more. She thinks he has gone away. The woman goes to Hawk's house, there is nobody there. She looks all over the house. She finds a hole in the top of the house. That is where he got out. Then the woman circles the house outside looking for tracks. She finds tracks. She follows the tracks. She sings as she goes. She wishes for rain to come. She thinks if it rains, Hawk will have to stop and she can catch him. It rains, he stops, and she catches up with him. Hawk says, "You go back home." She says, "No, I don't want to go back. There is nobody there any more. I don't want to go back." But Hawk insists that she go back. Hawk says, "Somebody will kill me and then I won't be alive." The woman says, "All right, I'll go too." Finally he agreed and said, "All right, let's go. You go one way and I'll go another. Don't follow me."

The woman is singing. Hawk is singing too. Each goes different ways. The woman is singing for snow, wishing for snow. Snow comes. She meets a lot of old women. They are digging roots. Hawk gets there too. The old women told how when their folks came there, someone killed them. Pigeon Hawk was killed and eaten. "That's too bad. There's a bad man has his camp near here. When you get there this bad man has a big basket and he hits you in the leg with it and breaks your leg. When you get there and he hits at you, you jump up. Next time he goes to hit at you, you lie down on the ground. All right, now, go."

Hawk goes and he sees that goblin man. Snowbird goes too. Gopher and Woodpecker go with them. Hawk walks along and meets him. He has the basket in his hand and he hits at Hawk. Hawk jumps up. Next time he hits at him, he hits higher up and Chicken Hawk lies down. The old women told him not to go in the bad man's house. "There is a hole inside the house, you would fall through." The man invites Hawk to come in. Hawk says, "No, I won't come. I'll sit down right here." The old women had warned Hawk not to eat the food the man would give him. "It's no good, it has human blood in it. Tell him, 'Oh, I'm not hungry. My aunts gave me something to eat.' " Gopher is the one who gave Hawk the good advice. The man knew somebody had warned Hawk.

At night the man went looking for Hawk. He says, "You sleep." He is going to kill him while he's asleep but Hawk says, "No, I'm not sleepy. I never sleep." So the man says, "All right. We'll play early in the morning." The man watched all night to see if Hawk goes to sleep. Every once in a while he says, "Are you asleep?" and Hawk says, "No." The old woman had warned Hawk not to go to sleep.

Daylight comes. The man eats breakfast. They are going to play Kick Ball. "Let's go." The old woman had said to Hawk, "You stay behind all the time, don't get ahead of the man." Gopher said she would dig up the ground and make it rough. Woodpecker said he would make holes in the tree. They go. They are both singing. Gambler, the man, is ahead and Hawk is in back. They go up to the hill. They come to the place where Gopher made holes and Gambler's ball went in the hole. Hawk's ball went up high, went through those holes in the trees that Woodpecker made. Gambler said, "Look at my hills." Hawk looks up and he sees a little cloud. He says, "You look at my mountain." But Hawk's clouds cover up the mountains. They come down, they are quite close. Hawk comes fast, very fast, and he gets there first. He wins.

Then Gambler comes and says, "You can't win me. I'll give you my stuff. I have lots of stuff. You can have my stuff." Hawk says, "No, I don't want your stuff. I didn't gamble for your stuff, but for you. You won my folks and killed them and now you die." Gambler has a servant who fixes his house, Roadrunner. Hawk says he is going to kill this slave, too.

Pigeon Hawk's wife is there. Gambler had left her by the fire. If he had won, he would have killed her. She was tied up and Hawk frees her. He says, "All right, I'm going to kill that Gambler."

Roadrunner takes a knife and tries to kill Gambler, but he uses the back of the knife, not the sharp edge. Hawk is watching and says, "What are you doing? Cut him up." Roadrunner was just pretending to hurt the Gambler. So Hawk goes up there and cuts Gambler's throat. He kills him. No more bad man.

There is a man at the house who is all broken, his legs are gone. He is Coyote. Hawk goes to the house and the man says, "Make me a leg." So Hawk makes a leg for Coyote. There are bows and arrows there and Coyote takes them and goes and shoots Gambler's family. He kills them all. Hawk fixes up all the people, makes their legs better. Pigeon Hawk isn't there, Gambler had eaten him. Hawk looks all over for him. He looks in the Gambler's feces for Pigeon Hawk's bones. He finds the bones there. He brings him to life again.

—BILL DOC
Beatty, Nevada

Easy or Difficult Life

The animals and birds used to be the first people. Badgers made the mountains.

Coyote and his brother, Wolf, were going to have a meeting to talk things over with all the people. They all got together and talked about women. Wolf spoke first. "There will be a big fandango and a man will try to catch hold of a girl's hand. If he catches her she will have a baby on her finger. When she shakes her hand the baby will drop off and be standing there."

That didn't suit Coyote. "That won't do," he said. "You can lie between a girl's legs and it feels good. That's the way to do it."

Wolf spoke again. "When a man dies he will come alive again. He will die twice." That didn't suit Coyote. He said, "Man dies once and he's dead."

Soon Coyote's son got sick and died. Coyote went to Wolf and said, "Did you say that man was going to die two times?"

Wolf answered him, "You said if a man dies once he's dead and he won't get up again. That's the way it's going to be."

So Coyote fell back crying and wailing. If he'd taken his brother's word his son would have lived again. Wolf had made a good speech all the way through but Coyote wasn't satisfied, so women have to have babies the hard way and death comes only once.

—JIM TYBO
Battle Mountain, Nevada

Theft of Pine Nuts (2)

Crow was on his way north. There were lots of people going. They
went a long way. They were going to Austin. When they got there
they made camp. There are hot springs there and they camped by
them. From Austin they went on their way north and camped by
the hot spring at Beowawe. Then they went on their way again.
They found another hot spring and camped there. Then they went
on their way again. They came to a camp where there were a lot of
people. Crow is going to the place where the pine nuts grow. The
people they met were playing Hand Game and they gambled with
them. After that they found lots of pine nuts.

Coyote and his brother, Wolf, had come with the Crows. They
sent Mouse to look for the pine nuts while they played Hand Game.
Mouse found the nuts and told his people he had found them.

That night they danced fandango, they danced for pine nuts.
The pine nuts were high up in a tree. They didn't know how to get
them down from the pine tree. Coyote tried to get them but he
could not reach them. So they got two woodpeckers, two different
kinds of woodpeckers. They tied their tongues together. They
have long tongues. They knocked down the pine nuts with their
long tongues. When the pine nuts came down, Coyote caught
them. (This place was southwest or south of Owyhee. There used
to be lots of pine nuts there, now there are none.) There used to be
no pine nuts down south till they brought them back from the north.

They started back with the pine nuts. Some of the people from
the north chased them. They looked back and saw the dust of their
pursuers. They went south through Beowawe, they returned the
same way they had gone north. Their pursuers almost caught
them. Then they caught up with them. Coyote tried to hold them
back. The others went on while Coyote tried to hold them back.
Crow was carrying the nuts. The pursuers killed Coyote. Then
they killed some of the others. They kept on going and killed them
as they caught up with them. Only two were left, the others were
all killed. Only Crow and Crane were left.

Crane was chasing Crow. Crane had been the owner of the
nuts until Crow's people took them. Crow was very tired but he
went on. Crane's long legs carried him quickly. Crane caught up
with Crow and kicked him. Crane killed Crow, that is, Crane
thought he killed Crow, but Crow wasn't really dead. Crow put the

pine nuts in his broken leg and the broken leg ran off with the pine nuts. Crane's children were coming on behind him. Crane told them to cut Crow to pieces and look for the nuts. They couldn't find them though they looked and looked. Then Crane thought about the missing leg and thought that must be where the pine nuts were. Crane sat down and looked around on the mountains and he saw the smoke of lots of fires. They were cooking pine nuts, that is where the smoke came from. Crane went to his people who were cooking nuts. Three of them went, Crane and two bluebird brothers. They found lots of people there roasting pine nuts. The people looked and saw Crane and the Pine-nut Jays coming. One old woman put the bad nuts on the side where Crane was to sit. Then Crane sat down and picked up the nuts by his side. They were bad, wormy. The Pine-nut Jays sat and ate lots of pine nuts, they didn't sit by Crane. Crane never found one good nut, they were all bad. Crane sat awhile and then he said, "I'm going to go back north to my own country." The jay brothers said, "We don't want to go back, we like it here. We'll stay and live here. The pine nuts taste good."

That same old woman got ready. She took a big long stick. Crane was ready to get up now. When Crane started to fly up, the old woman hit him with the long stick she had. She hit him in the tail and broke off some of his feathers. That is why Crane hasn't much of a tail. Then Crane made a tail out of his legs. When he flies he pulls his legs up and turns them backwards, like a tail.

The place where the pine nuts used to be was about eighty miles from Owyhee, a big timbered mountain.

Crow choked on pine nuts. They got stuck in his throat. That is why he has that funny call, "Kaw, kaw." That is why they call him "hai."

—JIM TYBO
Battle Mountain, Nevada

Chicken Hawk

Chicken Hawk's mother lived with him. The boy always went hunting. He found a little bird, Snowbird. He shot it. He hit it in the wing and broke the wing. Then the boy tried to chase it and catch it. The bird told the boy, "Did you know your father got killed? They killed your father over east." His mother had never told the boy how his father was killed. When the boy came home he asked his mother how his father had been killed. He kept on asking but she wouldn't tell him. The boy had heard the truth from Snowbird.

The boy said he was going after the people who killed his father. The boy made a net out of some string. He made a long net, about twenty-five feet long. The boy said, "If somebody kills me, then the net will break. If the net breaks you will know I am dead."

Then the boy set out. He met Gopher, an old woman. She told the boy that Meadowlark, the bird with a yellow breast with little black spots *(hittoo),* was the one who killed his father. Gopher told him that Hittoo had a kind of wild bear for a dog. She said this bear was coming after him and the boy jumped up. And the bear ran right under him and missed him as he jumped up. Then the bear turned and ran back but the boy jumped up again. The boy was too quick for him. Bear always killed people, he didn't usually miss. Gopher told the boy about how Bear caught people. The boy was too quick for Bear, Bear couldn't kill him.

There was a Crow tied back of Hittoo's house. The boy got close to the house. He looked in the door. Hittoo told the boy to go in the house, to go way far in. But the boy wouldn't go in, he stayed right by the door. He sat down outside by the door. Hittoo made a pudding out of people's brains. He made it inside the house. He put pine nuts on top of this pudding, the brains were way inside. So the boy just ate off the top of the pudding. He said he wasn't very hungry. He didn't eat the brains, just the nuts. Gopher had warned him about the pudding, that is why he didn't eat. If he had eaten the pudding he would have died. This was how Hittoo killed people. If Bear didn't kill them the pudding did.

Then Hittoo told the boy they were going to play a game— hoop-and-pole game. (If you go through the ring with the pole it counts five points. If the ring lies against the pole it is one point.) The boy won the game. He made more points than Hittoo. A game is usually twenty points. Hittoo said, "We'll play a different game now, kick ball." Hittoo had a ball made from a skull. He gave that to the boy for a ball. Then they started to play. They put the ball on the ground and kicked it as far as possible. Then they ran after it and kicked it again. The course was about a mile. The boy kicked the ball and it just spun around, it didn't go ahead. Hittoo's ball went ahead fast and far. Hittoo had four daughters. His four daughters were watching the game. The girls laughed; their father was ahead of the boy. Hittoo was way ahead. When they were halfway, Chicken Hawk took his own ball out from where it was hidden under his arm and played with that. That ball kicked well, it kept a-going, it was light. He caught up with Hittoo. Then he passed him and got ahead. They went around a stick that was the halfway mark and then started back to where they started from. The first one back to the starting place won the game. The boy got around the stick ahead of Hittoo. Hittoo was way behind and the boy was way ahead, kicking his ball. The boy won. When he got close to the end, the boy picked up his own ball and put down the one Hittoo had given him to play with. So Chicken Hawk won the game.

Hittoo said, "Let's try another game. Let's go to that big rock." It was a high cliff. From that long cliff hung a long sharp knife. Hittoo was way on top of the cliff, sitting on top of the knife blade. The game was to slide down the sharp knife. Hittoo got down all right, he wasn't hurt. Then he sent the boy up to slide down. The boy was about to try it. He sat on the knife and he slid down it. He got down all right, he wasn't hurt. This was one of the tricks by which Hittoo killed people.

Hittoo said, "Let's try another game." They made a big fire. They got a forked stick, a long one. They stretched a rope across the fire over the top. Then they had to jump over the rope. They told the boy, "You go first." The boy jumped right over, he didn't catch fire at all, he was light and quick. Then the boy said to Hittoo, "You go now." Hittoo started. He tried to jump but he got caught in the rope and tangled up. He fell in the fire. The boy took his forked stick and held Hittoo down in the fire with it. He pinned him down. Hittoo burned up. Hittoo told the boy, "Pick out the best of my daughters. You can marry her." The boy went back to Hittoo's camp. He started in to kill all the girls. Hittoo had killed his father and he was getting revenge. He killed Hittoo and all his family. Then the boy opened up the Bear's mouth and saw some of his father's hair sticking to Bear's teeth. He pulled them out and he packed that hair home to where his mother was. He went back to his mother.

When he was close to the house the net broke. The boy made it break just to tease and scare his mother. The mother cried and fell back when the net broke. Then the boy came in and picked his mother up. He brought out his father's hair. They went to bed. The boy put his father's hair close to his mother's hair. In the morning they woke up and saw the father.

—JIM TYBO
Battle Mountain, Nevada

Origin Tale (2)

Coyote lived by himself. He was making a rabbit net and while he was working, a girl peeked in the door. She was pretty. She didn't say a word, but left right away. Coyote thought that she was beautiful, so he left his net and followed her. He chased her but he couldn't see her—he just followed her tracks. He almost caught up with her but she kept ahead of him going over the little hills. When they came to the water, Coyote caught up with her. She told him to get on her back and she would take him across the water. Coyote wouldn't sit on her back very well but kept slipping down. So the girl let him slip off into the water.

Coyote turned himself into a water-strider and swam ahead of her, he got way ahead and got to the girl's mother's house before her. The girl told her mother, "I let Coyote go and he fell in the water. He didn't behave himself." Her mother said, "Don't talk so loud, Coyote is already here sitting in the house and he might hear you." The women cooked some ducks for supper and they ate outside while Coyote ate inside, lying on the bed.

He heard a great crunching of bones outside and Coyote thought maybe they had a dog. So he made a dog and sent it outside to see what all the noise was. The dog came back quietly, so Coyote knew that there were no dogs outside. The women were throwing the bones underneath them and there was something there chewing the bones. Coyote saw them through a little crack in the house. After a while they all went to bed in the house and the women stretched a net around so that Coyote couldn't get out. Coyote wished for a pocket gopher so he could chew the net.

They all went to bed and fastened the door. Coyote got in bed with the daughter. He felt something between her legs with teeth in it. He stuck his thumb in there and jerked it back quick when the teeth snapped. Coyote got scared and ran outside. They wanted to kill him but he was too smart for them. He hunted and found a pestle to put in there. He stuck it in and when the teeth snapped, it broke them all off. Then he went over to the old woman and did the same thing and pulled all the teeth out of the hole. So they had a good time when they got into bed again. The next night when they all went to bed nothing bothered him and he did what he liked. When they got up the next morning the girl was already swollen up big. In two or three days they had young ones. The old woman gave Coyote a jug to go fetch some water in. He went down to the springs but the jug leaked, so he had to put it in the water to soak until it would hold water.

After a while he brought the water home but he was too late. The children were all grown. The women had divided them into two bands and had taken all of the handsome ones and gone away. Coyote kept the band of ugly kids. They were Shoshones. The others were other kinds of Indians. That is where the Indians came from. Coyote is the father of the Indians. Coyote put the Shoshones into the water jug and started for his home with the jug on his back. Soon he heard a lot of racket in the jug—laughing, hollering, and raising hell. He was tired of packing the jug, so he set it down and opened it. Some of the littler ones got out and ran away. They were in Arizona and they speak just like Shoshones. The rest of them stayed in the jug and Coyote brought them home, washed and cleaned them and let them go.

The woman that Coyote followed was called Paa Naipi, Water Girl.

—Jim Tybo
Battle Mountain, Nevada

Coyote and His Daughter

Coyote and the people had long winters. Coyote wanted his daughter to go hunting with him. They made a trap with his net for rabbits and he told her to watch the net and he was going to chase the rabbit into it. He told her, "You catch those rabbits with your skirt." He went out and drove the rabbits into the net. One rabbit ran straight to the net and got caught, so the girl held the rabbit down. Coyote said, "Did I tell you to do it that way?" She hadn't done it the right way, so they let the rabbit go. He told her again to stoop over and catch the rabbit with her skirt over her head. He went back to chase more rabbits. Another one ran into the net and this time she caught the rabbit with her skirt as she stooped down. Coyote ran over and jumped on her and fell to the ground and broke her backbone. He went to get a doctor for her. He got two hummingbird brothers who were doctors. They doctored her and made her well.

—JIM TYBO
Battle Mountain, Nevada

Theft of Pine Nuts (3)

Lots of people were playing Hand Game. Crow lay down on top of a big rock and watched them play. Soon he smelled something. Crow fell down. Some who were watching said, "Crow fell down. He is dead." So they went to see. Blood was coming out of Crow's mouth. Somebody who was a doctor sang and doctored him. Soon Crow got up. He said, "I smelled pine nuts, coming from the north. I think I will go north and see those pine nuts, see how they look."

Next day Crow went up north. He ran. He went west of Owyhee. He looked. He went a long way. There were people there. They were having a dance. Then they played football. Crane was the boss of these people. Crow played against Crane. All the old women said that Crow was too short, that he couldn't win the pine nuts. Crow thought about it. Everybody was watching. Crow got another ball and when nobody was looking, he hid it. Crane had a human head, a skull, for a ball. Crow wouldn't play with this. He said he had his own ball. When the old woman wasn't looking, Crow took out his ball and ran fast. Crow played and won for two or three days and won the pine nuts. Crane didn't want to give him the nuts. Crow demanded them. Crane refused, so Crow went home.

After Crow got home he called everybody together at night and told them how he had won something but that Crane had refused to give it up. "Who can guess what I won?" Everything they guessed Crow said, "No, that's not it." Finally Crow said, "Go get Coyote. He is smart. He can guess." So they got Coyote and he said, "All right, I'll go after a while." Then he went. He sat down and talked awhile. Then he said, "Maybe Crow meant pine nuts."

Next morning Coyote said, "Let's all go up and get the pine nuts. So they all went north to get the pine nuts—Snake, Mouse, everybody went. Woodpecker went, two kinds of woodpecker. It took four or five days to get up there. Crane's people were having a dance. Then they played Hand Game. Coyote watched them. Coyote played Hand Game and he bet his hide. Twice he lost. Then he won and won and won. Coyote was glad. He had cried when he lost. Woodpecker found where the pine nuts were hidden and toward morning he took them. They stayed five days up there.

They took the pine nuts home. Crane's people tried to make pine-nut gravy, but it wouldn't cook right. Then they said, "Crow took the pine nuts." Everybody ran and chased Crow's people. Crane saw them. They went down south by Cortez. Crane caught up with them and killed them. Crow escaped and ran to the mountain. Crow ran to his home and said, "I have the pine nuts!" They made a fire. They scattered pine nuts all over. Soon there were pine trees all over with nuts on them. Crow said, "I've got pine nuts, I've got pine nuts," and he laughed. Crow cooked. Crane came and sat down. He wouldn't eat. He was mad. His people ate, however, and said, "Tastes pretty good." Crane went back north. Some of his folks stayed down south. They said, "We'll stay here and eat pine nuts."

—MINNIE LEACH
Battle Mountain, Nevada

Origin Tale (3)

Coyote had a wife and children. He played in the water. His wife told him to get water and wash the children. But Coyote played in the water and didn't come back. When he came back he had only a little water. His wife was angry and she kicked him out and gave him some of the children. That is why the white men are Coyote's children. "That's all right, someday you'll fight well." The children that the wife kept are different kinds of Indians. The Shoshone are Coyote's children.

—MINNIE LEACH
Battle Mountain, Nevada

Rabbit hunters, Battle Mountain, ca 1920. Courtesy Beverly Crum.

Tso'apittse (4)

Two men were hunting cottontail rabbits in the mountains. There was snow. Cottontail was hiding under brush. Tso'apittse tracked the two men. They didn't see Tso'apittse. Tso'apittse came near them and the men saw him and ran away. Tso'apittse was crying up there. The men ran and ran and ran and they got home. Tso'apittse ran after them. When the men got home they told an old man, "Tso'apittse is tracking us." The old man is a doctor. He sings and sings. Then Tso'apittse comes but because the doctor sang he couldn't catch the men. So Tso'apittse went home.

—Minnie Leach
Battle Mountain, Nevada

Another Tso'apittse Tale

There was a man who fought with his wife. Soon Tso'apittse came to this man because he fought with his wife. Tso'apittse carried him off in his basket. When they went under a tree, the man caught on a limb and climbed out of the basket.

Tso'apittse went home. His children came out to meet him.

Tso'apittse said, "Go look in my basket and cook what's there for my supper. We will kill him." The children look and say, "There is nothing in there."

"Go and look again. He must be someplace."

"No, there is nothing there." Tso'apittse went and looked but there was nothing in the basket.

By this time the man was home. He had a big stone knife. Tso'apittse tracked him to his home but the young man took his stone knife and slit his hands down from his fingers. Tso'apittse stayed there at the man's house all night. It was cold. He waited outside for the young man to come out. He fell down, it was cold, he died. The young man came out and saw him. He got a stick and poked Tso'apittse's eyes out with it. Tso'apittse died. Next morning the man went to Tso'apittse's home looking for the Tso'apittse children. They were crying from hunger. He killed them.

—Minnie Leach
Battle Mountain, Nevada

Bat (3)

Bat went up to the mountain to hunt deer. Mouse went with him. Mouse went inside a deer, through the mouth, and killed the deer. Bat said, "We'll go to my house and eat that deer."

Coyote was watching. He went up there and called to them. They were way up on the mountain and Coyote couldn't go up there. Coyote was hungry, thin and poor. He tried to make a trail up the mountain to the place where he saw a fire. Mouse was Coyote's uncle. It took Coyote a month to make a trail up the mountain. Coyote called to Bat and Mouse, "I'm hungry, give me something to eat." Soon Mouse said, "My uncle says he is hungry, he is going to die." Bat said, "Give him some bones." So they threw bones down at Coyote. Coyote ate the bones and choked on them. Then Coyote went home. Bat and Mouse laughed and laughed when Coyote choked on the bones.

Next night Coyote is home. He felt good—he sings and laughs because he has lots of bones. Next time he was hungry he went up there again. He had eaten all the bones they had thrown him. Bat said next time he and Mouse were going to watch a dance.

Bat says the enemy is coming. There is a dance that Bat is
watching. He said, "The enemy is coming soon and will kill all of
you. Better run away." Mouse went. Soon the enemy come and all
the dancers are killed. Bat strikes two women in the breast, cuts
them, flies away, returns, strikes them in the breast again, and kills
them.

—Minnie Leach
Battle Mountain, Nevada

Origin Tale (4)

This is a story about Coyote. He came upon a place where a woman
and her daughter were living. They were eating, so he sat down.
The women would eat the meat and then crack the bones with their
vaginas. After he finished eating, Coyote went out and tried to figure out how to get at them. He got a bone and wrapped it in
leather. After they were asleep he sneaked in and slipped the bone
in the daughter. She snapped down on it and broke her teeth. She
cried, "Mother, he's got my teeth." Then he went over and did the
same to the old woman. Then he got them both pregnant.

He stayed there and the girl had some babies. Coyote went out
to get some water in a willow canteen. Every time he got some water it all leaked out. So he put it to soak and then he slid on the
grass and mud. While he was gone both of the women were making
babies. When Coyote got back he heard lots of crying. The girl had
taken all her babies and had gone east. The old woman was there
and Coyote washed her babies and said, "You aren't so good-
looking as those that went away, but you'll get along on this side
and make your way in the world."

He brought the babies farther out west to his uncle's place.
Uncle was Hummingbird. He was rich and made rings. All the
people would come and have rings made. One Hummingbird told
Coyote to take all the rings around to the people that ordered
them. So Coyote went along and tried one on his finger to see the
stone sparkle. Then he put them on all his fingers and he danced
around looking at his rings. One of the stones dropped out and
while it lay on the ground it grew bigger and bigger and started after him. Coyote got scared and jumped over a ditch but it kept after
him. Then he broke through a willow thicket. Then he started going uphill, but the stone was still coming after him. So Coyote took

all the rings off and threw them in all directions. Then the stone quit coming after him. That is why there is gold in these hills—because Coyote threw the gold rings and jewels all around.

Then Coyote started away. Hummingbird knew he wouldn't deliver the rings anyway because he was always in mischief. Hummingbird was a magician (doctor). Coyote was going along and he heard two rocks talking together. He went over and looked at them and they still talked. He put his hand down and the rocks came together and pinched his hand. Coyote yelled, "Uncle, help me, I'm caught." Pretty soon the rocks came apart. Hummingbird was doing all this to punish him.

After he got loose he started out again. He came upon a bunch of girls picking wild potatoes. The girls started to whisper, "That Coyote is a wild-looking thing." Coyote heard them. He went over and put his tail in the ground and pulled out a small root. Then he put it in a little deeper and got a bigger one and then he put his tail way down and got stuck. The earth kept pulling him down farther and farther. He yelled, "Uncle, help me." But he went down until he was blowing dust. Pretty soon he was pulled way under and through the ground till he came up in some sand hills. His uncle was doing all that.

When Coyote came out in the sand hills he was close to his brother's place. He went over. He was all scratched up and lean and hungry. Wolf fed him deer meat, wild potatoes, and pine-nut gravy. His brother would pick up his bow and arrow and go out and pretty soon come back with a deer. Coyote asked, "Where do you get the deer?" But Wolf wouldn't tell him. So Coyote stayed there and got fat. He kept asking where Wolf got the deer. After a while Wolf said, "Oh, I've got a corral of them. You ought to go out and get one." So he went out to the corral and saw the deer. They didn't have any ears or nose-holes. Coyote went running around to make the deer run, so he could shoot at them, but they just stood there like cows and wouldn't move. They just looked at him. Coyote said, "What kind of deer are these anyhow?" So he broke an arrow in two and started poking around and he poked two holes for ears and the same for the nose. "It's no fun trying to kill anything so tame." After that they smelled him and started out on the run. Then he started shooting at them but all he got was a little fawn. He went back to his brother's place. "Here's a mouthful," he said. His brother knew what he had done because he was so long coming back.

Ruby Valley, 1936. Northeastern Nevada Museum.

Then he asked Wolf where he got the other stuff he was eating. He was always bringing in stuff already cooked. Wolf was going
out and he told Coyote not to touch the bag that hung in the room.
So Coyote just lay around there and every once in a while he went
out and shot a rabbit. He wondered why Wolf didn't want him to
touch the bag. He wondered about it for days. He lay around for
days, just singing to himself, and finally he couldn't stand it, so he
picked up a stick and poked at the bag. He poked it harder and
harder but nothing happened. So he gave it a hard jab and everything went dark. So he just stayed there. It was dark all the time after that. He almost starved. He would go out once in a while. He'd
make a torch of rabbit fur and when a rabbit ran by he'd touch it
with the torch and shoot at it while it was on fire.

After a while he couldn't stand it, so he yelled for Wolf. He
heard him way off, so he started out after him. After quite a while
he came out into daylight and saw his brother. Wolf knew he would
do that, so he just left him there with the bag.

That is how the night was made, and deer made wild, how gold
was put into the mountains, and how people were made—by Coyote monkeying around.

—Minnie Coutchem
(Tommy Stevens, translator)
Elko, Nevada

Coyote Learns to Fly (2)

Coyote was getting some willows to make a basket, or anything he could think of, a basket to put seeds in. The world wasn't like this, then. Everything grew nice. Coyote saw some geese flying overhead and he started dancing. He thought he might become a doctor. He talked to the geese. He hollered to them and told them to come down and give him wings so he could fly north with them. He asked where they were going. They said they were going north, to a dance up there. They gave him feathers, two or three from each of them. They told him to try out his wings. He tried it for half a mile and they told him to land, but he kept on flying. Then he fell and cracked his head and all his brains fell out. He started eating his own brains. The geese left him and Coyote started to follow them. He put pebbles in his head for a brain. He started walking off. The geese hunted on their way—rabbits, deer, lizards—with their bows and arrows. At night they rested. Coyote stopped and ate what they had left over. He slept there and then went on his way in the morning. He kept on following the geese for ten days.

The geese went to a camp where there was a dance and killed all the people there. The geese came back south after that. They met Coyote. They stopped there and told him all about the people they killed. Coyote asked them if there was a woman there who was pregnant. They said there was one that they killed. Coyote started going. He got there. He cut the woman open with a flint knife. It was a baby girl and he took her out of her mother's body. He then made himself into a woman. He made himself breasts out of clay. He put on some hot water to drink.

Her hair grew long and she braided it. She slept there one night and then she was talking to herself and said, "Any woman who has a baby shall do this way: The first day, sleep on a hot bed, it makes the baby and mother healthy. After the baby is born a woman shouldn't chew for five days. This keeps her teeth good and keeps her face from getting wrinkled. She shouldn't touch her face with her hands. This keeps her from getting wrinkles. She should not scratch her hair, but use a scratching stick—this keeps it from getting coarse and split." Then she started off toward her brother's place. The second day she slept there, boiled hot water, and fixed the hot bed and followed the rules she made before. After five days Coyote became a man again. He washed off the clay breasts, cut off his hair. Five days after childbirth a woman can chew. After a month she can eat meat with sagebrush. The period for following the rules is over.

In one day the baby grew as much as most babies do in a year. Then the baby started sitting up and Coyote started talking to the baby. He said, "You're my sister. You are sitting up now." Then the baby started to walk. The baby grew. Now the girl is about fifteen, sixteen years old. Every day she grew a year. Coyote wanted her to marry him. He asked her to sleep with him. She said, "No, you told me I was your sister." Then Coyote cried every night. Then he threw dirt in his face every night. Coyote kept on begging her to sleep with him. She started singing about Coyote's brother's place (Wolf's). Then Coyote sang about his brother's place, a big mountain. This is near Tonopah.

They were traveling and were almost to that place. Coyote asked her how she knew about his brother's home. She told him she knew it was his brother's home. The girl had grown to be a woman now. Coyote asked her to marry him. She told him, no, that he had told her she was his sister.

When they were about ten miles from Wolf's place, Coyote told the girl to stay there, to hide. Coyote went on to Wolf's place. Wolf's name is "Bias." Then Wolf told his brother, Coyote, to get some deer meat and cook supper for him and the girl. Coyote said there was only himself. He did not want to tell Wolf he had the girl with him but Wolf already knew it. Coyote wouldn't get supper ready. Wolf asked him again, but Coyote just stood there. Then he said, "How did you know, brother, that there were two of us?" Then Coyote told his brother, Wolf, that they had a sister now. Wolf told him to go get the girl. Coyote went and got the girl. When they got to Wolf's place they ate and stayed there that night. Wolf went hunting the next morning, as they were out of meat. He had a lot of deer in a cave, and he killed only one at a time. Every time they were out of meat Wolf went to the cave and killed one deer. He hung it on a tree. Wolf came back to his place and told Coyote to get the meat. Coyote wanted the girl to go with him. So they both went to where Wolf had hung the deer. Coyote told the girl to climb up the tree and get the meat. She said no, she wouldn't go up. Finally she climbed up. She did not have any pants on. A little blood from the deer meat dropped down. Then Coyote threw the blood back at the girl and it went in her. Then he told her not to touch the meat because she was menstruating. That is how menstruation started and Coyote made the rules about it. Then Coyote got his brother and told him that the girl was having her monthly period.

They started washing her with cold water, tied her hair back and told her not to touch it with her hands, not to eat meat, drink hot water, made her work hard so she won't be lazy, whipped her with sagebrush for two days. They whipped the weariness out of her body. She should follow these rules for five days. She got some dried sagebrush and piled it up. This is to keep busy so as not to become lazy. They told her not to eat meat for a month (this is just after the first menstrual period). Then Coyote put a tall tree (representing a man) and told her not to look at it. Coyote made all these rules. (All are kept today except the tree one.) Coyote told her not to sit down, to keep busy all the time. At night he put a stone under her head and told her not to go to sleep. Every time she fell asleep, her head would roll off the rock and she would wake up. (This rule is followed for the first period.)

Coyote's brother, Wolf, was mad about all this. He did not like Coyote making the girl menstruate. Wolf told Coyote that the girl was too young for this and said it was Coyote's fault that she menstruated. They quarrelled about it. Wolf did not want women to have monthly periods, but Coyote did.

Wolf went out in the field. He raised *ap uap* [eappih?] and *wai* and *wata dambu,* three different kinds of seeds. Every morning he went out to look them over. He had acres of them.

The girl's first month was over. She washed herself, put hot stones in the fire, took them out, put water on them, and used sagebrush to wash herself in the steam.

The girl lived apart from Wolf and Coyote during this first month after she first started menstruating. She lived about three or four miles away. When the month was up, she returned. Wolf was glad when she came back. Then Wolf told his sister to go gather the seeds. She told him no, that she would rather go at night. She made herself into an animal, a kangaroo rat, and she went to the fields at night. It took her three days to cut the grain. She carried the seeds in the little pouches in her cheeks.

One morning she asked Wolf for *mumi.* Wolf got her the head of a deer. The girl said, "No, I want a *mumi."* Wolf said he did not know what she meant. She kept on saying she wanted a *mumi.* Then he went and got a mountain sheep, a young male yearling. He carried it on his back and took it to his place, where he dumped it off. Then Coyote took the hide off it. Coyote was glad about it. The girl cut the hind feet off. This was what she had meant by *mumi*. Wolf knew what she wanted. She made moccasins out of it. That is what the kangaroo rat has on the bottom of its feet now. It took her three days to make these moccasins.

She was going to store the seeds for winter. It took her two days to winnow the seeds. She made a little hole for herself. That is how the kangaroo rats live, in holes. She took half the seeds and stored them away and left the other half for the brothers. She put them on the other side of the entrance to her house.

In the deep part of the hole she stored the seeds. On the other side she had her nest. In the middle she has a little thin dirt cover. She can go out through this easily.

Kaan kwaisi kwaiyakkwa. Weeppukkankikku. (The rat's tail came off. It was dangling.) The end.

(You always say that at the end of a story. Coyote and Wolf turned into a wolf and a coyote and the girl turned into a kangaroo rat.)

—MARY STANTON
(Judy Gibson, translator)
Ely, Nevada

Si-ets

Mary knows the story of Si-ets carrying off the boy in a basket and his escape by pulling himself out on a limb. She says this happened over at Strawberry Valley, about twenty-five miles from Ely. You can still see the witch's body. It is a big stone.

—MARY STANTON
(Judy Gibson, translator)
Ely, Nevada

The Cannibal Bluebirds

It was in March. There grows bitter onion and *yampa* (Indian carrot). Two people came to dig the onions and carrots. This was all they had to live on. The carrots and onions grew on the side of a mountain, Mt. Wohang-gada (a mountain near here). The other mountain where the people lived was Timping gada (big hill). They walked over to the mountain. They had moccasins made of sagebrush. They were naked except for rabbit blankets. They had bows and arrows.

One morning they set out for this mountain to gather onions and carrots. On a little summit they saw Condor. One of the men fell under a sagebrush bush. There were four condors. One of them caught the man who did not hide under the sagebrush. The man saw the birds take his partner and saw the birds fighting over him. The ankle and moccasin fell from the man who had been captured. The condors ate the man. The other man ran but he was too scared to run fast. He ran to their home. When he got to camp he told the people what had happened to his partner. They did not believe him because they had never seen any condors there. So he took them and showed them the ankle and moccasin that the birds had bitten off. Then they believed him after they saw the ankle. At night they did not make any fires at their camp. They were scared.

A couple of years later there was a flock of great big bluebirds. One night the people heard the bluebirds saying, "Kai ya." They were scared and went south to where there were a lot more people. When they got there they told about the condors and about what they heard the bluebirds saying. They stayed there dancing with their hosts. Then the bluebirds came to where the dance was. They had big bills and killed all the people with their bills. Only one person escaped, a woman. She got in a big carrying basket. The birds did not see her. The bluebirds ate the hot coals from the fireplace. The hidden woman watched them. They stayed there one day and ate all the people they had killed. The woman stayed hidden in the basket.

Then the birds went away. The woman got out of the basket and came over here to Eureka (not far from Ely) and told her grandfather what had happened down at Tonopah.

The people at Eureka did not believe the woman's tale, so she showed them a feather from the big bluebirds that she had picked up. They said the feather was from a *datawi*, a bird almost as big as an ostrich. These birds travel through the sky in December when the sky is foggy. You can hear them sometimes. Half the sky is dark, the other is blue. The people are scared when they hear these birds. Since the white people came they are not scared.

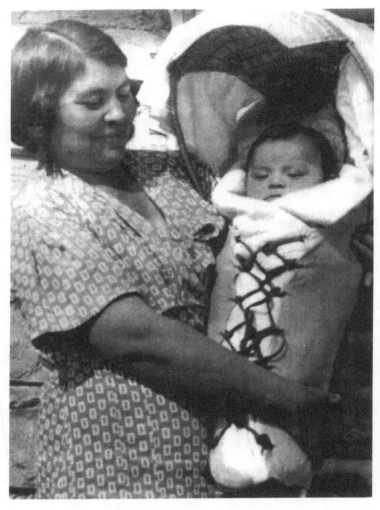

Shoshone woman and baby, ca. 1930. Northeastern Nevada Museum, Elko.

This is a true story. It was told to Mary's father's grandfather. Some of the woman's descendants still live near Austin.

—MARY STANTON
(Judy Gibson, translator)
Ely, Nevada

Watoavic

There was a family, with their children. The children were playing.
It was at sundown. They had a little fire there. Watoavic (Si-ets) is
a man made of stone. If you hit him, you can't hurt him. But he has
pitch all over him and if you throw fire at him he will burn all over.

The children were dancing the circle dance when Watoavic
came. He got in the circle of children and when he got out he
started walking on his hands. He went over a little hill and the children followed him, all except one little girl. The children who followed Watoavic were killed. The little girl who didn't follow him
went back to camp and told the people how the children followed
this man and how all the children walked on their hands just like
Watoavic had done.

Then all the people went to this place. They had cedar-bark
torches with them. They found the children all dead, their lower
halves missing, and sand in their ribs. Then they looked for
Watoavic but they couldn't find him. Next morning they tracked
him. Watoavic had a big fire and was sleeping with his back to the
fire. They shot at him, but they couldn't hurt him. He just pulled
out the arrows that shot him. They couldn't find the right place to
shoot him. Then one of them shot him on the bottom of his feet.
This was the only fleshy part on him. He jumped up and ran toward
water. This happened at Steptoe Mountain. He ran down the valley
and fell dead there. The people followed and tore him to pieces.
They took a great big stone and pounded him. This is a true story.

—MARY STANTON
(Judy Gibson, translator)
Ely, Nevada

Water Babies (2)

Tom Nephi has seen water babies. He lives on this hill right near
here. Some of the water babies live in the water, some on land.
You can see its trail. It cries just like a baby when something is
going to happen or someone is going to die.

At White River, Water Baby swallows the baby and gets in the
cradle, then swallows the mother's breast. She calls other women
and they cut off her breast. They can't kill Water Baby.

When you see a red light at night, that is a water baby. When you hear a water baby crying, it makes your hair stand up and you can't speak.

A Pony Express rider saw the water baby.

There is a water baby like a woman with long hair.

Over near Clover Valley there is a peak between Clover and Star Valley from which you can see a big hole, big enough for a wagon to go through. That was where Snake used to look out to see if any enemy was coming. This monster had eyes like sparkling glass. When you see it, it kills you. There is a big mound by the highway in Clover Valley, which is the grave of the monster.

—Mary Stanton
(Judy Gibson, translator)
Ely, Nevada

Theft of Fire

There were four animals and Coyote was the chief. There was Porcupine, Stink Bug, and Pack Rat. These four decided they would have a meeting and gather their people together and tell them that they were going south to get fire from the people down there who had fire. They said they were cold and needed a fire in their land.

They started on their way. Coyote said they were to disguise themselves, so Coyote made himself a wig out of bark from a tree. He gathered it and made it look like hair and he put it on his head. The others did not put on any disguise. They went on their way. It took a long time. When they got to where the people were, they found them having a dance. Porcupine and Stink Bug stayed outside during the daytime and Coyote and Pack Rat joined the people. They walked around and enjoyed themselves. When evening came, all four of them came in and joined the others. Then they all started dancing the Circle Dance and the dance kept up all night. Just before dawn Porcupine and Stink Bug ran out and they stayed in their own camp all day. They didn't show themselves in the daytime. The girls thought they better hunt for these two—they danced with them at night but they never saw them in the day.

The girls hunted for them and found their camp, but all they saw was Porcupine's quill dress, which was lying in the mud. At night it looked so pretty that they didn't recognize it when they saw it lying there. [Laughter.] They saw a hole—that was where Stink Bug was sleeping. The girls didn't find the two.

At night they all danced again. Porcupine and Stink Bug came out and joined the dance. The Stink Bug jumped up and down and made a funny noise that attracted the attention of the girls. They wanted to see what he looked like in the light. So they made a cedar-bark torch and went over to Porcupine and Stink Bug. They saw an old black insect and they thought, "He's not good-looking. We won't dance with him again." [Laughter.] The same thing happened with Porcupine. So they danced with Coyote and Pack Rat. They had not danced with them before because they had seen them in the daylight and knew they were not handsome.

It got near dawn. Coyote danced close to the fire. The people told him not to dance so near the fire or his hair might catch on fire. Just at dawn his hair caught on fire. Coyote told his companions he was ready. Coyote and Pack Rat started running, and Stink Bug and Porcupine ran after them. The people chased them. They caught up with Stink Bug first. Next they caught Porcupine and killed them both. Coyote and Pack Rat kept on running. They ran a long time. The people got close to them and Coyote took his burning wig and gave it to Pack Rat to carry. The pursuers killed Coyote. The Pack Rat carried the fire under his belly and kept on running. It was a charcoal he was carrying. He ran toward his nest. When he was almost there (he lived in rocks near the cliff), he jumped up toward the cliff. He was going to divide up the fire. He put some fire in his nest and then he put fire in all the different directions—that is why all the wood burns. That is how they got fire to keep people warm. From now on all wood will burn.

—Mary Stanton
(Margie Stark, translator)
Ely, Nevada

Cottontail Shoots the Sun

Cottontail's name in stories is Dav Nadz Gwi Ingup. He got this name by killing the sun. This is what they called him after that.

At that time the sun was traveling low, close to the earth. It was human then. It was too hot. Everything was so dry it got all scorched. Nothing would grow, it was too hot and dry. Cottontail was lying down. He couldn't do anything, it was too hot. He lay on his belly with his back to the sun. Sun wanted to play with him. He thought Cottontail was doing something funny. Sun had a cane that he used to kill things with. He took this stick and poked Cottontail in the back. He did this every day. The cane was hot and Cottontail got burned. So Cottontail thought, "How can I destroy Sun?" Cottontail's back is marked now where Sun poked him. So Cottontail made his plan to kill Sun. He made a bow and arrows. He worked on the flint for arrowheads. He used deer horn to sharpen the flint. After he got the points all sharp, it was a long time. He baked the points with poison. (Poison is the blood of any animal, plus snake poison, cooked together in an earth oven with stones.) He baked the poison all night and in the morning he rubbed the points in the poison. Then he started making bows. His bow was made of *ho gup* (like cane). He straightened that for a day, worked on a hot stone to make it pliable. His bow string was made of sinew. It took a long time to get things all ready. He used feathers from Gopher Hawk for his arrows. Then he had to get a coyote hide to make a quiver. He used two sticks for the frame of the quiver and buckskin thongs for the carrying straps. He made several quivers.

The Sun was so hot you could smell how everything was scorched. When everything was done, he looked to see in what direction Sun was going. He had to find out where Sun came up. This was the first day.

The next day he went over to the spot where Sun got up. He dug a hole to hide in. He made a lot of side-holes in his tunnel to hide in so he could keep from getting scorched. Sun began to come up but he rose in a different place from where he usually did. It was on the other side of the mountain. Cottontail watched him.

Then next day he went to that place and made another hole. Cottontail didn't get any sleep, he watched the Sun. Then the Sun began to rise. Every day Sun came up in a different place and Cottontail would go to the spot and make a hole there.

Then Cottontail started on his journey. He came out on a flat plain. It took him several days to cross the plain. He couldn't find a mountain where he could hide in a hole. Then he saw what seemed like a skylike place—it was the ocean that he saw. When he got close he saw it was water. It was before dawn then. Then the water began to boil and Cottontail ran back and forth. He didn't know what it was. He said, "Huhunugugup"—this means in his own language "I am scared." Soon the water boiled, made steam. The Sun jumped on a tree on an island in the water. Sun sat there on the top of the tree and scratched his head. Cottontail watched. Sun was eating his lice. He stayed there quite a while. Cottontail sang to himself. [A song was sung here.] He said, "Sun is easy to kill, he is a human being."

Cottontail thought he would wait another day before killing the Sun. He started making his hole. He made it quite deep. He made a roof of branches to shelter him. He thought he would practice to see how fast he could dodge into the hole and hide in the curve in the hole, and he would practice aiming his arrows at the tree. He practiced all night, he didn't get any sleep.

Then the water started boiling. Cottontail knew it was the Sun coming up that was making the water boil. So Cottontail sang again. Cottontail got his weapons all ready. Soon the Sun came out and got on the same tree and started eating his head lice. As soon as he jumped on the tree, Cottontail started shooting at him. The first arrow went just a little way, then it started to burn and fell. Then he got another arrow and it burned, too. This happened to all his arrows. They all burned up. So Cottontail had nothing left but his quiver. He thought he would use his quiver. He made an arrow out of one stick from his quiver, dampened it by putting one end in his mouth. Maybe his saliva put poison on it. He took a good aim. He shot it at Sun. It went a long distance and it hit the Sun. Then Cottontail ducked into his hole. Part of him got scorched, he wasn't quick enough. You can see on Cottontail today where he got scorched. These are the brown spots.

The Sun fell into the water and it started boiling hard. Then Cottontail got into the curved place in his hole. The ground was hot. Cottontail wanted to cool it. So Cottontail called the North Wind. He wished the North Wind would come. So it started to hail. Cottontail was in the hole several days. It kept on hailing and snowing, but the ground didn't cool off very much. Then it gradually began to cool. The ground began to lose its heat. So Cottontail thought he would come out and see what it was like outside. When he got out, it was dark—there was no Sun. Cottontail's eyes are like cat's eyes, he can see in the dark.

He went to the water to drag out the Sun. He laid him on the ground. Then he started to skin the Sun just as though he were game. It took him a long time to skin the Sun. It was dark all this time.

Then he started to cut up the Sun. He took him apart and looked at all the pieces. He put the pieces of Sun in a pile. First he cut the hands, wrists, upper arms apart and piled them up. Then he started to cut up the body. Then he wanted to make a new Sun. He took the gall bladder off the liver and threw it up to the sky. He said, "You are going to be the Sun and stay up there forever. You are not going to hit people's backs. You are not going to be too hot. You are going to make things grow and ripen and help things on the land." Then he took out Sun's rain-bags (kidneys—where the water is). He said the rain bags will be the moon. Then he said he was going to name the months. He started from July and named all the months, twelve of them. Then he said that after twelve months it starts over again. He said the rain-bags will be the moon.

July	Rye-grass moon, *wa bi mi ha*
August	Little summer, *na ga ha da thun*
September	Rabbits' digging time (they dig the grass), *ka mu bi ma di huwa dan*
October	Little moon, *na ga ha mi ha*
November	Deer-breeding time, *bia mi ha*
December	Very cold moon (blizzard), *goa mi ha*
January	Snowflake moon, *bo sidj mi ha*
February	Coyote has a baby, *ija duʳru wa mi ha*
March	Moon with the green edges (things start getting green), *bwi k makandi mi ha bi ma du ruwa wa no an mi*
April	Moon when the mountain sheep have their young, *dimbi wa sopita*
May	Moon when the antelope have their young, *gwa d na bi ma ndarua wa n an mi ha*
June	Moon when the deer have their young, *dihi ya bi ma du nua wa no'an mi ha*

So Cottontail named all the months. He said all this to the rain-bags, "From now on, you will be here twenty-five days, then you will vanish and appear again in the east. When you renew, you must wash yourself. It will rain in summer at that time, and snow in winter. When you are up there, if you want the weather to be dry, you will sit in a straight curve ⌣. When the weather is going to be wet, you will sit like this)) ." Then Cottontail said that from now on whoever lives on the land will know when it is going to be dry and when it will be wet. Every bit of grass and the humans will be healthy and live well. "You will help the people. The grass and animals and people will be healthy because of the Sun and the Moon." This is what he said to the Moon. Then he threw up the rain-bags way up in the sky, to the west. It is a new Moon in the sky now. The Sun travels east and west now. It is doing very well.

When Cottontail had finished making the Sun and Moon, he started talking. He took the Sun's body and is going to name the parts. He named all the parts of the sun's body, he named the fingers, arms, legs, and all the rest. Then he took the kidneys and called them his Sun Rock. Then he started talking to the Sun and Moon again: "You listen to me now. Whoever lives in the land will have a good brain because of you two. You help the people. People will have brains and they will invent things like Sun Dance, healers, and so on. The first people in this land will have all their knowledge in their heads. They will have no papers, no writing."

He said to Sun, "You will give light to the whole land." He told the Moon he should give a light at night.

Now Cottontail started talking to the Ocean. "You will be salty because Sun fell in you. No one will drink you. You will stay salty." In some parts of the world they will have warm springs, boiling water. They will stay that way. These hot springs are the tears that the sun shed when he was shot.

Now Cottontail was going to start back to his home. It took him a long time to journey home. He went over the plain and over the mountains. Finally he came to a little wickiup. He saw an old woman sitting there near her place. The old woman started building a fire. He asked her why she was doing that. She said she was expecting Cottontail. *Dava nai di wa sugin* (this means Cottontail is killing people on his way, after he killed the sun). Cottontail asked the old woman what Cottontail was going to do. She said first thing Cottontail would do was to jump over the fire and she will hold him in the fire, where he will roast. She didn't know it was Cottontail to whom she was talking. He was changed from being scorched. Then Cottontail said, "We might as well try it." The old woman said, "All right." They went a little way from the fire. The old woman said, "You run to the fire first." Cottontail did. He ran to the fire and jumped over it. The old woman didn't get a chance to kick him in the fire, he ran so fast. Then Cottontail told the old woman to try it. Cottontail said, in his language, "You go now." Then the old woman ran to the fire. When she was not far from the fire Cottontail was right behind her. He kicked at her heels. She stumbled and fell into the fire. [Laughter.] Cottontail held her down in the fire with a forked stick until she was dead. Her bones popped and crackled. Then he knew she was surely dead.

Cottontail went on his way. He looked around while he was traveling to see whom he could see. He came upon another old woman. She was making a big water jug out of willows. She was working as fast as she could. She told him she was expecting Cottontail, who killed the Sun, to come. He asked her what she was going to do when Cottontail came. She said, "When he arrives, I'll let him get inside the big jug and then I'll crush the jug and jump on it." Then Cottontail said, "Let's try it now." (She didn't know he was Cottontail.) So Cottontail said, "Let's try it," and he got in the jug and the old woman got on it and jumped on it. She heard him squeaking inside. She thought he was killed. But Cottontail came out and said, "You be next now. You go in." So the old woman got in the basket and Cottontail jumped on it and trampled the old woman to death. [Laughter.]

Cottontail went on his journey. He looked around to see whom he could see. He saw a lot of logs laid up in tipi shape. He looked inside and saw a big stone hanging up in there. He started saying, "Hun hun u i" (it means he is scared). There was an old woman sitting outside. Cottontail asked her, "What is that for?" She said she was expecting Cottontail, who killed the Sun. Cottontail said, "What is Cottontail going to do with that?" She said, "When he comes we both go inside."

"Then what?"

"When Cottontail is inside, I will shake the rock and it will fall on Cottontail and kill him." Cottontail said, "Let's try it now." They both went in and she loosened the rock and ran out. The rock shook the log house and the old woman heard Cottontail's squeaky voice inside. She thought he was dead. Then she no longer heard the rock rumbling around inside. Cottontail appeared at the door and said, "It's your turn next." They both went in and Cottontail shook the rock and ran out. The rock went for the old woman and killed her.

Cottontail went on his way. He traveled a long time. He came upon a field of *i'apih* (a kind of seed). It was a large field. He thought, "I am hungry. I'll stay here awhile." There were lots of little cottontails there. So Cottontail stayed near the field. *Ba nan dika di* (looked like Chinamen) lived there. A lot of children and their sisters lived nearby. It was their field.

One of the girls (the oldest sister) went out to see how the field was. She discovered there were a lot of cottontails there. She went home and told her brothers there were a lot of cottontails there. "They are ruining the field." Then the brothers started to go and get rosebushes to make bows and arrows. They started making weapons to kill the cottontails. They went out to the field and killed a lot of little cottontails and started home with them. They looked at them. The littlest boy told his brother they had seen a cottontail sitting under a bush. They tried to catch that cottontail. They shot at him, but they could not hit him. This was Cottontail. When they shot at him he blew at the arrows and the arrows did not reach him. They tried to catch him in their hands. They made a circle around him and started to close in. Then they started making a noise, "Hun hun u i."

Cottontail sat there and waited until they got close. When they were almost touching him he jumped through their circle and ran away. He went into a hole and traveled underground. He knew their home was not far away. He came up above the ground and started walking. When he was near their home, he saw a spear leaning against a tree. He thought he would do something to make these people helpless. He blew out the pith from the spear so that it was very light and wouldn't hurt anyone. Then he went into the tipi and saw the sister sitting there. She was waiting for her brothers. Cottontail sat down and thought he would disguise himself. He asked the girl if she had any paint. She said she had a little, which she gave him. He put it on his face. It sounded as though the boys were coming. Soon they came. Cottontail heard them talking about the spear, wondering how it got so light. They knew something was wrong with it. They stopped at the doorway to the house. The leader stared at Cottontail. He looked strange with the paint on his face. When the others saw Cottontail they stopped too. They froze in their steps. They said, "Hun hun u i." All the brothers backed out of the house. It was about sundown. It was getting cold. The sister told Cottontail, "You better wipe that paint off your face and let my brothers in. They are getting cold." Cottontail was sitting by the door. He wiped off his face. The boys came in and told Cottontail to move over. He moved over close to the sister.

They divided up those rabbits they had caught. Each got one. They gave one to Cottontail. When he got it, he threw it in the hot coals. Then he shot an arrow at it and lifted it up with the arrow. All the people watched him and thought they would do as he did. They imitated him, even the sister. She used her poker to lift up her cottontail. Her little rabbit fell all to pieces.

They ate their supper. Then they all went out to play with their spears. Cottontail stayed in. Then they came in to bed. Cottontail sat up. He sat there till they were asleep. He started to tie them with their own hair. He tied all their braids together. Then he went over to the sister. He wanted to sleep with her, he didn't want to destroy her that way. He had intercourse with her and soon her guts were coming out of her mouth. Then he knew she was dead. Cottontail set fire to the house and went outside. He stood and watched the fire. He heard the people inside making a noise. They were frightened. They were tied up and were helpless. They all burned to death. When all was quiet, Cottontail knew they were all dead.

Then Cottontail went on his way. He was walking slowly, looking around. He met a Rockchuck, like a groundhog. They lived in a rockslide. They were calling Cottontail names. They knew it was Cottontail. They said how bad he looked, said he was wearing his mother's blanket. He looked bad. They made fun of him. Cottontail got very mad. He thought he would destroy these people. He started picking tree bark and gathered dead branches from old trees. He covered the holes that led to their burrows with this stuff. He made sure all the holes were covered with brush and bark. Then he set the brush and bark on fire. He watched to see that they smoked well, so that the smoke would go down into the holes. He did this all day. He went back and forth from hole to hole, seeing that his smudges kept going. He heard the Rockchucks crying. When there was no more noise he knew they were all dead.

Then he went on his journey. He walked on for some distance, several days. He went slowly and looked around to see whom he could see. He was getting close to where his aunts lived. He stopped at the place where they stored their food. They buried their food under the ground. He took one of the sun's kidneys and put it on top of the place where the food was stored. He left it there and went on. When he was near their house he tied a piece of rabbit-skin blanket on his leg (trying to be funny) and then he ran to the house. The aunts saw him and recognized him. They said, "Our nephew is here." He ran away from the door and then came back. They called him "nephew." He liked that name, so he did not get mad. Then he went into their house. They told him to make himself at home. They gave him seed (*poina*). He did not have enough, so he told them to get some more. So the women went out to get some more. When they came to the place where the food was stored they found a big rock on it. They tried to move it but they couldn't. So one woman said to the other, "Go get our nephew to move the rock." So she went and got Cottontail. She said to Cottontail, "There is a rock on top of the food. We can't move it. You better come." So Cottontail went with her to the big rock. He told the two women not to look at him while he was lifting the rock. So they covered their eyes with their hands. When he started lifting the rock, he poked his rear end up in the air. One woman said to the other, "Look at him, he is putting his rear end up in the air." Cottontail heard her and told them not to look. Then Cottontail lifted up the rock and when the women opened their eyes there was no rock there. It had vanished.

Then Cottontail told them to take out the seeds and they did. They all went back to the house. They fixed some more food for him because he was still hungry.

After they ate they all went to sleep. They slept all night. In the morning, after breakfast, Cottontail went on his way again.

He went slowly and looked around. He met two wildcats sitting by a fire. The fire was just a white stone, that was all they used for fire. Cottontail told them he was cold, they better build a fire. He told them to go get cedar wood to make a fire. The wildcats told him it was dangerous to touch the wood. When they went to pick it up the wood hit out at them. So Cottontail said, "Go get some. I'm cold." The wildcats would not do it. Cottontail asked them again, "You better do as I say." So the wildcats went a little way. They tried to pick up a limb but when their hands started to touch the wood, it moved. They ran and the wood ran after them. When they got near to Cottontail he got up and he took out Sun's kidneys for a weapon and threw that at the wood. It stopped running and fell down. Then Cottontail told the wildcats to try again to pick up the wood. They picked it up and it was all right now. Cottontail said to

the wood, "Wood should not be like this. From now on you won't
be dangerous." So they made a fire and Cottontail got warm. They
sat there awhile and then Cottontail got thirsty and told the wildcats
to go get some water. They told him the water was dangerous and
chased them. Cottontail told them to get water. So they went over
to the spring and tried to dip their willow cup in. Just as the cup got
near the water, the water started splashing at them. The water ran
at the wildcats, who ran away. When they got close to Cottontail he
threw his Sun-rock at the water and said, "Water shouldn't be like
this. From now on you won't be dangerous." Then Cottontail told
the wildcats to get some water. They went and got some and Cottontail drank.

Cottontail stayed with them overnight. These two wildcats
were his cousins. That is why he didn't harm them.

In the morning he went on his journey. He walked slowly and
looked around. He found two boys, Sky Boys. When he got to their
place, one boy said to the other that he better feed Cottontail. So
he did. He fed Cottontail some strange food that he had never
eaten before. It was white and hard, sky sweet. There was just a
little of it and Cottontail wanted some more. He liked this food. He
asked the boys where they got this food. They told him that they lie
down and sing before they get it. When they sing and look at the
sky, then the food appears in the sky and comes toward them.
When it gets near the ground they break off a piece of it. So Cottontail said, "I want some more of that food, we better do that
now." So the boys lay down and sang and looked up at the sky. Cottontail lay down at the end of the row on the south side. [Song
given here, "This Sky Sweet is coming down toward the earth."]
There was noise like thunder, then the sweet was coming down,
the candy cracked. It came slowly toward the earth. When the
candy appeared Cottontail started shivering, he is scared. [Laugh-
ter.] The boys kept on singing. Cottontail got up and ran around.
When he looked up, it appeared white. Cottontail was scared.
When the food was halfway between earth and sky Cottontail was
very scared and he thought he would destroy it. He threw his Sun-
kidney-rock at it and it hit the food and it broke all to pieces. Cottontail started to pick up the little pieces that fell. Then he said,
"Food shouldn't be like this. Food should be on the land, not come
from the sky." He said to the pieces, "You shall remain on the land
and be a plant that bears sugar, in a ball form (ga'phia). You shall

have little insects (aphids) on you. You shall be sweet, sometimes on the sagebrush and willows and on pine trees." Then Cottontail started telling the two boys they could not remain on the earth. "You will go to the sky and remain there. That is where you shall live." Nowadays when anybody thinks they see these Sky Boys, they faint. An old maid might get lovesick and imagine these boys and get sick. They did not turn into stars, the boys just went to the sky. There is a hole in the sky, that is where these two boys live. When Cottontail finished talking, the two boys flew to the sky.

Then Cottontail went on his way. He went slowly and looked around. He came to a swampy place. He looked to see whether anyone lived there. He walked a little way through the swamp. Then he changed himself into the form of a boy. He saw two girls there, that is why he changed. The two girls found him. They were glad to see a boy. They took him to their house. They had come out to get wood, but they left the wood there and picked up the boy and carried him home. When they got home they fed him *nappeh*, a food like sweet potatoes, roots that grow in the swamp, cattails. So Cottontail ate that. Then they went to bed and he slept with the two girls. He started feeling around these two, he felt their breasts. He said he was hungry, he wanted to nurse them. So he did that. In the morning they got up and they had breakfast. When they finished, the other people went out to gather the roots in the swamp. The girls and Cottontail followed them. They went to where there were a lot of these plants. The girls showed Cottontail how they gathered roots and helped him get some. Then after Cottontail learned how to gather the roots, the girls left him.

Then they all went home. They had supper. At night Cottontail slept with the girls—he was acting like a man now. [Laughter.] The girls were scared because he had turned into a man. In the morning they didn't feed him as they had when they thought he was a helpless little boy. The rest of the people suspected that these two girls must know something. "It seems queer that these two girls don't feed Little Brother."

The two girls left Cottontail home and joined the rest of the people when they went out to gather roots. When they got to a place where there were a lot of plants they all started to gather them. Cottontail was walking around at the edge of the river. He got a little stick and poked it under the ground. It went under the place where the people were. They knew something was happening, the whole swamp shook every once in a while. Cottontail kept on poking his stick from the bank where he stood. He walked around.

The two girls went home but the others stayed there. After the girls had gone, Cottontail poked his stick under the swamp and turned it upside down. The people were all buried underneath the swamp and died. It was about sunset now. Cottontail gathered up the digging sticks that the people had been using and set them on fire. He gathered some of the plants and started home. He reached home. The girls asked him where the rest of the people were and Cottontail said, "The people have got big roots now." He said the people won't return, they are going to stay there for a while. They are peeling the skin off the roots. That is why they have made that big fire you can see (this was the fire he had made of the digging sticks.) He said to the girls, "Don't worry about those people. They will come back later." The girls believed him.

They had supper and then they went to bed. Cottontail slept with them and killed them by having intercourse with them. He poked their guts out of their mouths.

Then he turned into a cottontail. He became an animal forever.

—Mary Stanton
(Margie Gibson, translator)
Ely, Nevada

[Mary Stanton says you can't start a story today and
finish it tomorrow. Once it is started you must go on to
the end. Stories should only be told in winter.
Telling Coyote stories (except in winter) brings on
a cold winter. —Anne M. Smith]

Antelope Hunting

Margie Stark's grandfather was a shaman, a doctor. When anyone was starved, his people would go to him. They would ask him to get meat for them. They had a meeting. They all agreed, and he went out and started singing. He went where the antelope are—he knows where they are. First he tells his people they must build a corral, fix trees on top of each other like a corral. He tells them to make a circle with wings—like this ʃ͡ʔ . Then when everything is ready they must start singing and sing for five days. When they finish singing, he starts on his way. Then they have to pick out one person, the doctor selects him. They get the antelope spirit right into the corral. So now the antelope won't be so scared. They will know the way and come right to the corral.

The doctor stays at the corral and he sends out the chosen man. He must be a strong, healthy man with a good mind. He must not have any bad ideas. The doctor sends this man out to bring in the antelope. It takes him several days to bring the antelope to the corral. They come slowly. There are lots of them. When they get close to the corral, the chosen man makes a fire to notify the doctor that he is coming with a big bunch of antelope. In the morning all the people come. The chosen man stands at the entrance to the corral. The antelope all go in the corral. Then they shut the gate. Then the doctor chooses the best shot and tells him to shoot the leader of the herd. This man must not miss or the herd will all escape. They never killed an animal less than two years old. They let the yearlings go.

They count up the people, then they see how many antelope there are. Usually everyone gets two antelope. They count the people first and kill two apiece. The doctor and the chosen man get only two, just like the others. The women get a male and female skin. The male skin is for her moccasins and the female hide for her dress.

The best shot kills the leader. The other antelope are killed by the mind of the doctor. When they cut open the antelope they find a white thing like an egg in their guts. This is the thing from the mind of the doctor that kills them, but if the best shot hadn't killed the leader, the doctor would have been powerless to kill the others.

After the antelope are skinned, they take the hides and meat out of the corral. Then they let the yearling antelope out and drive them north. They take the meat home, tan the hides, and make jerky out of the meat.

The name of Margie's grandfather was Pu Ju.

—ANNE M. SMITH

Afterword

At an earlier period of time, Shoshone myths played an important part in the lives of the Shoshone people. They were passed down to each generation through the oral tradition. Many Shoshone myths are hilarious, even when they touch on grave human problems. Also, Shoshone myths taught one how one should behave, but they did this without being preachy. I would like to share the following with my reader: (1) some comments about Shoshone myths, (2) my mother, the storyteller, (3) a Shoshone myth written in Shoshone, and (4) a free English translation of that myth.

Some Comments about Shoshone Myths

Was it Magpie or was it Deer that broke its leg, and then sat licking its marrow? I remember having mixed feelings about the mental image this presented. The broken leg and the wounded one licking its marrow and discovering that it was good to the taste. I was very young at that time and this was my first introduction to the animals that talked and acted as humans.

As I grew older, listening to an adult tell these stories became an enjoyable experience. It always seemed that they stopped too soon. In our family both my parents took turns telling stories.

By the time I was about nine years old, I had heard many of the stories that are included in this book. Seeing these stories written on paper is a new experience for me. It is an isolating experience because in a "live setting" the whole family listened and responded vocally to the storyteller. We would say "ha'a" (yes) periodically, at the appropriate times. And the storyteller would answer questions if you asked.

Tom Premo, 1965. Courtesy Beverly Crum.

Sometimes my father would interrupt my mother, if she were telling a story, to add a phrase or a song she might have forgotten. My mother did the same thing when my father told a story. I miss this group participation.

As a group we laughed together at some of the hilarious stories. And as a group we were saddened when some of the story characters did things that were bad. Shoshone stories taught one how one should behave, but they did this without being didactic. For example, in some stories Coyote treats his daughter in a wicked way. The message of the story is that proper Shoshone fa-

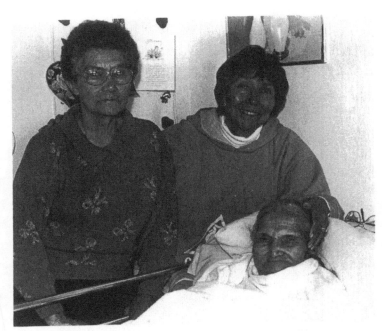

Anna Premo with daughters Mildred (left) and Beverly, Elko, 1990. Courtesy Beverly Crum.

thers did not treat their daughters as Coyote treated his daughter.

However, even when the stories touched on grave problems, they still had a humorous way of presenting it. For example, in one story Coyote's wicked treatment of his daughter caused him to appear utterly foolish. He went to extreme measures to deny his crime.

Also, different age groups responded differently to these stories. As a child I heard things at a child's level. I understood only those things that I had experienced. For example, I understood how Mouse felt as he sat shivering, saying, "Brr, I'm so cold!" I could identify with his situation because, along with my two brothers and a sister, I had to wait for a school bus during the cold winter months.

When I questioned my late great-aunt Kikih, who was 108 years old at the time, about Shoshone myths, she said this: "Aten kwa'i nanatekwinappeh maanankuhten kuhnaikkanten. Ne sukka oyokusen nankaten, apaisen tan naappeha. Ateen peaittempehneen pehnah sakka te'ahwai'iten naappehkante. Tommo taka u te'ahwai'iten, tommo taka" ("Shoshone myths are lengthy. I have heard about all of those things that happened a long time ago. The old people used to tell them. They told them only in the winter").

And so it was in our family. When the daily chores were done and everyone prepared to settle down for the night, the storyteller began his, or her, story. Because some of the stories were lengthy, often it was the last thing a child heard as he or she drifted off to sleep.

My Mother, the Storyteller

Several years ago my mother suffered a stroke. We celebrated her 101st birthday in a nursing home in 1989. She has since died. Even though she was physically helpless, her mind was clear and active. She loved to visit with friends and family, and she had a wonderful outlook on life. She had a tremendous wealth of knowledge and understanding of her own culture. In past years she shared this knowledge not only with her family but also with anthropologists, such as Nan Smith and Julian Steward.

Both my mother and father, Anna and Tom Premo, translated many Shoshone myths into English for Nan Smith's collection of Basin Area mythology.

My mother, in 1967, told me the story I have called "Coyote and Mouse." As she told it in Shoshone, I wrote it down in English. Nineteen years later, at the age of 98, she again told me this same story. Only this time, I wrote it down in Shoshone. However, before she told the story, I read her the English version we had done nineteen years ago.

—BEVERLY CRUM

COYOTE AND MOUSE
ITSAPPE MA'AI PO'NAIH

Himpaisen, ekisen utihi newe niweneku, Itsappe· ma'ai Po'naih nawaka nanaahka. Kaisen ta tahmato'iku soteweh wahateweh, nanatei neweh, kai kammui ta'utta. Pahupekkanna peweh. Itsappe

Po'naiha semmai niikwinna, "Taweh takkanaito'i. Taweh tukama tenippuiyihto'i. Tahi tenippuiyihka imaa supai soon takkapainto'i."

Itsappe tenippuiyihteki, "Wewesiwuu, wewesiwuu, appo wekkutti, appo wekkutti," mai niwennakinna. Imaa nanku Itsappe tenimmatenkahtekisi po'naiha semmai niikwinna, "Maittenkahti puiku. Himpaikanti takkapa'i?"

Po'naih pinnah kai uman nanka tesumpiteten natsattemahkasen koniniisi semmai u naniwaikiannu, "Ne kwitappeha wewehekittsi paika'i."

Itsappe teittse nankasu'annusi nittnaittseh, "Wewesiwuu, wewesiwuu, appo wekkutti, appo wekkutti!"

Napaisi'i tenimmatenkannusi tea Po'naiha semmai niikwinna, "Ma puiku himpaika'i takkapin?"

Po'naih tea kammuhyenkasen koniniisi kai nanah maittenkahti puikkanten Itsappea naniwaiki'a, "Ne kwitappeha wewehekittsi paika'i."

"En ha tokaisen?" mai Itsappe u tetepinna. Teittse nankasu'a, "ne puha tukuh kai tapuinna," mai suanna. Wihnu Po'naiha kai tokain nankasuankanten pensen maittenkahti kuhuyampiteku. Itsappe kwiya'annu akka takkapitta soonti puittsi. Wihnu takkwihtihkuttsi sukkuh takkapa's hapikku.

Po'naih pen isanainna tan nanka sumpaatuhka te'eyapekkasi apai pehen tookkahnihka watsimpiteku.

Itsappe yetsesi pehen kahnihka yuakku semmai tuhusuahkanten, "Hakappun soten wene? Ne witsa nanah u wekkumpahku!" Po'naiha nimma'ikkiyu, "Hakani mai'ukka taweh naahanto'i? Soon takkapa'i naketsa. Kai hakanikku taweh kammui nayaawa'iyu." Itsappe tuhupekkahkanten pehen kahni kuppaihti weppa'innukkikwainna, Po'naiha wettekwanto'i, mai suakkanten.

Napaisi, tuhuwaisi Itsappe maittenkahti kuhuyahka. Akkuhku maanankuhku teaihtettsia takkap'ai nukkikkinti puinnu. Po'naiha puisumpana'ihka, soten u antappun nukkiyu. Itsappe u paitsenkakkiyu, "Koihki; en settiyainnuhi."

Po'naih kai u nankapittsianten antasen nukkikkinna. Akkuhtum manankuhtuttsi toyamantun nukkikkinna u sumpanainna, u ata, Yehnettsi sukkuh kahnikanten. U suwakanten mi'aten.

Mi'aten wihnu waseppehnii puinnu. Soteen akkuh pa'attsi, kai takkakantenka yekwikka. Po'naih wemmihkanten settiyaihkanten sakku tento'isi uteen kemahka katennu.

Uteem piapeh, wahatti tutuakanten, Po'naih man tesumpitennu. "Hakanai pite'ihkanten aisen siten teihtettsi?" mai pen teteyannii tetepinna.

Po'naih sekkwippikanten semmai, "Eitse eitse, ne eitseinna," mai.

Uteem piapeh semmai u niikwinna, "Maikku ne ahnatukka yu'ai."

Po'naih wihnu nittunaitsehka, "Ne eitseinna!" mai yekwiten. Soten wihnu uteem piapeh pemmen appea semmai niikwinna, "En witsa ma yu'ainka." Soten wihnu uteen appe tetteha u puisunkanten pen ahnatukka u tekinnu.

Napaisi wihnu Po'naih yu'aisi, sukkuh mannai mi'annu.

Ei mananku nukkikkinten Po'naih wemmihikanten piteku. Attunti puhaisi pen ata Yehnettsia puinnu. Soten akkuh pa'a waamman katte. Po'naih namasen taikkwakinten semmai, "Ne u wakanten tento'ihkwanto'i." U wakanten wihnu tento'ihku.

U tento'ihkinku u ata u puinnu. "Isen hattun hakannai pite'ihkanten," mai suanna.

Yehnettsi Po'naiha nanasumma tetepinna. Po'naih semmai, "Ne ma'i Itsappea namanukkikki," mai.

Yehnettsi wihnu u naniwaiki'a, "Saikkih ne waka naakkanten yu'ahka."

Napaisi wihnu Po'naiha tsaanku eppeaihka, Yehnettsi pen kahnihkatti u te'ahwainkanna. Waseppitta amattampeh, u ohainnankuhten, sukkuh neewainihka. Un nanku teasen semme un tepitsi nankuhten neewainhka. Yehnettsi sukka tsittsukaahkanten semmai, "Aisen ne kwitakkahni," mai.

He'e hapikkanten Itsappe, Po'naiha nayaaten, sukkuh piteku. Attunti ekkwikkinten Yehnettsian tepaikkappeha ekwinnu. Itsappe sukkuh waatukka weneten Yehnettsia paitsenkakkiyu, "En tepaikkappeh manti ne maka. Ne pahupekkanna."

Yehnettsi Itsappea tuhuihka, Po'naiha u miankahtaihka. Pen kwitakahni Itsappea tsittsukankasi semmai u niikwinna, "Ikkah himpehpai. Ukkuh ma tukka wene. Makki ne tsappaikukka ma yaawikkwannekki. Maikkuh panai mattutua." (Supai kwa'i waseppeh tepitsi piayu, aten un amattempeh natiam petteyu.) Yehnettsi sukka amattempeha tsappahaikku. Itsappe pa'anten pahaikkusi u takkitsa'ahku.

Itsappe Po'naiha paikka pite'ihkanten pensen napaikkannu.

Yehnettsi wihnu Po'naiha semmai niikwinna, "Taweh en woho'a paikkannu. Maikkuh saikkih toyaman nahannekki tepai tek-kappehpai. Soon tutuanaihannekki saikkih kahnipainten."

Kaan kwasi kwai'akku!

COYOTE AND MOUSE

A long time ago when animals talked and were relatives and friends, Coyote and Mouse lived together. Spring hadn't come yet and the two friends couldn't find rabbits for food, and so were hungry. Coyote said to Mouse, "Let's make snow. Come, let's sing all night. With the two of us singing, then in the morning there will be lots of snow."

Coyote started to chant: "Wuwuseewoo, wuwuseewoo, appo wukootee, appo wukootee," he was saying. Towards morning Coyote stopped singing and said to Mouse, "Look outside. How much snow is there?"

Mouse, disinterestedly, went no further than the door and replied, "It's only the height of the shadow of my droppings."

Coyote, feeling bad hearing that, chanted even harder, "Wuwuseewoo, wuwuseewoo, appo wukootee, appo wukootee!"

Later on, his singing finished, again he asked Mouse, "Go look how much snow there is."

Again, Mouse went as far as the door and not even looking outside, said to Coyote, "It's only the height of the shadow of my droppings."

"Are you telling the truth?" Coyote asked him. Feeling bad, Coyote thought to himself, "My medicine must not be strong." And doubting Mouse's reply, he went and peeked outside himself. Coyote was astonished that he saw so much snow outside. Then suddenly he slipped and fell flat on his face there in the snow.

Mouse, frightened because his lie was discovered, hid in the walls of their winter home.

Coyote picked himself up and went into their house, angrily thinking, "Where is he? I could just swat him down!" He called out to Mouse, "What are we going to do now? There is just too much snow for us to track rabbits in." Then, in a wild rage, Coyote ran around hitting the walls of the house, hoping he would hit Mouse.

Later on, when Coyote's temper had cooled down, he again peered outside. Far off in the distance, he saw a tiny little object running along over the snow. From the tracks, he recognized that it was Mouse running away from him. Coyote called out to him, "Come back! You'll freeze to death."

Mouse, not believing him, kept running away. He was heading there to a faraway mountain where he knew somebody; his uncle, Porcupine, lived there. It was to him he was going.

As he traveled along, he saw some mountain sheep. They were sitting there high on a ridge where there was no snow. Mouse, tired and nearly freezing to death, climbed up there and sat down beside them.

The mother mountain sheep, who had two young ones, noticed Mouse and asked her companions, "Where did this little thing come from?"

Mouse, shivering, said, "Brr, brr, I'm so cold."

The mother said to him, "Well, warm up under my arm."

Mouse, even more insistent, said, "I'm cold!"

So, the mother mountain sheep said to father mountain sheep, "You'd better warm him." The father mountain sheep, feeling sorry for him, put him under his arm.

Later on, Mouse, having warmed up there, left them setting off again on his journey.

After traveling a long ways, Mouse finally arrived very tired. Looking around there, Mouse finally saw his uncle, Porcupine. He was sitting high up there on a cedar tree. Mouse said to himself, "I'll climb up to him." So he climbed up.

As he climbed up to him, his uncle saw him and thought, "Wherever did this little fellow come from?"

Porcupine questioned Mouse about various things, and Mouse answered, "I've been running away from Coyote."

To this Porcupine replied, "Well, stay here with me and warm yourself."

Later on, after Mouse was well rested, Porcupine explained to him about his house. From one limb hung the left side of the ribs of a mountain sheep; next to it also hung the right side of the ribs of a mountain sheep. Porcupine, pointing to that, said, "This is my toilet."

After a few days Coyote, who had been tracking Mouse, arrived there. Sniffing around, he smelled Porcupine's kill. Coyote, standing there under the cedar tree, called up to Porcupine, "Give me some of your food. I'm hungry."

Porcupine, feeling spiteful because Coyote had chased Mouse away, pointed to his toilet and said to Coyote, "You can have this stuff. Stand right there under it. When I drop it, you should grab it. Now then stretch your arms up." (At that time the mountain sheep were very large, and the ribs were very heavy.)

Porcupine dropped the ribs; he dropped them on Coyote, crushing him. Coyote having come to kill Mouse, was himself killed.

Porcupine then said to Mouse, "We have killed your enemy. Now then live here on this mountain, and have pine nuts for food. You must have many children while making this your home."

Rat's tail broke off!